THE COMPLETE
HOME RENOVATION
MANUAL

THE COMPLETE
HOME RENOVATION
MANUAL

SMITHMARK

This edition first published in 1993 by SMITHMARK PUBLISHERS INC.,
16 East 32nd Street, New York, New York 10016

SMITHMARK books are available for bulk purchase for sales
promotions and premium use. For details write or telephone the
Manager of Special Sales, SMITHMARK PUBLISHERS INC.,
16 East 32nd Street, New York, New York 10016 (212) 532-6600

Editors: Mike Lawrence and Derek Bradford
Designer: Bob Burroughs
Editorial Director: Pippa Rubinstein
Art Director: Dave Allen

ISBN 0–8317 1588–X

Typeset by Bookworm Typesetting.

Printed in Spain

CONTENTS

INTRODUCTION   6

1: THE PROPERTY   8

Moving or improving   10
Staying put   11
Checking it over   14
Stepping inside   17

2: PLANNING THE WORK   20

Making the house sound   22
Working on the inside   23
Working on the outside   26

3: THE STRUCTURE   28

Types of house   30
Walls and their problems   35
The roof structure   38
Chimneys   44
Structural timbers   45

4: RENOVATING THE EXTERIOR   46

Roofs and gutters   48
External walls   62
Wall insulation and damp-proofing   70
External doors and windows   80

5: RENOVATING THE INTERIOR   92

Floors and staircases   94
Working on the walls and ceilings   110
Fireplaces and chimney breasts   126
Organising the kitchen   138
Bathrooms and showers   150
Creating more space   162

6: WORKING ON THE SYSTEMS   170

Lighting   172
Heating and ventilation   180
Insulating the home   190

7: WORKING ON THE OUTSIDE   202

Garages and carports   204
Porches   210
Patios   214

CONCLUSION   218

INDEX   221

INTRODUCTION

The challenge of completely restoring a dilapidated property into a home of your dreams is an exciting one. Just conjure up the scene. You are replacing the final roof shingle while down below your partner is fixing ornate trellis work to help the roses trail around the door.

Then it's a quick shower followed by coffee on the patio, before returning refreshed to complete painting those gleaming white window frames. It's certainly a romantic scenario, but unfortunately not too realistic.

There may be times when things seem to be going well. But more often than not you are likely to find yourself up a ladder in the pouring rain struggling to get a canvas on to a wildly leaking roof, while down below your partner is desperately trying to shut a warped window. At best, refreshment is likely to take the form of a mug of coffee and cookies as you sit on an old box with your socks and shoes still soaking wet from a puddle you stepped into.

A pessimistic outlook? Perhaps. But a large-scale house restoration job is not for the faint-hearted or the disorganized. But, whoever you are and whatever your capabilities, provided you know what to expect and have laid your plans carefully, you will be able to shrug aside the bad days – even enjoy them – as you get the satisfaction of succeeding with some other task.

This book has been designed to help you chart a smooth passage through the choppy and stormy waters that lie ahead. It will educate you in every aspect of house improvement so that you are fully conversant with each stage of the work. With its help, you will be able to formulate a strategy to take you from initial hopes to final realization of the dream.

It does not matter whether you are a complete novice to do-it-yourself or whether you have already cut your teeth on home improvement work. In either case, you will find the information and advice in the following chapters invaluable.

Although, in essence, the book is aimed at helping you to do as much of the work yourself, it recognizes that many people would prefer, for all sorts of reasons, to let professionals tackle certain aspects of the work.

Whereas doing it yourself is the key to greatest economy, you may decide to employ a mason, a roofer or a plumber to do individual jobs. Perhaps you feel incapable of achieving

complete success, you want a job to be finished quickly or you have not got a head for heights. No matter what the reason, at the end of the day the decision is yours. The most important point to remember is that whichever way you go, the work must be done correctly.

Keeping complete control over the whole project means following an outline timetable and monitoring your budget throughout. Time and money are two of the most important elements of house renovation.

As you work your way through the initial sections of the book, you will become aware of how to assess the condition of a property, how to plan the work, how to establish what are the priority jobs, how to draw up a realistic schedule and how to decide on who is to do the work at each stage.

Before you go house-hunting, familiarize yourself with the initial sections. Take in all the advice offered so that you can come up with a practical judgement of what you are capable of or are prepared to take on. The idea of renovating a really run-down house has to be assessed alongside the alternative of improving a fairly respectable property.

Much depends on a whole host of individual factors, the most important surrounding your

own family and lifestyle. It is generally true that an individual or a couple without children to consider are going to be able to dedicate much more time and money to the task. A family obviously occupies considerably more time and tends to create unexpected demands on effort and resources.

If the objective is to make as much money as possible from your endeavors, then a really dilapidated property is the most likely bet – provided that the initial purchase price is right, the condition is evaluated correctly and you get all the numbers worked out. However, a property in better condition, available at a bargain price, might be the more lucrative venture to tackle in the long run.

From the outset, treat the whole question of renovating as a business. Run the project on sound, practical principles. Keep a file, which should contain all correspondence with surveyors, architects, contractors, suppliers and financial establishments.

It may seem tiresome to do this, and taking the trouble to get everything down in writing can be time-consuming. But in the end it can literally save both time and money, particularly if a dispute should later arise over what was or was not said earlier.

Very often it is the small contractor who is the least efficient with correspondence – usually because of pressure of work. However you must get all bids and estimates in writing and if any amendments or alterations to the initial agreement occur then these must be formalized if disputes are to be avoided.

If a contractor is reluctant to put it in writing, then find another one or type it out yourself and get him to sign it. It is much better to have a clear understanding at the outset.

Contact suppliers to find out how much notice you must give for a delivery and order everything – scaffolding or staging, ready-mix concrete, lumber and so on – in good time. Keep a diary to remind yourself to confirm orders.

Once you have a thorough grounding in the planning work, then you can move through the rest of the book to find out what you might encounter in terms of repairs and restoration to walls, ceilings, heating and the rest. The sections are arranged in the order that they should be tackled, although there are circumstances where this may have to vary.

There is also a section where you can gain sound advice on improving the quality of family living by up-dating those hearts of the home – the kitchen and bathroom – and finding ways of creating more space and generally improving the amenities in your new home.

THE PROPERTY

Home renovation is more than just a weekend hobby for millions of people nowadays. Some are updating and improving the properties they already live in, while others are seeking their ideal home – the run-down property they can just afford to buy and then turn into the home of their dreams. This opening chapter describes what to look for when planning to improve your own home or to buy another house.

MOVING OR IMPROVING?

To move or improve – that is the question. It is a dilemma that most homeowners have to face at least once a lifetime. Comparatively few people remain in their initial house forever; too many changes – expected or unexpected – occur over the years for that to be the rule.

We change our homes for many reasons – sometimes simply because we want to, sometimes because circumstances dictate. The traditional pattern (if such a thing exists) is for a couple to progress from a first-time buyer's property (an apartment or small starter home, perhaps) to a three- or four-bedroom duplex or single family house as a family is started. If careers are successful or money is inherited, then for some there could be another move or two to more prestigious detached properties. Equally, a move could be brought about by a change of job or location.

That, of course, is a carefully orchestrated scenario. For some, social circumstances, financial changes or simply the desire for a change of environment can be the motivating factors. Equally the prime mover could be investment with an eye to capital appreciation. Those involved in this activity are as much, if not more, concerned with houses as opposed to homes for living in.

During the booming 1980s the new housing market was in a dramatic upswing. In the lucrative real estate market of this decade, people could count on getting high resale values for their houses and, using this collateral, could confidently plan on borrowing more money to move on to bigger and better houses. Jobs were plentiful and incomes seemed to be on a continuing rise. It was generally a very comfortable situation, with a healthy real estate market and a confidence that created a stable market and a steady turnover of properties.

In the early years of the 1990s, however, the housing market has been particularly volatile. Fluctuating mortgage interest rates, escalating labor and material costs for new construction and uncertainty about the mortgage banking industry in general conspired to depress the new housing market. In this state of persistent economic depression the will and means to build new houses becomes questionable. Ironically this has led to another increasingly viable option – that of staying put and improving the house you already own.

This has created a totally different situation. No-one can possibly predict with any certainty what will happen to the economy in one year,

let alone in ten. This naturally reflects on the state of the housing market.

The result is a new attitude and approach, where homeowners now tend to look more at the possibilities of improving their existing home. And those looking to buy will pay greater attention to the potential of a particular property in terms of renovation or future extension to accommodate later requirements such as a growing family or ageing relative.

There are also those who are not necessarily concerned with extra space but who see the potential of an older property and want to enjoy the aesthetics and conveniences that come through renovation or modernization.

■ In town or in the country, every individual house poses its own exterior renovation problems, from brick chimneys to metal gutters and downspouts, roof shingles to windows and shutters. In addition, many older-style houses have unique period architectural features which may require specialist renovation techniques.

■ Wood siding is one of the most widespread materials for covering exterior walls, and can be horizontally lapped to emphasize the length of the building or fitted vertically to give an appearance of extra height. Timber species such as cedar and redwood can be left to weather naturally, while pine, hemlock and spruce are generally given a painted finish.

sunniest, which are an inconvenient shape, where there are awkward areas that could be put to better use and so on.

Possibly you have neighbors or friends with similar houses where improvements or alterations have already been made that you particularly like. Doubtless, with their help, you can also build up a fair picture of the kind of work and therefore budget involved.

Assessing a strange property is a different matter altogether. For a start, in a normal housing market you may not have the time to ponder carefully the pros and cons of a particular place or get contractors in to give you bids or estimates of what might be involved.

Unless the market is stagnant or the property difficult to sell for whatever reason, you will be fortunate to get even a week or two to make a decision. If the property is particularly desirable or priced as a genuine 'bargain', you will almost certainly find you have to make an instant decision. In this case, a good grounding in being able to evaluate property quickly could be a priceless asset.

STAYING PUT

Assuming that your house is more or less suitable for your needs but you feel its layout or facilities could be improved – and it is in need of a good overhaul in certain departments – what are you going to do?

In general terms, there are some basic jobs that can be done immediately with few skills and a simple toolkit. Take the doors in a room, for example. Are there too many? Would it be more convenient if one opened outwards into a hallway rather than into a room? Could a pocket or folding door instead of a hinged one save valuable floor space?

Such jobs, involving some ability in the use of wood and sheetrock (drywall) needed to block off a doorway or basic screwdriver and chisel work to alter the type or operation of doors, cost very little to do. Even blocking off a window to create a complete section of wall for extra storage requirements is not going to over-tax your pocketbook or your do-it-yourself capabilities too greatly.

The problem you will face in altering walls will depend on whether they are simply of a partitioning or load-bearing nature. The former, especially in a modern house, where many interior walls are of sheetrock (drywall) construction, is simple to remove. On the other hand, removing a block wall serving as a partition can be a daunting task for anyone not used to heavy demolition work.

Such people have to ask themselves a whole set of different questions in order to assess whether it would be financially viable to bring their existing home up to the desired requirements or whether a move would be more practical. They also have to bear in mind how much work they are prepared to do – or are capable of doing – themselves to keep costs within the available budget.

It is always far easier to assess how much it would cost to pay for alterations to your present home – especially if, as is likely, you have lived in it for a few years. You will already have a good idea of how you would change it, since you will know, for example, which rooms are the

If the block wall is load-bearing – that is, supporting part of the house structure above – then it requires expert building knowledge to decide on the correct replacement support to insert before it is demolished. With any work of this sort you must get professional, on-the-spot advice before you do anything.

Conversely, if you need an extra room, it could well be possible to partition off a large room to create two smaller ones. In this case, building a partition wall is essentially a 'hammer and nails' carpentry job that most capable people should well be equal to.

The problem with planning alterations on this scale is being able to take a detached, clinical view of a house you have grown used to. It is sometimes impossible, for example, to imagine that closets or a large piece of furniture could be moved to an alternative location in a rearranged layout. We tend to become comfortable with familiar surroundings.

Before resorting to paying for the advice of an architect or engineer, you need to get all your ideas down on paper. In other words, make a scale drawing of the complete floor area you want to alter. This does not have to be elaborate, but it should be accurate – so use graph paper and work to a convenient scale.

On the plan, mark the outside walls of the house and the position of all doors, windows, drains and other service pipes and electrical runs. The interior plan should show whether walls are load-bearing or not. In addition, you must indicate precisely the position of doors and windows, pipes and electrical runs inside – in fact, put down as much information as you think will be relevant.

It is only when you have the facts spread out in front of you that you can really begin to understand the existing layout of your house – and, most important, the possible opportunities available for change.

The relevance of marking on doors, windows, services and so on is to let you see at a glance where potential problems may lie and how difficult it is going to be to make particular alterations you may want. For example, a bathroom can pose problems since it has to function entirely around the supply and disposal of water. You cannot simply move it to the other side of the house as you might, say, with a dining room.

Even at the end of this exercise, you may still be baffled as to what can be done. If so, a professional should be able to come up with a series of possible options. Architects and engineers usually work within a similar scale of fees and at least you should be able to get an

■ Classical influence can bring a sense of grandeur to house style, with decorative features such as pediments, porticoes and simulated stonework masking a conventional structure.

■ Georgian style in the late 18th and early 19th centuries favoured ornate entrances and multi-paned sash windows, scaled down in size as the storeys rose.

■ The Georgian style also spread to smaller homes, allowing the porch to become the focus of the façade. Windows are still carefully placed to enhance the overall symmetry.

■ Solid brickwork has a massively solid feel which no wooden-framed building can ever aspire to. A coat of paint can disguise alterations or cover up discolored bricks and pointing.

idea of what the cost is likely to be simply by making a telephone call to individual practices; they should be able to give you at least approximate fee figures.

You are unlikely to be charged an enormous amount for an initial visit, consultation and outline suggestions. Should you decide to take the matter a stage further and have proper plans drawn up for yourself or a contractor, then you must ask what the fee for this will be.

You can run through the same process if you are thinking of buying a property and there is no pressure on you to make a quick purchase.

However, you may not have sufficient appreciation or knowledge of building work to make a swift, accurate assessment on a particular property where there is a line of interested parties considering buying as well. In this situation, you can take your professional adviser with you when you make your visit to get an immediate expert reaction.

Your initial response to such a suggestion may be that this is a waste of money. But imagine what it could be like to buy a house believing it to be possible to make certain alterations or improvements, only to find out a few months later that you cannot do what you want – or that the cost of what you plan to carry out is likely to be quite prohibitive.

Even in a lively market, most vendors understand that a potential purchaser will want an architect's or engineer's report on the building. You can take this opportunity to get the professional to include renovation or alteration possibilities in the report. This could possibly involve an additional fee, which again you can ascertain in advance.

CHECKING IT OVER

The advantage of planning wholesale improvements to a house in which you have lived for a couple of winters is that you have a pretty thorough knowledge of its hidden weaknesses and potential problems.

You cannot, for example, spot a really cold, drafty corner when making an inspection of a strange house on a hot summer's day. Equally you will not know that the boiler makes strange hissing sounds as it warms up or that mold tends to grow on the wall inside a closet in the middle of winter.

When you inspect any property, you will be looking for the same things and searching for the obvious faults. But it is only with your own home that you will have a complete picture.

In some cases first impressions can be a good indication as to the overall state of a house.

the price you are paying for the property, then you can consider yourself as having got a considerable bargain.

None of this, of course, takes into account such major faults as settlement, termite damage or serious rot, the extent of which will only be revealed by expert inspection. If such conditions exist and prove to be serious, you may be facing a no-go situation.

FIRST IMPRESSIONS

When you go to look at any property you are considering buying, the first and most obvious thing you will notice is its general paint condition. Paint peeling from walls, doors and windows, exposed woodwork, rusting gutters, cracks in the stucco, algal growth or siding that is in a poor state of repair – all these will be

Although it is not uncommon to see somewhere with gleaming paintwork and a neatly tended garden that is in need of vast improvement inside, it is rare to see an eyesore with an overgrown garden that is immaculate and fully modernized inside.

If the house is run-down outside, expect the worst inside as well. You will probably find an antiquated electrical system and plumbing to match, few modern services and a lot of dampness. Real estate agents often describe such a property as being 'in need of some improvement'.

What they are in fact saying is that there is an avalanche of work to be done and it would cost a small fortune to employ contractors to tackle the jobs required. If you are capable of doing some or all of it yourself and the house is being sold reasonably cheaply, then you could look forward to some return for your labors in the years to come.

Unless you are up-to-date with materials and their prices, then you should take a trip to a builders' supply company or speak to a few manufacturers to see how much, for example, a new garage door would cost – or new plastic guttering, a replacement window, bathroom fixtures or custom kitchen cabinets.

Make a list of all the obvious, larger items you think you are going to need and then add on an extra 50 per cent for smaller items, decorating materials and so on. At least this will give you a rough figure to work on. It is not going to be totally accurate, but it will prepare you for the worst. And it should avoid the nightmare of seeing, halfway through the work, your budget turned upside down. If the cost of the improvements you would like to see is then reflected in

■ Rowhouses soon became the accepted form of building in towns, whether adorned by all the trappings of Georgian style (top) or more simply broken up with projecting bays and dormers in later times (above). Basements reached from below the front steps were a popular way of creating extra living space within a restricted floor plan, and can often be converted into garages.

clearly visible to the naked eye.

No straightforward painting job is beyond the capability of anyone prepared to wield a paintbrush. All the preparation work, such as removing rust, filling cracks, replacing glazing compound and so on just requires a little easily gained knowledge and certainly no great degree of skill or ability.

The only possible drawback for some people is that you will probably have to scale the heights to do part of the work. Not everyone is happy working from a ladder. Nowadays, fortunately, you do have the option of renting some scaffolding or staging from which you can work safely and comfortably at heights.

You may decide it is worth buying such a kit if there is a lot of work to be done and you are prepared to undertake it on an on-going basis. After all, exterior painting and maintenance can be a never-ending task. You could even share

■ 19th-century houses reflected the pretensions of their owners, who referred to them as villas rather than houses. Stock features were the projecting two-storey bays and the recessed arched entrances, often featuring decorative stonework.

the cost of the kit with a friend or neighbor.

If you feel reasonably confident about painting yourself, then do it. If you need persuading, then just get a bid from a professional company and you will see the reason why!

'All that glisters is not gold', wrote William Shakespeare. And that could well apply to a house with fresh paintwork. A quick spruce-up before placing a property on the market is an established practice. It is also one way of covering up a multitude of problems, including rotting wood or rusty metal.

You cannot, of course, inspect every inch of exterior woodwork. But a strategic prod here and there around door and window frames with a sharp pocket knife will reveal if there is a trouble spot lurking behind a fresh coat of paint.

LOOKING UP TOP

You can check the condition of the roof and chimney stack at a glance, and the age of the house will help you to complete the picture. A wood shingle roof should, with care, last at least fifty years without major problems apart from the occasional shingle cracking or slipping out of alignment. These can be replaced or reset without too much difficulty. It might also be wise, even for a relatively sound roof, to consider a fresh application of sealer/stain/fire retardant liquid. This will make the shingles look better and provide greater longevity.

Asphalt shingles are much the more common form of roof finish. Under normal conditions they can last up to twenty years before they begin to crack, split or curl. Adding a new layer of class A triple-tab asphalt shingles is a good way of reviving a tired roof and of changing the

color and appearance at the same time. The new layer can be laid directly over the old . . . once. If there are already two layers it is time to strip the roof down to the sheathing and start over again with a new application of shingles.

The real key to knowing whether an apparently sound roof is watertight is whether any damp patches are showing up on ceilings or whether attic timbers or insulation are wet. The best time to detect this is obviously on a rainy day. Get into the attic and use a flashlight to search for any leaks. Make sure you trace them back to the trouble area, since water will often drop some distance from where it gets in.

■ Late 19th-century houses began to develop decorative idiosyncracies of their own, from decorative bargeboards to ornate chimneys. The more complex the external detail, the more difficult authentic renovation can be.

You can make a reasonably thorough inspection of the roof from the ground, using a pair of binoculars. Look for broken or missing shingles; loose or damaged flashing, where the base of the chimney stack meets the roof; and damage in valley gutters. The chimney itself, especially if disused, can be a prime source of dampness. So check that the brickwork pointing and stucco are sound and the cap itself is solidly fixed in mortar.

You need to have a good head for heights, a proper roof ladder and, if necessary, correct scaffolding or staging to get on to a roof for a closer inspection or to carry out repairs. There is no reason why you should not be able to complete most remedial work, although many

■ Brickwork may be just a decorative veneer on modern period-style houses (above and below), whereas the external walls are of load-bearing masonry on this 19th-century single-family home (above right). Areas of stucco on the walls provide additional visual interest.

are understandably reluctant to take it on. If you are prepared to, you will save yourself a lot of money. If you are not, get a reputable company to do the work for you.

Flat roofs are notorious for leaking. Unfortunately a visual inspection may not reveal anything untoward, even though the roof leaks like a sieve. Loose or missing flashing will be self-evident, as will cracks in the roof covering. However, external inspection may not reveal any obvious faults; only the occupier will know whether it is sound or not. Age is a clue to condition. With any flat roof, after 10 or 15 years you are generally living on borrowed time and you must expect early failures.

If you are happy to work on a flat surface, then it would be worth your while to re-cover a small roof yourself. Leave large roofs to a specialist roofing contractor.

TAKING A SIDE VIEW

Normal cracks and holes in masonry walls are cheap and simple to fill in. However major cracks could indicate some much more drastic problem, such as the need for underpinning foundations. Very often you will have no realistic alternative but to call in professional experts to do the job. It is one type of work that could prove costly and very disruptive.

Patches of loose stucco can generally be tackled quite successfully by the amateur. Larger areas or complete walls, however, really need good building skills.

The job of replacing doors or windows is relatively straightforward, provided you are using the same size units. If you want to enlarge an opening, then you need to know what you

■ Occasionally, architects hark back to traditional styles, using features such as decorative siding, dormers and verandahs to disguise the basic box structure.

few days, possibly in just a weekend. Care should be taken with metal guttering however, since it is fairly heavy and quite awkward to handle when working at a height.

If you detect only the odd leak or patch of rust in your metal guttering, a little first-aid work will give it a new lease of life.

STEPPING INSIDE

It is most unlikely that you will move into a house and like the decor sufficiently to leave it as it is. So it is of no great concern if the wallpaper is shabby or the paintwork faded or chipped. Nine times out of ten you will want to strip the paper off or paint over the walls or woodwork as soon as you can.

As a general rule, however, the shabbier the existing decorations, the more preparatory work you will have to do to get things ready for

■ The post-second World War period saw the development of modernist styles for many homes. The main features were bland picture windows and the absence of any relieving decorative features save for a boxy front porch.

are doing. It is quite possible that you would have to install a longer header to support the wall above, which is a major operation.

Metal gutters and downspouts that need replacing should not pose any particular problems. The former are held in place with brackets screwed to the fascia boards (in the case of gutters) or to the rafter ends, while the latter are fixed direct to the wall. Using the plastic versions, which do not suffer from rust, you can put up a new system in a matter of a

redecorating. And it is also possible that behind old wallpaper lurks another problem, such as deteriorating plaster and possibly damp.

Whatever the overall condition, however, this is not normally an aspect of a property that should cause too much worry. The one advantage here is that if you can live with the existing decor, initially at least you will be saving yourself valuable time and money to spend on other more important or urgent jobs.

It is far more crucial to look at the services, starting with the electrical installation. An inspection of the distribution board should reveal all, since this is where old systems normally originate. Tell-tale signs include the old-fashioned fuse box and probably a jumble of cables, which may even be rubber-covered. Look around the house for outlets that look really old-fashioned, are mounted on base-boards or are broken or scorched. Switches mounted on wood blocks are another sign of old age, while ceiling fixtures suspended on frayed cable provide another giveaway.

If any of these conditions are present, then you need to have the old wiring ripped out and new power and lighting circuits installed. These should run from a modern distribution box to an adequate number of 15-amp outlets in each room, g.f.i. units for kitchen appliances, flush wall switches, plastic-coated ceiling roses and other modern electrical fittings.

This is expensive but essential work, which requires expert electrical knowledge plus some basic preparation – such as fishing down walls for cable runs, lifting floorboards and making holes to receive outlets. If you are competent, you can undertake your own rewiring. But you must get the local electrical inspector to make the final inspection and the local utility company to make the final electrical connection to the house distribution board.

Plumbing covers not only the pipework but the units themselves – sink, bath, wash-basin, toilet etc. If you find modern units, then you can reasonably assume that any old lead piping has been replaced by new copper or plastic versions. A look under the kitchen sink unit and behind the bath panelling will tell you all you need to know.

Find out the age of the central heating system. Generally you can tell if the system is old and out of date by looking at the boiler in the basement. Older systems were fired with coal (or wood in some areas) and will probably have been switched over to oil or gas more recently. In many instances this was done by converting the existing heating boiler to the newer fuel. These hybrid systems can still work reasonably well, but it might be time to convert fully to the newer, more compact and much more efficient boilers that use oil or gas as the primary fuel.

GETTING THE WRONG FEELING

If you detect a musty smell in any of the rooms you visit, if the air feels moist or there are stains on walls or ceilings, then dampness is getting into the house. This could be caused by rainwater penetrating porous walls, particularly adjacent to leaking gutters, in which case the problem is quite easily remedied.

Rising dampness, on the other hand, is much more serious. This is caused by a faulty or non-existent damp-proof membrane. If you come across dampness on the ground floor above baseboard level and extending upwards, then you should call in an expert to check the extent of the problem.

Dampness can, in turn, lead to the even more

■ The kitchen is the hub of both domestic and family activity, and will most strongly reflect the taste of its occupants. Cottagey homeliness or the clinical style of the operating theatre are largely matters of personal taste; what is more important is whether the kitchen functions well from a practical point of view.

■ The entrance hall of any house makes an immediate impact on the first-time visitor. Its size and shape are less important than the sense of providing a welcome, which depends more on factors such as lighting and decoration than on shape and size.

serious problem of wet and dry rot. The former is not quite as bad, since the rot remains localised. But dry rot can find its way through walls and ceilings and eventually attack all the structural timbers in the house.

Dry rot is identifiable by cracks both with and across the grain, where the wood literally crumbles away when touched. It can be devastating – and so, too, can be the cost of eradicating it. Normally any work should be left to a specialist company, since it must be totally cleared and all affected areas sterilized.

Nearly every property is to some extent affected by fungus and insect damage. Termite infestation can be especially serious and will lead to substantial structural damage which can be very expensive to repair. If evidence of insect damage is readily visible, it is vital that a full-scale professional survey is conducted to determine the extent of the damage. In fact, most mortgage loans are conditional on the submission of a formal termite report prepared by registered termite control company. You cannot tackle the treatment yourself, since many of the chemicals used are controlled by state environmental agencies and are available only to licensed operators.

■ The bathroom has come a long way from its early Victorian beginnings, when space for bathing and washing was not regarded as a high priority. As a result, much ingenuity is often devoted to cramming a quart into a pint pot during later renovation work.

PLAYING SAFE

All this may give you the feeling that suddenly viewing a house you are considering buying has become a daunting prospect. What you must remember is that, whatever its age, no property is going to be in perfect condition. What is important is that you are able to recognize what is serious and what is acceptable – and, of course, have a reasonable idea of what costs might be involved. Only then can you put a realistic value on the house and decide what it is worth to you to buy.

It is an obvious word of warning but one that can all too easily be ignored that 'when in doubt, walk away'. You may, for a variety of reasons, feel you have found the 'ideal' property and therefore try to convince yourself that any problems can be overcome – or, worse, that they do not exist. But it pays to be critical and careful. And if, by doing so, you fail to make the purchase, don't despair. There will always be another 'ideal' property round the corner.

PLANNING THE WORK

Once you have chosen the course your home renovation project is to follow, you need to decide on job priorities so you can start drawing up detailed plans, schedules and timetables. At this stage you must also decide whether you will need some extra help from the professionals in the home renovation business – people such as architects, builders, plumbers, electricians and other specialists.

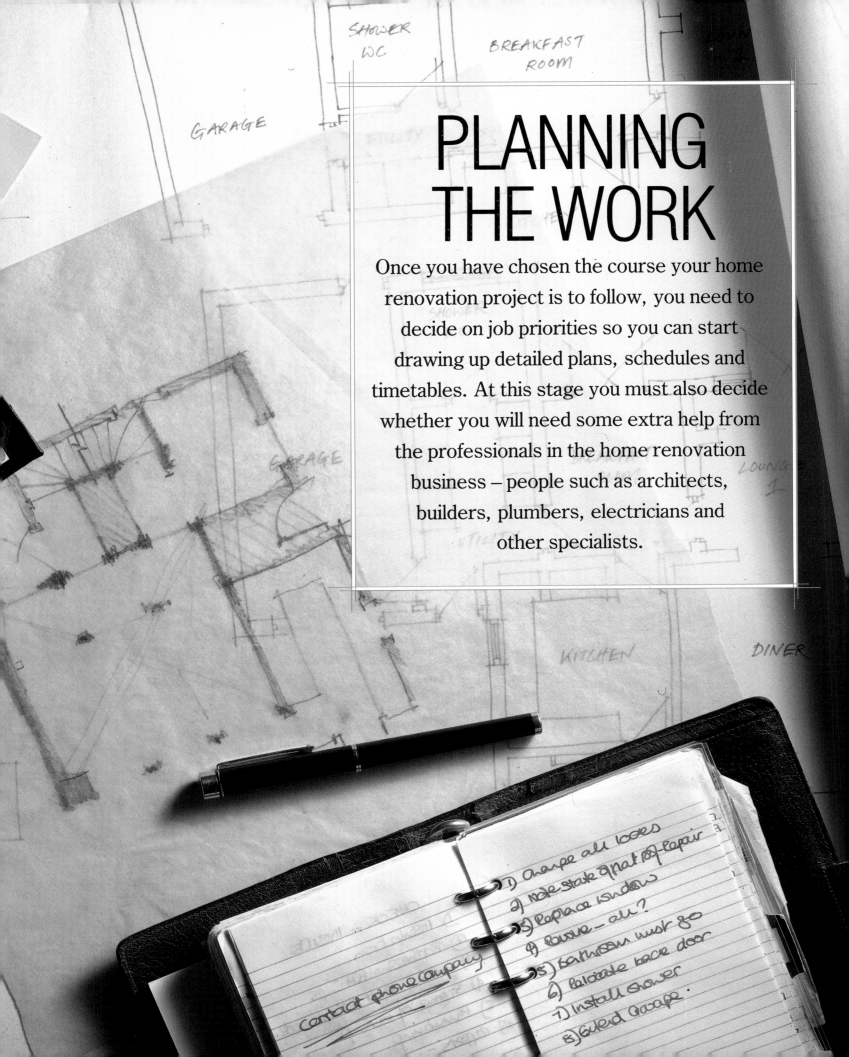

The value of careful appraisal and ascertaining exactly what renovation work has to be done to a property will be reflected in both time and money saved. But even those can be wasted if you do not plan each stage properly. Without organizing the correct order of jobs, you can easily find yourself having to cover the same ground over again.

An obvious example is with electrical work, where you may decide you want to install wall lights after you have decorated a room. Since this involves cutting into the wall to run in the new cable to the lights, you will then have to redecorate afterwards.

Equally, in the kitchen it makes no sense to move a built-in appliance to the other side of the room after you have discovered it is not in the most convenient place. To change the location at this stage will involve extending the run of both supply and drainage pipes.

So you need to take your time to decide exactly what you want and then to draw up a blueprint of when and how each job is to be tackled. Unless you have very fixed ideas of what alterations or improvements you want to make to your 'new' home, it will certainly pay you to live in it for a few months until you get to know it a bit better and can be sure of what you want to be done and where.

Even after a short period, you may well alter your views considerably. You will also then be in a much better position to judge existing shortcomings or problem areas.

There are many factors that can influence how you arrive at your final plan. Is there major building work to be done? At what time of year

■ Making sure the house is weatherproof is always a top priority. Loose or missing roof tiles or shingles allow water to get at the roof timbers and penetrate ceilings below, while blocked gutters will cause damp penetration lower down the building. Outside walls in poor condition will also allow rain and wind to penetrate the structure.

is it best to do a particular job? Should you start inside or outside? Are there priority jobs? Are there any financial restraints? If you have had a professional report carried out on the house, what were the findings and were there any comments within it that would affect your own preferred timetable?

MAKING IT SOUND

The first essential is to ensure that the roof is waterproof and free of rot. If the roof is leaking or the gutters are overflowing, causing dampness in any of the rooms, or there is serious rot or insect damage to treat, then make these the first things you tackle.

In the case of anything involving structural timbers in the house, upheaval is unavoidable. Rooms will probably have to be cleared of

furniture while floors are taken up. The attic may have to be stripped of its insulation and all the items in it stored somewhere else while extermination treatment is applied.

Dealing with a bad attack of dry rot can cause an amazing amount of devastation, with plaster being hacked off walls and complete joists and floors being replaced. So this type of work is something that must be done immediately –

even if it means having to put up with makeshift accommodation for a while.

It goes without saying that these jobs are always better done during the summer, since the house inevitably becomes a building site and doors and windows have to be kept open all the time. If for any reason you have to schedule any of it for the winter, the best advice is to get it over with as quickly as possible.

■ Rot is public enemy number one, closely followed by insect attack. Both can cause extensive damage to timber.

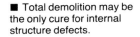

■ Total demolition may be the only cure for internal structure defects.

WORKING ON THE INSIDE

Where the house is basically in sound condition, it is a good idea to turn your attention first to any interior structural work you want done. Alterations affecting the inside should ideally all be done together to minimize the unavoidable inconvenience.

If you are knocking down walls, replacing ceilings or installing doors to the outside, for example, get the work out of the way so that all the resultant debris can be dumped and then cleared in a single operation. This can be done through the rental of a dumpster, which you will want filled and removed as quickly as possible – not hanging around for weeks on end.

Equally, thinking ahead, you may have some major garden remodeling projects planned where debris could be used to help with the landscaping. Therefore you will want to save any material you are removing and store it in a convenient pile somewhere outside.

Should you be planning any major building work, than it would obviously be an advantage to have this completed early on. Putting up a single-storey extension, for example, does not necessarily mean that too much mess will spill into the house itself. But it is still better to get the major upheaval over as soon as possible. One advantage is that it would then provide you with valuable temporary living accommodation

■ Many older homes have bathrooms and WCs that have gone unimproved for decades. Not only will the visible components need replacing; the underlying services such as water supplies and waste disposal may well need full-scale modernising too.

■ Similarly, the revolution in interior design may have passed the kitchen by, with washing, food storage and preparation facilities a picturesque relic of a bygone age. One particular need is often for a better electricity supply to cope with the multitude of gadgets now regarded as essential in a modern kitchen.

when working on the main rooms in the house.

On the other hand, an attic conversion or a two-storey addition will certainly affect the inside of the house, since walls must be broken through, existing windows blocked up and new staircases built.

Any alterations or additions to the essential utilities – water, gas and electricity – will inevitably result in considerable disturbance to floors and walls. Such work should therefore be planned with this in mind and all of it completed at the same time.

Pipes and cables are the lifeblood of any home and their efficient operation will add enormously to the well-being and peace of mind of the occupants. Plenty of hot water, warmth

from radiators, ample outlets and light switches that work will justify the necessary inconvenience any installation or repair work causes.

All these jobs take time – weeks and possibly months, depending on their extent, the ability of the individual and what time is available to carry them out. Since you really cannot move on to general improvements and decorating before they are complete, you might decide that employing professionals for all or part of the work might be the sensible option. On the other hand, you may be happy to live with any inconvenience for as long as it takes to complete all the required stages.

As far as utilities are concerned, the most important rooms in the house are the kitchen and bathroom. Cooking, washing and bathing facilities are essential and you will need to have at least the basic minimum facilities in operation all the time.

If you have to replace the toilet, bathtub or stove, then make sure everything is arranged so that the work can be done speedily. You cannot afford to have these vital facilities out of action for any length of time.

If you have a family, particularly with babies or young children, it may well be sensible to arrange for them to stay with friends or

■ Hot water on tap was a luxury until early in the 20th century, and was generally provided by a gas-fired geyser over the stone sink. Many have survived in working order for far longer than their original installers could have dreamed possible at the time.

■ The inexorable rise in demand for electricity has in many older homes led to a piecemeal extension of the original wiring system well beyond the bounds of safety. Installations such as this must be a top priority for total replacement.

relatives temporarily while the major part of the work is being carried out.

Cooking facilities are, perhaps, the least critical in this situation. Arguably they can be out of action for a few days without causing too many headaches. Cereals, salads and fruit, for example, form a perfectly acceptable diet. Alternatively, if there is a local fast-food take-out, you can at least make use of it for the short period necessary. Whatever arrangements you can make, never forget to have hot drinks readily available, either by use of a camping stove or a regularly filled thermos, which hopefully you can get a neighbor to supply.

It is always a good idea to have at least one room set aside where the family can escape to and relax in some degree of comfort, especially in the winter. As long as it is furnished to a degree and has a carpet – however temporary – it will provide a welcome sanctuary.

WORKING ON THE OUTSIDE

Apart from any essential repairs you need to carry out to make the fabric of the house sound, you can leave exterior decoration until last – unless you cannot stand the idea of your place not looking as good as the house next door!

Remember, however, that if you intend any alterations that will affect the exterior later on, such as changing the position of windows or doors, this could upset any work you do now. You may, for example, have to install new clapboarding around the new frames to make good any damage caused when the old ones are removed, and then repaint it.

For anyone who has not tackled exterior painting before, be warned! Depending on the size of the house, its design and overall condition, it can involve you in months of work. Bearing in mind that most people will only have summer evenings and weekends at their disposal, to paint a large family house with wooden trim can take all summer.

Estimating how long a job is going to take is never easy, especially with larger projects where so many unexpected problems can arise. The sensible approach is always to over-estimate – and be realistic. Nothing is worse than falling behind your schedule. This can cause a feeling of anxiety to creep in needlessly and encourages jobs to be rushed, so that standards of workmanship fall badly – and possibly disastrously.

The best advice is never to plot an exact schedule. Your plan should basically give you an order in which things are going to be done and the optimum time of year to tackle them. Be realistic in allocating time to each stage, and make allowances for unforeseen delays. Illness or family and work commitments, for example, can all conspire to interfere with progress from time to time.

FINANCING THE WORK

Not everyone is in the fortunate position of having sufficient funds readily available to provide them with complete freedom of choice over when particular jobs are going to be done. Some will have to plan what they are going to do around savings and future borrowing.

The ideal solution is to borrow sufficient money when taking out a mortgage to cover the cost of essential improvements as well – and all of them if this is possible and practical. So you must first find out what financial arrangement your bank is prepared to offer you. It is absolutely essential that you allow for the availability of money to cover every stage of your work plan.

In certain circumstances, of course, you may well be eligible for an improvement grant – for insulation, for example, or if you have bought a property in an historic zone. Obviously you will need to check this out and determine when any funding is going to be available. This will equally have an effect on your timetable.

Careful budgeting and purchasing can save you a lot of money, particularly if you are renovating a large proportion of your property. The overall cost will run into thousands – at least – so any savings along the way can help significantly in relation to the final total. There are several useful principles you should get into the habit of adopting.

First, especially in times of inflation, buying as soon as possible should represent a considerable saving. Buying in bulk is sensible, too. Even tiny items such as nails and screws should be bought in large boxes, not expensive little packets. You'll use them up eventually!

Shop around for the best prices. Large builders' supply companies are normally very competitive. But do not forget the small hardware store, where there are frequently excellent bargains to be had as well.

Finally, if you are going to employ an architect or engineer, you must first consider what you want to do. Even better, prepare a rough drawing – however simple – since this should greatly reduce the final costs involved. If you can at least give an overall picture of what you want, it will save a lot of time and money paying the professional to experiment with different ideas.

DECIDING WHETHER YOU NEED EXPERT HELP

Assessing the job

Whether you decide to tackle a particular job or project yourself will depend on a number of questions which only you can answer, since they relate to individual factors such as the nature of the work, your personal level of skill and technical knowledge, the time and money you have available and your level of personal commitment to getting the work completed. Check how each of these points applies to the project you are tackling before making your decision.

Personal skill

Start by deciding whether you have the *ability* to tackle a particular job. You may have done it before with considerable success, or you may have watched someone else do it and felt that you could soon pick the skill up. Be honest with yourself about your ability, however; contractors hate having to undo someone else's bodged work, and would rather have been called in at the beginning.

Remember that larger projects will often require a range of skills. In this case, break the job down into its component parts and assess each one individually. For example, you may decide to leave the structural part of, say, an attic conversion to a contractor, but to do all the internal fitting out yourself. This is a perfectly acceptable way of tackling many projects, so long as the contractor is aware of your intentions at the outset.

Technical knowledge

Next, ask yourself whether you know what is involved in carrying out the work from a technical point of view. For example, jobs such as doing your own wiring or plumbing work or creating a new opening in a wall are not difficult in terms of the level of skill needed, but it is essential that you have sufficient knowledge to ensure that you make the right electrical connections, choose the correct pipe sizes or use the appropriate type of header to bridge the new opening you are constructing. In some cases, getting expert advice may be all you need to do before you actually carry out the work yourself; in other situations the whole job may simply be too complex for the layman to tackle without enlisting some professional assistance.

Rules and regulations

Many home improvement projects have to comply with the requirements of various pieces of legislation that are intended to ensure that such work is carried out safely and to satisfactory standards. These rules obviously apply mainly to major structural work, but alterations to things like staircases or the disposal of waste water may also be covered. It is therefore vital, before even planning or starting work on any home improvement project, to ascertain whether any official permission is needed and also whether the work must comply with local building codes. Just because a job needs official permission or approval does not mean that you cannot do it yourself, but you must obtain permission first and ensure that what you do complies with the codes throughout. Contact your local zoning and building departments for advice on how to proceed.

The time available

Next, consider how long the job is likely to take to complete. You will usually take longer than a contractor to carry out a particular task, and on larger projects you must weigh up the advantage of calling in an expert and getting quicker completion – at a price – against saving some money but having a longer period of disruption around the house. Other factors, such as having the house open to the elements during the winter, may also be relevant when you are deciding which course to adopt.

The cost

Cost is often the most important factor in deciding whether to carry out a particular job yourself. At first sight the thought that your own labor is free may seem very appealing, and on many jobs the cost of materials represents only a tiny fraction of the overall real cost. For example, having your house painted by a contractor will cost between five and ten times the price of the paint and other materials; the rest is his labor charge. However, you must be sure not only that you can finish the work in a reasonable time, but also that you can do it properly.

When you are pricing a project with a view to doing it yourself, remember that professionals can buy materials at lower prices than you can, as well as working more quickly. Balance these points against the cost of your own time. To get a proper picture it may help you to have a couple of bids from the professionals (see below) which will cost you nothing and will help you arrive at a decision.

Choosing a contractor

Personal recommendation is the best way of finding a contractor. Otherwise, it is safest to pick individuals or companies with membership of the relevant professional or trade organization, and to check that the membership is genuine. Once you have found two or three suitable contractors, get written bids so that you can select which firm to employ on the basis of the materials specified, the time the work will take and, of course, the price. When you have made your decision, accept the chosen bid in writing so that you have a legally enforceable contract should any future dispute arise.

THE STRUCTURE

Before you can start work in earnest, it is vital that you have a clear picture of what you are up against, by finding out all you can about the structure of the building and examining it closely for obvious and potential trouble spots. A guided tour round the house is the best way of assessing what is there and what needs attention.

TYPES OF HOUSE

Whether you are thinking of improving your existing home or considering purchasing a house in need of renovation, you must check out the basic fabric of the property to appreciate what essential repairs might be required. Once the structure is sound, you can start making whatever other alterations and modifications you want.

Houses are very individual, even on a speculative development. Each one has its own unique circumstances that could result in specific structural problems. For example, a house on a corner plot could be more susceptible to problems caused by the weather than an identical one in a sheltered situation.

Each house has its own set of ground conditions, too. Tree roots in the foundations and back filling of the site can make one house more prone to subsidence and settlement than a similar neighboring property.

Probably the most important factor in the structural stability of any property is the actual type of construction itself and the materials used. This section is dedicated to looking at the various types to help you make a quick assessment of the property you either own or are considering buying.

Apart from the period and style of the property, which may carry their own interest problems, there are other factors to watch out for. Unseasoned wood, for example, can make one house deteriorate much quicker than another. Dampness in a masonry wall and an unsuitable choice of material can lead to damaged brickwork, where the surface of the bricks crumbles away due to frost attack.

Of course, a house is very much a hand-made construction. As such, much of its structural stability depends on the quality of the work involved. Two builders working from identical sets of plans can produce two very different buildings. So you must be on the look-out for faulty construction, such as poor quality brickwork or inadequate or non-existent damp-proofing.

Understanding the type and style of property is critical in trying to analyze possible faults. You must be able to know what you are looking for and recognise trouble when you see it.

Wood-framed walls

The vast majority of houses built since the twenties are of wood-frame construction. Older homes have walls about 6in thick, consisting of a series of 2 × 4in studs spaced at 16 or 24in

The 19th century urban rowhouse

■ The urban rowhouse evolved steadily throughout the latter part of the 19th century, collecting details from earlier styles while trying to comply with the demands of ever-increasing building code legislation.

The roof was traditionally covered with slates or clay tiles. Ridges and hips were protected by molded tiles, often with decorative finials, and valleys were lined with lead gutters.

Projecting bays with gables above provided extra floor area in the primary rooms, as well as giving the façade additional grandeur.

External walls were generally of solid brick, often laid in ornate banding and intricate patterns with decorative terracotta plaques and other features built in.

Sash windows were still the norm, with lintels and sills generally of stone in better properties; brick soldier arches bridged window openings in many more humble dwellings.

Entrance doors were generally recessed within an open porch, which was often surmounted by a decorative arch or portico.

stone lintels and sills

projecting front bay

cast-iron rainwater system

tiled porch

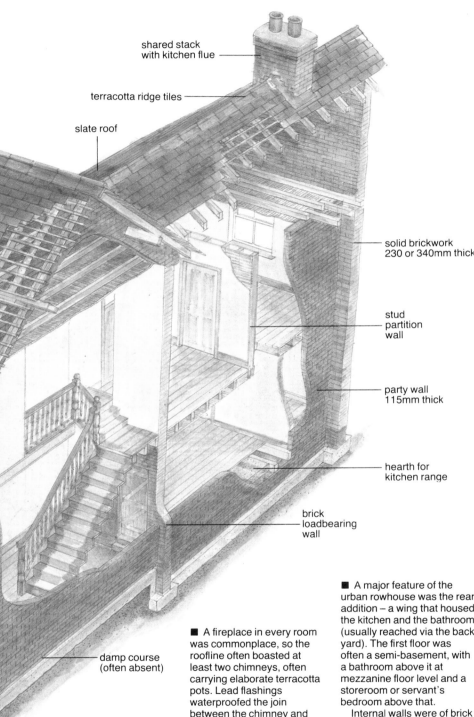

shared stack
with kitchen flue

terracotta ridge tiles

slate roof

solid brickwork
230 or 340mm thick

stud
partition
wall

party wall
115mm thick

hearth for
kitchen range

brick
loadbearing
wall

damp course
(often absent)

brick footings
on concrete
foundation

■ A fireplace in every room was commonplace, so the roofline often boasted at least two chimneys, often carrying elaborate terracotta pots. Lead flashings waterproofed the join between the chimney and the roof slope.

Floors were generally the suspended type to keep dampness at bay, although kitchens and sculleries at semi-basement level usually had solid direct-to-earth floors of necessity.

■ A major feature of the urban rowhouse was the rear addition – a wing that housed the kitchen and the bathroom (usually reached via the back yard). The first floor was often a semi-basement, with a bathroom above it at mezzanine floor level and a storeroom or servant's bedroom above that.

Internal walls were of brick if loadbearing, or of lath-and-plaster on timber studding otherwise. The foundations were also generally of corbelled brickwork; concrete did not come into common use until around 1900.

centers. The exterior is usually finished with sheathing consisting of ½in thick boards laid diagonally, to which a decorative exterior finish such as shingles or clapboards are nailed.

Alternative exterior finishes include brick or stone veneer and, on less grand houses, asbestos shingles. Removal of the latter is strictly controlled by the asbestos abatement regulations at both state and federal level, so specialist demolition and disposal contractors may have to be employed to deal with them.

On the interior, the typical wall finish will be either lath and plaster (late 19th and early 20th century houses) or, in more recent houses, ½in sheetrock (drywall) nailed up with taped joints.

More modern homes may have the wall thickness increased to 8in by the use of 2 × 6in studs at 24in centers. The main reason for this is to allow the fitting of a full 6in of foil-backed fiberglass insulation batting in the cavity, and so to reduce heat losses through the house walls. The exterior sheathing is CDX plywood, ⅜in thick on studs at 16in centers or ½in thick if they are at 24in centers. Sheetrock (drywall) is the standard internal wall finish.

Most wood-framed homes are built using the platform framing technique. Each floor is a platform, resting on the sill plate at first floor level and on the top plate of the first floor walls for the second floor above. The subfloor – diagonally-laid boards in older homes, plywood sheathing in newer ones – extends to the edge of each floor platform.

Some two-storey homes were also built using the balloon framing technique, which is seldom used nowadays. The studs, usually 2 × 6in wood at 16in centers, run the full height of the building (to a maximum of 20ft) and the second-floor joists lap the studs and rest on a continuous ribbon let into the studs to provide additional support. The one advantage of balloon framing is that there is less vertical movement in the wall than with platform framing, which is a bonus if external brick veneer or stucco finishes are used.

Solid brick walls

Solid brick walls are found in some older houses (pre-1920) and are distinguishable by having headers (half-bricks) as well as stretchers in the face of the wall. This type of brickwork is usually 9in thick, although a 13½in thickness is also quite common. You can check the thickness of the walls at door and window openings. But remember to make allowance for the thickness of the internal plaster – usually about ¾in thick.

Old solid walls can give quite a few problems,

particularly with regard to dampness. Many were built without a damp-proof course (dpc), which allows dampness to rise from ground level, and footings or foundations were often rudimentary.

Such foundations could be stepped bricks laid directly in a trench, in comparison to the concrete footings used nowadays. If these footing bricks have crumbled due to the length of time they have been underground, then the house may have settled. This is evidenced by out-of-square door and window openings and cracks in outer walls.

However, this kind of settlement often occurred many years ago and has since ceased. So it is quite common to find out-of-true walls, floors, roofs and ceilings in old properties where movement has stopped and there should be no danger of further troubles.

Cavity brick walls
Cavity wall construction involves the building of two withes of masonry with a cavity between the two; the withes are linked with metal ties for stability. Brick is used for both withes in older homes, but concrete or clay masonry units may be found in more recent houses. Except at the corners, only stretchers (length-wise) bricks will show on the surface of the wall. If the walls are stuccoed, you will probably be able to tell if it is a cavity wall by measuring its thickness at a doorway or window opening. Such walls are usually about 11in thick.

If built properly, cavity walls suffer few problems. The wide cavity provides sufficient circulation of air to prevent penetrating damp-ness. Such walls should be warmer than solid walls, particularly if insulation has been instal-led. If the house has been fully insulated, it is likely that the cavity has been filled with insulation material. You may be able to see this insulation by looking into the cavity from the attic, if it has not been properly sealed.

If the house was built within the last four or five years, it is likely that the cavity would have been filled during the construction with fiber-glass insulation batts (slabs).

Cracking and bowing can occur (see below) and if damp patches appear on the wall after rain, this can indicate that the wall has been badly built, possibly where mortar has been allowed to fall into the cavity and form a bridge by which damp can cross the wall ties.

Dressed stone walls
Houses built of stone will vary both in appear-ance and durability, according to the type of material used – usually of local origin. Dressed

The 1930s duplex

■ The 1930s duplex is a hybrid of many architectural styles, but the features common throughout the boom housebuilding period between the two World Wars were the hipped main roof, the symmetrical pairs of bay windows and the recessed porch. Inside, the biggest change from pre-war times was to an essentially square floor plan, with a rear living room giving onto the garden instead of the bleak back addition looking onto an enclosed yard.

■ The roof was generally tiled, initially in plain clay tiles but increasingly during the 1930s in curved pantiles, or covered with shingles. Tiled hips and ridges are finished with plain half-round tiles.

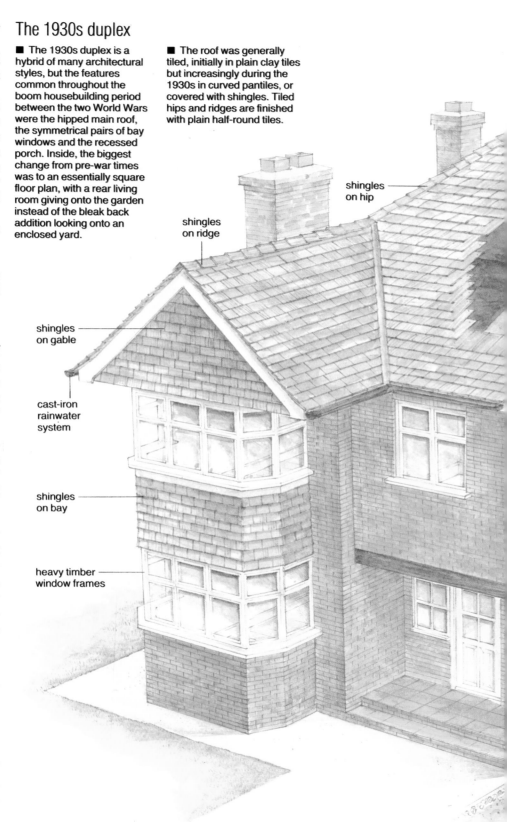

shingles on hip

shingles on ridge

shingles on gable

cast-iron rainwater system

shingles on bay

heavy timber window frames

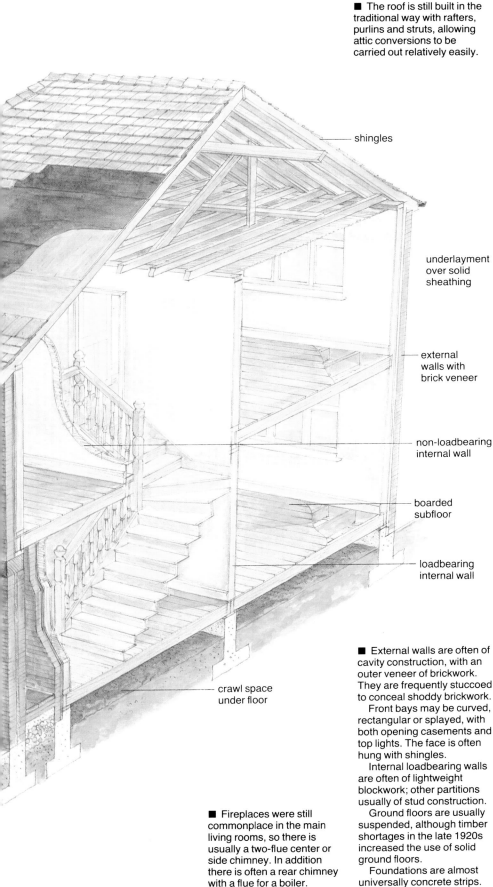

■ The roof is still built in the traditional way with rafters, purlins and struts, allowing attic conversions to be carried out relatively easily.

shingles

underlayment over solid sheathing

external walls with brick veneer

non-loadbearing internal wall

boarded subfloor

loadbearing internal wall

crawl space under floor

■ Fireplaces were still commonplace in the main living rooms, so there is usually a two-flue center or side chimney. In addition there is often a rear chimney with a flue for a boiler.

■ External walls are often of cavity construction, with an outer veneer of brickwork. They are frequently stuccoed to conceal shoddy brickwork.

Front bays may be curved, rectangular or splayed, with both opening casements and top lights. The face is often hung with shingles.

Internal loadbearing walls are often of lightweight blockwork; other partitions usually of stud construction.

Ground floors are usually suspended, although timber shortages in the late 1920s increased the use of solid ground floors.

Foundations are almost universally concrete strips.

stone blocks have a regular outline, rather like brickwork. In high quality houses, the stone can be very carefully cut with a dressed flat face called ashlar. More commonly, it has a split or rough projecting face.

Ashlar stone blocks are often backed with bricks and are plastered on the inside. Dressed stone walls are usually built in courses, like brickwork, and are normally of solid stone, bonded together with lime mortar (which is very soft) and plastered on the inside.

Modern 'stone' houses may be built with an outer stone veneer using pre-cast reconstituted blocks. In this case, the construction and any subsequent problems are exactly the same as with a modern brick veneer wall. The only difference is that, instead of an outer brick skin, stone building blocks are used.

Stone walls frequently suffer from dampness problems, while dressed stone has a tendency to crack along the mortar joints, like brickwork.

Natural stone walls

Some old cottages and houses are built with natural or 'random' stone walls. The material involved is used as found and is not dressed or cut to make uniform blocks. The stones are placed in a random style and the way the stones are keyed together depends entirely on the skill of the builder.

It is common for the spaces between the stones on the inner and outer walls to be packed with rubble. It is also quite usual for dressed stones to be selected to form corners.

Bricks may be used with natural stone walls where a regular building material is needed, such as at external corners (quoins) and for building chimney stacks.

Invariably, natural stone buildings were built on a foundation of stepped stones without a dpc. So rising dampness will be a likely problem and a definite candidate for early treatment.

Brick veneer walls

A modern wood-framed house with a brick veneer wall is strong and well-insulated, but has as much in common with a traditional building as chalk does to cheese! From the outside, it can look exactly like a conventional brick, stone or block-built house.

The main structural frame of this type of house is built as already described with 2×4in or 2×6in studs, faced with sheets of plywood, which provide stiffness and strength. The spaces behind the plywood sheeting, between the timber studs, are filled with non-combustible blanket insulation and the inside is faced with sheetrock (drywall). A moisture and vapour barrier of building paper is fixed to the face of the plywood sheathing and the exterior brick, stone or block cladding is built on the outside with galvanised metal ties screwed to the plywood sheathing to maintain a narrow cavity. This cavity ensures that if the brick outer skin becomes wet due to driving rain, any penetrating moisture does not reach the dry inner leaf.

Because sheetrock (drywall) is used for lining a timber-framed home, tapping the inside walls and listening for a hollow ring is one indication of this type of construction. Other tell-tale signs to look for are wide timber boards around window and door frame openings, while a visit to the loft may allow you to see the plywood-sheathed timber frame on the gable walls.

Hollow unit masonry wall

Another type of solid masonry wall is built up from hollow clay or concrete masonry units, laid with mortar like bricks. These are better insulators than brickwork, both because of the aggregates used to make them and because of the air pockets inside the blocks. They come in a range of sizes – lengths from 8 to 24in, heights of 4 and 8in and thicknesses ranging

from 4 to 12in. These blocks are also often used for the basement and foundation walls of wood-framed houses.

Walls built with these blocks can be a single block thick, but can also be made up of two or more units; if these are of different thicknesses the thicker block is laid on the outer face of the wall in one course and on the inner face in the next to improve the through-wall bonding. They are commonly laid horizontally in running or stretcher bond, but can be built up in stack bond (with reinforcement), or in ashlar bond (with alternating courses of 4in and 8in high blocks).

Reinforced masonry wall

House and apartment walls are sometimes built in brick or hollow unit masonry with steel reinforcement incorporated in the structure, especially if the wall may have to withstand extreme lateral wind or seismic loads.

The wall may consist of two withes of brickwork about 2in apart with horizontal ties between them, with both vertical and horizontal reinforcing rods set in the cavity; this is then filled with cement grout to bind the whole structure together. Alternatively, the wall may be built in hollow unit masonry with the cells in

■ **Below** The roof of a 1960s house is commonly finished in asphalt shingles. Its structure will probably consist of pre-fabricated trusses, making for ease of construction but causing difficulty in creating attic conversions.

External walls may be of cavity construction with a masonry veneer and a stud wall inner layer, set on concrete trench foundations. Parts may be covered in siding or shingles, or may have a plain stuccoed finish as a contrast to the exposed brickwork.

Internal walls are generally stud partitions clad with sheetrock (drywall).

Ground floors may be suspended or solid, with the former often given a sub-floor of plywood rather than diagonal boards.

There are generally no fireplaces, thanks to the widespread use of central heating.

The 1960s single-family house

■ The commonest features of the 1960s house are its low-pitched roof and the widespread use of bland picture windows. Garages are now an integral part of the design, frequently with a flat built-up roof linked to a boxy front porch.

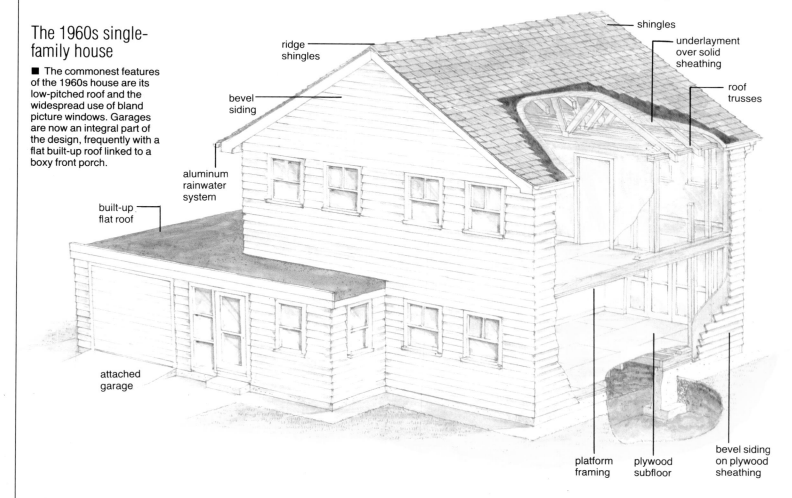

shingles

ridge shingles

underlayment over solid sheathing

roof trusses

bevel siding

aluminum rainwater system

built-up flat roof

attached garage

platform framing

plywood subfloor

bevel siding on plywood sheathing

The 1980s house

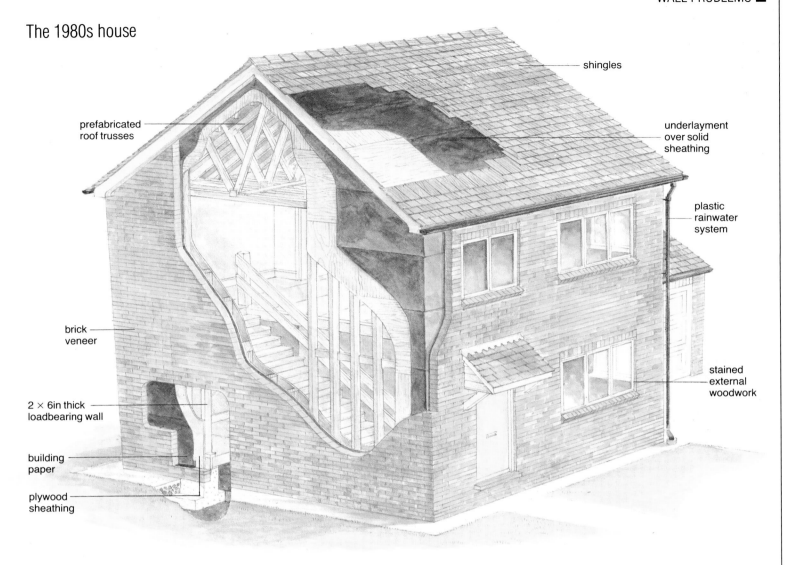

prefabricated
roof trusses

shingles

underlayment
over solid
sheathing

plastic
rainwater
system

brick
veneer

stained
external
woodwork

2 × 6in thick
loadbearing wall

building
paper

plywood
sheathing

■ The 1980s house is in direct line of descent from its 1960s predecessors, with its basically square plan. There is less external adornment for the most part, and more widespread use of woodstains instead of paint on exterior siding.

The roof is usually covered with asphalt shingles, on a structure of prefabricated trusses with a slope generally steeper than that of 1960s houses. Gabled and hipped styles are popular.

The external walls are load-bearing timber frames, often with a decorative brick or stone veneer.

Internal walls are generally wood stud partitions clad with sheetrock (drywall).

Floors are often solid or suspended concrete slabs downstairs, and suspended wood joists with a plywood subfloor upstairs.

the blocks aligned vertically and with reinforcing rods passing up through them; the cells containing the rods are then filled with grout. Extra horizontal joint reinforcement is also usually included in the structure.

WALLS AND THEIR PROBLEMS

Certain basic criteria apply to the walls of a house, whatever its construction, and you should check that your walls meet these requirements. For example, they should be straight both vertically and horizontally. Equally, there should not be any cracks or major deterioration of the building material from which the walls are made.

Make sure, too, that door and window openings are square. You can check this by measuring the diagonals. They will be equal if the frame is square.

Of course, with an old building you can expect the external masonry walls to be slightly

out of true. But there should not be signs of recent movement, such as fresh cracks. If you are considering a particularly old building it is certainly worth getting it checked out by a fully qualified architect or engineer.

Bowing walls

If walls are bowing outwards, this can indicate a serious fault. At ground level, it can mean that the foundations have moved, possibly due to settlement, and therefore underpinning could be required.

If the bowing is in the middle of the wall, then the problem is a weakness in the wall itself, probably caused by an excessive roof load. Either the framing or masonry used for the walls is not sufficiently substantial or the loading of the roof may be excessive. In the latter case, this could be caused by the use of a heavier replacement roof covering, for example.

You can usually detect a bowed wall by sighting along its surface. Because it tends to

fall away from the ends of the second-floor joists, another sign is a gap between wall and baseboard – or wall and floor – on the second-floor level of the house.

Specialist treatment will be required here, perhaps the insertion of steel tension rods at second-floor level or even the complete rebuilding of the wall.

If the bowing is outwards at the top of the wall, the problem is likely to be caused by a spread in the roof timbers, perhaps because the ties – that is, the ceiling joists – linking the rafters at attic-floor level or collars linking the rafters in the attic space have failed. This is usually associated with a sag in the ridge, so look for this fault too.

Again, this is a problem about which you must take specialist advice. Partial rebuilding of the roof and walls may be required, and this is likely to be both expensive and highly disruptive to your renovation schedule.

Cracking walls

If you discover any cracks in masonry walls, you must first decide whether the cracks are in the wall itself or are just in any decorative covering on the wall, such as stucco.

In the latter case, it is best to chip off a section of the cracked stucco to see if the crack extends to the base frame. Cracks in stucco are not too serious and can be repaired quite easily.

Fine hairline cracks in masonry that follow the mortar joints in a stepped diagonal line are usually unimportant, especially if they radiate from the corners of door and window openings, which are often weak points in a wall.

Cracks more than about ⅛in wide could be significant and may be an indication of more serious structural damage, such as settlement of the foundations, vibration from traffic, settlement, heave caused by tree roots or drying out of the subsoil.

Such cracks could indicate earlier movement which has now stopped. But if they re-open after they have been filled with mortar, this indicates that movement is still taking place. This can be confirmed by fixing small strips of glass, about the size of microscope slides, across the cracks at two or three positions, using an epoxy resin adhesive or mastic. The glass should be fixed just clear of the wall. If it cracks after a few weeks or months, this indicates continued movement in the wall.

Seek the advice of a professional as to the

■ Clapboarding is one of the most widespread exterior wall finishes, with its strong horizontal lines helping to make the building appear longer and lower. Where the siding is painted, the householder's major annual chore is keeping all the paintwork in good condition.

cause and cure of the problem. If the trouble is due to roots, the offending tree must be removed. If the problem is inadequate foundations, then underpinning is required. This is an expensive job involving excavation of the foundations section by section and the casting of a reinforced concrete beam under them.

The type of crack is often a useful guide to the problem. A stepped diagonal crack along the mortar line, for example, often indicates comparatively harmless general settlement, while a near-vertical line can mean more serious problems like subsidence. And a horizontal line can be a sign of sideways movement and is often accompanied by bowing.

The length and depth of the crack can also help to indicate the seriousness of the problem. Long cracks are usually more serious than short ones. Those that are visible both on the outside and the inside of a wall can be a sign of major structural faults.

The location of the cracks can also have a bearing on the likely cause of the fault. A diagonal crack running down the wall from high up on a corner can indicate settlement of the foundations at the end of the building. Cracks that start at the base of a wall and converge

upwards can indicate localized settlement between them. A vertical crack down a wall close to a corner can indicate a failure of the roof ties, allowing a section of the wall to fall outwards.

A straight crack between adjoining properties can also be a sign of settlement, while cracks along the join between a building and an addition can indicate inadequate bonding of the new wall to the old. Another cause can be a failure in the foundations of the addition. A vertical crack down a wall containing a chimney can indicate problems with the flue, possibly due to the drying of the internal masonry and damage to the flue lining. The flue itself may need to be rebuilt.

Bulging walls

If you suspect a bulging wall, check first that it is not bowed. In the case of a bulge, this is normally where the wall is stuccoed and the surface is coming away. Tap the affected area to see if it sounds hollow and test the stucco over a wider area to ascertain the extent of the problem. Look also for cracks in the surface.

There is always the danger that rainwater will get behind the stucco, making the wall damp and the problem worse. The loose material should be chipped away and the wall re-plastered after being allowed to dry out. This is certainly a job for a specialist if a large area of repair is involved.

Damp walls

Dampness in solid masonry exterior walls can be due to penetrating or rising damp – or it could be due to condensation.

You can eliminate or confirm condensation by taping a piece of aluminum foil to the wall. If water droplets form on the surface of the foil, condensation is the problem. This can be reduced by improving ventilation and heating.

Water droplets on the underside of the foil indicate dampness in the wall.

If the dampness is near the bottom of the wall, perhaps shown by a line of white efflorescence along the lower part on the outside and damp and peeling wallpaper inside, the problem is rising dampness due to the absence of a dampproof membrane (dpm) – or a faulty one. Old brick or stone foundation walls are most commonly affected.

Look for the dpm, which is visible as a thin black line between brick courses. If you find one, make sure it is at least 6in above ground level and is not covered by soil. If there is no

■ Many old buildings have rudimentary stone or brick foundations (1).

Concrete slabs with thickened edges support many wooden-framed homes (2), and also buildings with an outer brick veneer (3).

Platform framing is built up off concrete foundations (4) or off 8in concrete blocks (5), while wood foundations generally have a compacted gravel base (6).

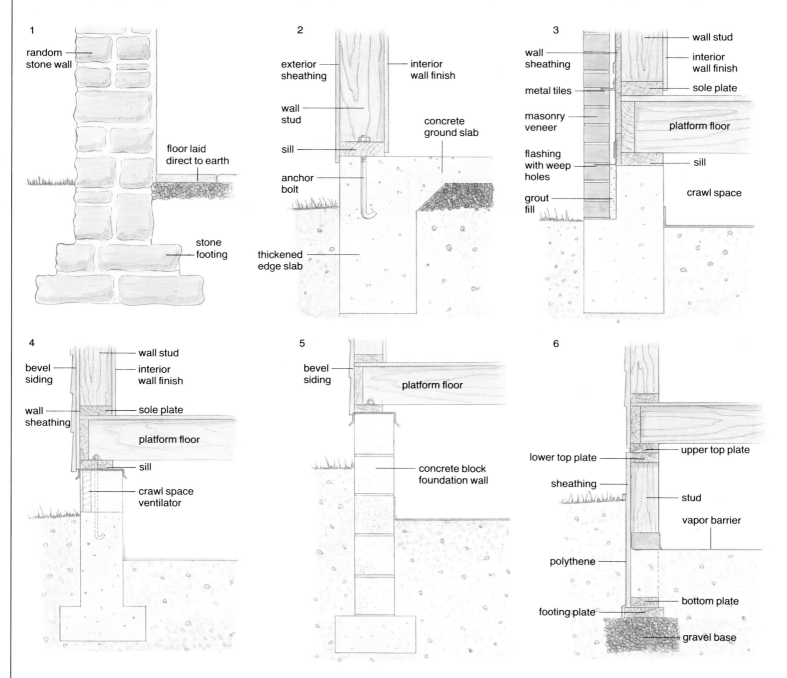

1 random stone wall; floor laid direct to earth; stone footing

2 exterior sheathing; interior wall finish; wall stud; concrete ground slab; sill; anchor bolt; thickened edge slab

3 wall sheathing; wall stud; interior wall finish; metal tiles; sole plate; masonry veneer; platform floor; flashing with weep holes; sill; grout fill; crawl space

4 bevel siding; wall stud; interior wall finish; wall sheathing; sole plate; platform floor; sill; crawl space ventilator

5 bevel siding; platform floor; concrete block foundation wall

6 lower top plate; upper top plate; sheathing; stud; vapor barrier; polythene; bottom plate; footing plate; gravel base

sign of a dpm, you may have to have one put in.

A conventional dpm can be inserted in a slot sawn in the bottom part of the wall. Alternatively a chemical dpm can be injected into the masonry. This work is usually best left to a specialist, although it is possible to insert a chemical dpm yourself.

Penetrating dampness is usually a problem with older brick or stone-built properties with solid walls and will show up worse after heavy rain. It can occur at any height. Look first for a leaking waste pipe or rainwater downspout and repair the fault where necessary.

Isolated damp patches are easily cured by painting the outside of the wall with a clear silicone water-repellent sealer. Larger areas, on the other hand, may require the addition of stucco, clapboarding or vinyl siding.

Rotting wood

With outer walls, rotting wood is obviously only a problem where you have a wood-clad or wood-framed building. The rot-affected wood must be removed and replaced with new wood, treated with preservative. If the rot is extensive, it is probably advisable to get a specialist carpenter to make the repairs.

Missing siding

Whether natural wood, aluminum or plastic is used for siding, any missing sections should be replaced without delay or serious damp problems and rot (in wood) could occur.

The damage could be the result of storms or other severe weather conditions. More likely, however, it is due to general deterioration, such as corrosion of the fixing nails, caused by water penetration. So be prepared for the fact that even a small amount of damage could indicate major renovation work.

Fixing up siding is a task that a competent handyman could quite easily tackle. If, however, large areas are involved, it may be better to call in a specialist contractor.

THE ROOF STRUCTURE

There are three aspects of the roof structure to consider – the shape, the structural framework (which you can see from inside the attic space), and the external roof covering (which you can see from outside).

The roof shape

Basically roofs are either sloping (pitched) or flat, the latter having just a slight slope to throw water towards the gutters. The majority of houses have pitched roofs, since these perform

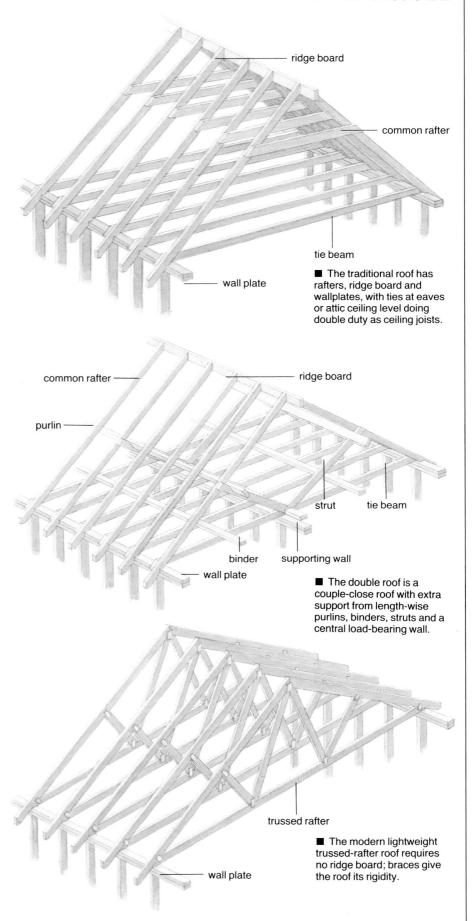

■ The traditional roof has rafters, ridge board and wallplates, with ties at eaves or attic ceiling level doing double duty as ceiling joists.

■ The double roof is a couple-close roof with extra support from length-wise purlins, binders, struts and a central load-bearing wall.

■ The modern lightweight trussed-rafter roof requires no ridge board; braces give the roof its rigidity.

best in potentially wet climates.

Flat roofs are cheaper and easier to build and tend to be used mainly for garages, home extensions, porches and some low-cost homes. Water does tend to collect on this type, however, and leaks are common. If you have a flat-roofed house, be prepared to spend quite heavily on maintenance.

The most common pitched type is the gable-end, where two sloping roofs meet at a central ridge which runs the full length of the roof. At each end a gable wall is built up to the ridge. On duplex houses it is common to have continuous pitched roofing running from one side of the building to the other.

With a hipped roof, the ends as well as the sides of the roof slope to the ridge, and the roof sections come down to the gutter level – that is, the eaves – all round. With a hipped gable roof, the hipped ends do not come down as low as the eaves and a part gable wall is formed.

A gambrel roof has a double pitch on each side of the ridge, thus forming a roof with two distinct slopes. Gables are formed on the end walls. With a gambrel hipped roof, the ends as well as the sides have a double pitch forming a gambrel roof all round the building.

A type of roof very rarely found on houses, but quite common on outbuildings, is the monopitch. Here the roof slopes from one side to the other. Lean-to roofs are found where one building, usually an extension, joins on to a larger building. The conventional lean-to is a monopitch type, but lean-to hip roofs are also found where the sides of the roof are inclined in the same way as the main roof section.

Carcassing framework
Flat roofs are usually formed by joists spanning two side walls with a decking of boards or plywood on which a weather-proofed surface such as mineral felt is laid. The basic problem here is damage or deterioration to the covering surface. If left for a long period without treatment, the resulting water leaks will penetrate the decking and cause an outbreak of rot in the roof joists.

Many methods of building pitched roofs have developed over the years. Single and double rafter roofs are found in very old houses and cottages. These roofs were carefully made using substantial timbers and, while it is possible to replace damaged wood, it is usually out of the question to contemplate an attic conservation or any other major structural alteration in historic roofs of this type.

From about the 19th century up to comparatively recent times, the traditional method of building ridged roofs with rafters supported by purlins and struts was used. With this type, it is possible to move the struts to allow for attic conversions, although the work must be carried out by specialists.

Such conversion is also possible with a trussed purlin roof. This type already has a clear space in the attic since there are no sloping central struts.

A collared roof is also built with rafters butting on to a central ridge. In this case, however, there are no trussed purlins. The rafters are supported by collar ties which brace the rafters quite high in the roof to give extra height to bedroom ceilings. In a roof of this type, there is sometimes insufficient headroom to allow for an attic conversion.

Modern houses are usually built with trussed rafters, where the trusses are prefabricated in a factory. There is no ridge board and no purlins. Diagonal braces are nailed (using metal plates) between the underside of the rafters and the top of the ceiling joists and the tiling battens are nailed directly to the upper surface of the trussed rafters. This type of roof is not suitable for an attic conversion because the trussed rafters cannot be modified.

ROOF COVERINGS

Depending on the age and style of the property and the type of roof construction, there is a whole range of covering materials you may find. So check what type you have, since the inherent problems they may have can vary from one roofing material to another.

Wood shingles and shakes
The best shingles and shakes are of red cedar, although white cedar and redwood are sometimes also used. Cedar has a fine, even grain and has natural resistance to water and rot. If left untreated, it weathers over the years to a silvery-gray color.

Sawn shingles are available in 16, 18 and 24in lengths and in three grades, and are nailed direct to spaced or solid sheathing. At ridges and hips the overlap alternates from one pair of shingles to the next.

Split shakes have one highly textured face, and come in 18 and 24in lengths. Because of their textured surface, they are nailed to the roof sheathing with asphalt felt interlayment between each course to prevent wind-driven rain or snow from penetrating between them.

Both shingles and shakes must be chemically treated to achieve the required UL class C rating for flammability.

■ The roof coverings on older properties show far greater variety than is found on modern buildings, and often reflect locally available materials such as shingles or slate (top). Even handmade clay tiles differ widely in color and texture from one area to another (center). Only with the advent of the machine-made and mass-produced shingle of today have roofs tended to monotonous uniformity.

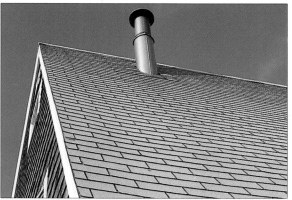

Fiberglass and asphalt shingles

These man-made shingles are formed in strips with two or three tabs in units measuring about 36 × 12in. Most have self-sealing adhesive or locking tabs to improve their wind resistance – vital if they are used on shallow roof slopes. Each shingle is usually nailed just above each cut-out, with a 5in exposure and 7in toplap.

Fiberglass types have an inorganic base that gives them excellent fire resistance (class A) as well as resistance to rot, moisture and curling, while asphalt types are only moderately fire-resistant (class C).

Plain tiles

These are sometimes found on older prop-

erties, mainly in urban areas. Usually made of clay, but sometimes of sand-faced concrete, they come with matching special units for finishing off at ridges, hips, rakes and eaves. The tiles are fixed over solid plywood shea-thing, with an under-layment of roofing felt to prevent draughts and water leaks into the loft space. Watch out for cracked, broken and frost-damaged tiles. These indicate that re-roofing is required. Old roofs with many missing, cracked or broken tiles will definitely need complete re-roofing.

Interlocking tiles

These tiles are sometimes used for re-roofing, especially as a replacement for old slate roofing. As the name suggests, the sides of the tiles – and sometimes the heads – interlock. Laid in single layers, the tiles will be lined with underfelt to eliminate draughts in the loft space.

Slate

Although very satisfactory when sound, slates can give problems when they get old. Nail sickness causes them to slip out of place, while natural ageing will give rise to delamination.

Slates may be nailed to battens or, in better quality housing, the roof may be boarded and the slates nailed directly to the boards. Old roofs are rarely lined, which causes the attic space to be drafty, dirty and cold. If you are re-roofing, you can fit underlayment beneath the slates to cure this problem.

It is worth replacing old slates with new natural or imitation slates to maintain the original style of the property. In recent years it has been popular to replace an old slate roof with interlocking concrete tiles. These often spoil the look of the house and are frequently out of keeping with adjacent ones.

Corrugated roofing sheets, which come in metal, fiber/cement or plastic, are mainly confined to use on outbuildings, although occasionally they are used for houses. Although functional, if found on a house they would be better replaced with another type of roofing material more sympathetic to the surroundings.

Roofing felt is widely used for waterproofing flat roofs. Usually three layers are used. The first is nailed down to the roof boards, while the second and third are bonded to the first using hot bitumen. The surface is liable to blister and crack and after about 15 years the roof may need to be re-covered.

Asphalt can be used as a covering and is normally applied in a layer about ¾in thick over underlayment. Working with hot asphalt is a

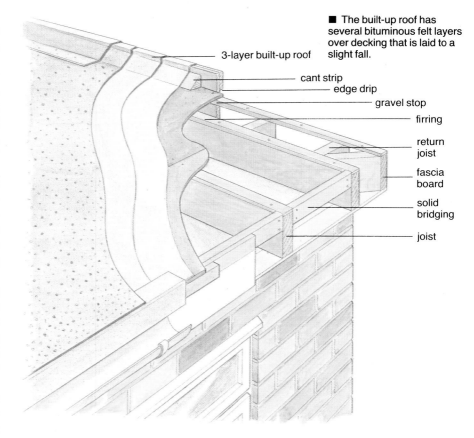

■ The built-up roof has several bituminous felt layers over decking that is laid to a slight fall.

3-layer built-up roof
cant strip
edge drip
gravel stop
firring
return joist
fascia board
solid bridging
joist

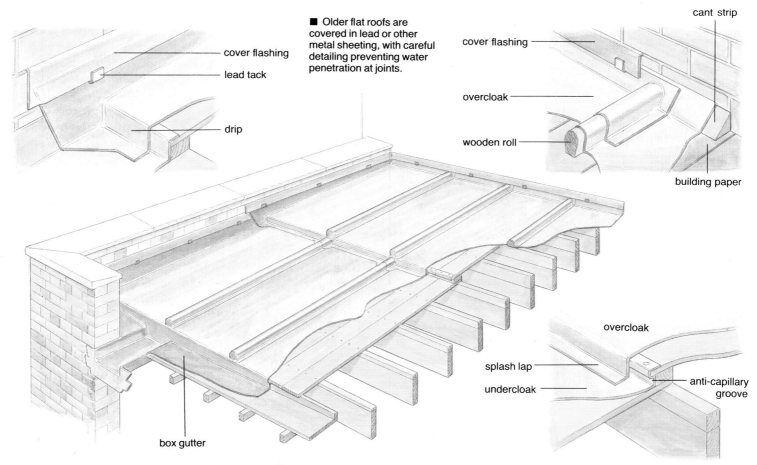

cover flashing
lead tack
drip

■ Older flat roofs are covered in lead or other metal sheeting, with careful detailing preventing water penetration at joints.

cover flashing
cant strip
overcloak
wooden roll
building paper

box gutter

overcloak
splash lap
undercloak
anti-capillary groove

skilled job. Although cracks, if they form, can be repaired with cold mastic, it is best to get a flat-roof specialist to carry out any major repairs with this material.

ROOFS AND THEIR PROBLEMS

Whatever type of roof you have or find on a property you are considering buying, there are some basic problems you should be aware of and look out for. They will, of course, depend on the construction itself and the covering used.

Sagging roof
If the roof is sagging, this could indicate serious problems, unless the property is very old and the original cause has settled down.

If the ridge is straight and the sag is confined to a saucer-like depression in the roof covering, it is likely that the trouble is the result of poor construction of the part of the roof. Probably there are insufficient purlins to support the rafters or the cross-bracing is insufficient. It is also possible that the rafters are too weak, so check that they have not rotted or been severely attacked by insects.

It may be possible to brace the roof to prevent the trouble getting any worse. In some cases it may even be possible to jack the roof back into line before re-bracing it.

If the ridge itself is sagging, and perhaps the roof covering too, then the trouble is likely to be more serious – and so more expensive to put right. It may well be that the roof timbers have been affected by rot or insect attack. Examination in the attic should reveal the extent of this problem.

If there is no sign of rot or insect attack, then look for possible insecure fixing of the roof timbers, which would allow the roof to splay outwards, or even movement outwards of the top of the wall. The latter is particularly serious. By dropping a plumb line down from the top of the wall at the eaves, you may be able to highlight the problem, which may well have been evident when you checked for bowing.

Hogged roof
This is a fault common to terraced houses. The roof falls away from the party wall, leaving the roof tiles or slates along that wall sticking up, with large gaps under them.

It is due to settlement of the foundations and, as long as the settlement has ceased, should not give cause for concern. It is, however, worth getting an architect or engineer to confirm this. A vertical crack between the front wall and the party wall should give cause for concern.

Rippling
Slight undulations along the ridge are sometimes difficult to spot, but they are a sign that the rafters have been spaced too far apart. If the rippling is in the roof surface, this also indicates that the rafters are too widely spaced.

A check in the attic space will confirm these faults and reveal whether rot or insect attack in the roof timbers is the cause. In the latter case, take steps to eliminate the trouble. Not much can be done about over-wide rafter spacing and there is no need to do anything unless the trouble gets worse.

Deteriorating coverings
If shingles, tiles or slates have cracked, slipped, delaminated, or are missing over a wide area, you have no option but to recover the roof. This is expensive, but does give you a chance to line the roof with underlayment, which will make the attic space drier, cleaner and warmer.

As a temporary solution, you can apply an all-over treatment, involving coating the roof with three layers of heavy duty bitumen liquid reinforced with fiberglass fabric membrane. This is much cheaper than re-roofing and can extend the roof life for 10 to 15 years. But it is not attractive to look at and eventually re-roofing will be required.

Faulty flashing
Flashings, which may be of metal (usually lead) or asphalt felt, waterproof the joints where the roof joins brickwork such as a house wall or chimney stack. Metal flashings corrode and felt flashings crack and pull away from the wall. In both cases, water can trickle down behind the flashing, resulting in damp patches on upstairs ceilings or walls.

Temporary repairs can be made quite easily and cheaply with self-adhesive metal-backed flashing strip. Ideally, new lead flashings should be fitted in the long term.

Rotting wood
Barge boards, fascias and soffits are made of wood and as such, are prone to damage and rotting from the elements. So check regularly that all the wood round the perimeter of the roof is sound.

They are fairly easy to replace, although highly decorative barge boards can be expensive to recreate using new wood. The job will usually involve erecting scaffolding, which is expensive, or using a platform tower; you cannot carry out the work safely from a ladder. Prise off the old wood section by section and nail up the replacements to the rafter ends.

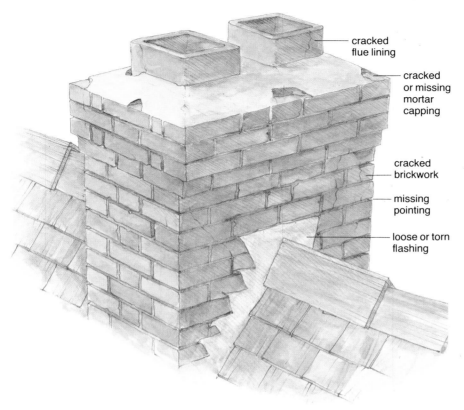

cracked flue lining

cracked or missing mortar capping

cracked brickwork

missing pointing

loose or torn flashing

CHIMNEYS AND THEIR PROBLEMS

Chimney stacks are particularly vulnerable to damage, being exposed to the elements and also to attack from the inside by flue gases.

Use binoculars to examine the chimney first from ground level. If it is leaning and still being used, you will have to have it rebuilt. If it is obsolete, you could have it capped, which would be cheaper. If the mortar joints in the brickwork are crumbling away, these must be repointed. This could be an expensive job if the chimney is difficult to reach and a lot of access equipment is required.

If the flue caps are cracked, leaning or missing and the flues are still being used, they must be replaced. The layer of mortar in which they are bedded must also be replaced to ensure that rainwater is thrown clear of the top of the chimney.

Faults with the flue caps are likely to indicate problems with the stack itself and with the flue lining, which may need to be replaced if the flue is still used. You can fit some types yourself, which will save some expense.

If the flues are unused, the best solution is to remove the flue caps and fit capping slabs to give ventilation to the flues to keep them dry. At the same time, the stack can be reduced in height by removing brickwork down to just above the roof slope if it is in poor condition.

■ Chimneys are very exposed to the elements and can suffer from a variety of faults (above), including cracked mortar cappings round the flue liners and defective pointing on the chimney itself, both of which can allow water to penetrate and cause damp in the masonry and rot in the roof structure.

As the deterioration continues, the chimney may start to lean (left) or to deteriorate alarmingly.

The other major weak spot is the junction between the chimney and the roof slope, which is traditionally waterproofed with stepped lead flashings (right). These can be lifted and torn by high winds, or may simply become porous with age. Their failure again allows water penetration.

STRUCTURAL MEMBERS AND THEIR PROBLEMS

All wood in the house must be inspected for wood rot and insect attack. There should be no visible signs of active wood rot in any house, regardless of its age.

In an old property it is common to find evidence of insect attack that has probably long since died out. This will be nothing to worry about if the roof or walls are not sagging, bowing or showing other signs of weakness.

In such houses, the wooden components were of sufficient size to allow for a certain amount of insect attack without causing problems – unless, of course, the extent of the attack was particularly severe.

Insect attack

There are several different species of wood-boring insects that can infest structural woodwork. They all eat through wood and leave round exit holes in the surface as they emerge.

In many cases attacks will have died out. But active infestation can be spotted by inspecting the woodwork (ideally during the summer months when they are most active) to look for fresh bore dust under and around holes. Clean wood inside the exit holes also indicates they are new and the attack is active.

If there is an active attack, the wood must be treated with the appropriate insecticide. At the same time affected floorboards, joists and roof timbers should be tested for weakness and any badly weakened wood should be replaced. This is a job for extermination specialists and, depending on the extent of the damage, it could be expensive work.

Wood rot

Basically, there are two types of wood rot that affect structural components – wet and dry. The latter is the more serious.

Wet rot affects wood in wet, cold environments and turns it dark brown so that it crumbles away when touched or probed. Often cracks form and these will be along the grain.

Dry rot also affects damp wood, especially where ventilation is poor. Once established, the wood can take on a shrunken, dry, cracked appearance, hence the name dry rot. Affected wood develops deep cracks across the grain, while the fungus itself produces grey conductive strands that can even penetrate walls to affect wood elsewhere in the building.

A distinctive musty smell accompanies a dry rot attack. Under floors, in roof spaces and in basements you may discover fluffy cotton-wool type growths and pancake-like fruiting bodies with reddish-brown centers.

All affected wood must be removed back to sound timber, brickwork must be treated with dry rot fluid and replacement wood must be treated with wood preservative. Repairs involving ceilings, floors and walls could be extensive – and therefore expensive.

■ Wood-boring insects can do considerable damage to structural timbers (left), especially if the infestation is not treated. However, the damage is rarely anything like as severe as that caused by dry rot (below left), which can completely destroy timber.

RENOVATING THE EXTERIOR

The obvious place to start work on renovating your house is with the exterior. There is little point in tackling internal improvements if the outer envelope of the house lets in the wind and rain. A top-to-toe overhaul is the solution, working from the roof downwards via the exterior walls, doors and windows, and culminating in a check of the building's resistance to dampness rising from below.

Roofs and Guttering

CHECKING THE ROOF

It is obviously vital to have a sound, well-maintained roof. If it is allowed to deteriorate, it will soon let in rain. This in turn will lead to damp patches on internal walls and ceilings and ruined decorations.

If that is not bad enough, by allowing a leak to go unattended it will not be long before the structure of the roof starts to decay, possibly leading to dry rot in the roof timbers and wall plates. This could spread over a wide area of the fabric of the house, necessitating very expensive remedial work which must be carried out by a specialist contractor.

The roof could also become a danger to passers-by. Injury to a third party caused by a falling shingle may result in legal proceedings, so make sure that the risk is covered by your homeowner's policy. The possible consequences could otherwise be very serious. So it is important to make sure the roof is completely sound before you make any effort to repair and restore the rest of the property.

With roofwork, it is definitely a question of prevention being better than cure. If you can reposition a shingle while it is only partially dislodged before it slides out completely – or replace one that is only cracked and not completely broken – you will prevent the formation of brown damp patches on ceilings and internal walls that will not only spoil interior decorations but also be difficult to cure.

The main problem with doing your own repairs is the danger of working at a height, which can be intimidating. Safety is a very important consideration. But even if you would not dream of working on the roof, being able to spot potential problems and knowing how they should be repaired will enable you to brief a contractor thoroughly and not be persuaded to accept substandard work. It is a sad fact of life that many homeowners are completely ignorant of what work is carried out on their roofs. As a result, the roofing business includes its fair share of con-men.

Knowing how your roof is constructed is the first step to being able to keep it in good condition, whether or not you carry out the repair work yourself. And carrying out regular checks on its condition is a practice you would do well to use. You can do this from ground level using a pair of binoculars.

cracked capping

cracked flue lining

defective pointing

damaged or torn flashings

rotten eaves trim

■ To check on the condition of your house roof, the next best thing to a bird's eye view is an inspection carried out at eaves level from a ladder. On pitched roofs, look for shingles or tiles that are cracked, out of position or missing altogether. Check too that ridges, hips and valleys are weatherproof. On flat or low-pitched roofs, make sure that sheet materials are intact and securely fixed.

Take this opportunity to check the condition of chimneys and flue caps – with binoculars if necessary – and also of gutters and eaves-level trim.

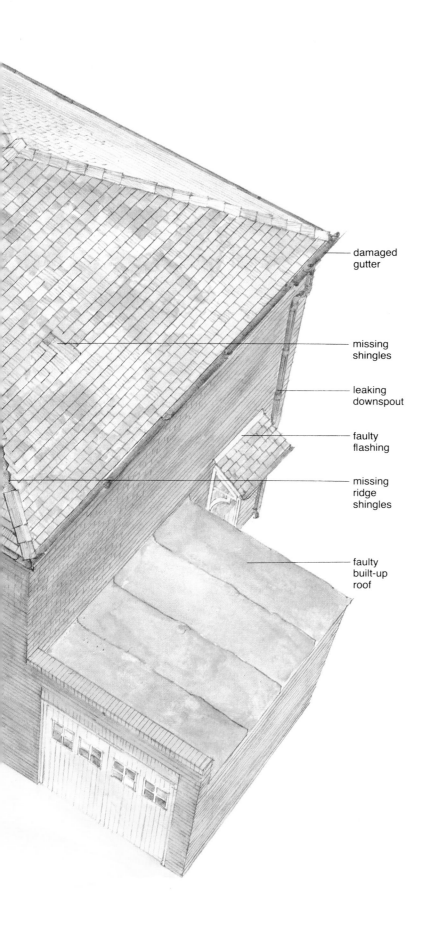

damaged
gutter

missing
shingles

leaking
downspout

faulty
flashing

missing
ridge
shingles

faulty
built-up
roof

Look for missing and cracked shingles and watch for damaged or crumbling pointing in chimney flues and parapet walls. Check also for cracked or leaning flue caps. The mortar around the caps should also be free of cracks and not obviously loose.

Flashing, which may be of lead or zinc sheet or felt, is used to waterproof the joints where a roof abuts an adjacent wall – possibly a house wall, parapet wall or chimney flue. This frequently cracks or pulls away from the cladding, allowing rainwater to trickle down behind it and eventually to cause damp patches to appear on internal walls or ceilings.

Check also that your chimney stacks are not leaning. If they are, you will need specialist advice since rebuilding a chimney is definitely not a do-it-yourself job!

On a wet day, it will pay to go outside and look at the guttering in case there are any leaks. These often occur at downspouts and at joints between gutter sections. Water dripping over the edge of a gutter can indicate that it is blocked by debris or that moss or other vegetation is growing there.

Also on a wet day, or shortly after rain, go into the attic and look for leaks. These will highlight cracked or missing shingles and possibly cracks in flashings and in lead or zinc-lined valley gutters.

As well as knowing enough to be able to tell a contractor the extent of the trouble, it is helpful to know the names of the various roof components in case you have to brief someone to carry out the repairs.

HOW ROOFS ARE MADE

It is best to start with a knowledge of roof construction so you will understand how your roof is made and therefore will be better able to carry out repairs on it yourself or get someone in to do the work for you.

Roofs basically fall into two types – flat or pitched – and it is quite common to find both on a property. For example, the main house may have a pitched roof and the garage or a one-storey addition a flat built-up felted roof.

Flat roofs
These are the simplest type and are often found on garages and home extensions and sometimes on house features such as bay windows. In fact they are not completely flat but slope slightly to one side or end to direct rainwater into a gutter.

They consist basically of a series of joists which span the walls at each side of the building.

The joists usually rest on a wall plate bedded on top of the stud wall. The joists are fixed to the wall plate by nailing.

With an addition, the joists are often notched on to a wall plate bolted to the house wall. Alternatively the joists are supported on that side by joist hangers screwed to the wall. They are covered with plywood sheathing and water-proofed with two or three layers of roofing felt. Cross ventilation via soffit vents is essential to prevent condensation from causing rot in the roof timbers.

Pitched roofs

This type slopes at varying angles. The simplest is the lean-to, which is widely used on single-storey additions and lean-tos built on to a house. It is constructed with rafters resting on a wall plate at one side and supported by a wall plate bolted to the house wall or by joist hangers, in a similar fashion to a flat roof, but at a much steeper angle.

Pitched roofs may be covered with glass or plastic where it is necessary to let in plenty of light. They can, of course, also be covered with any type of traditional pitched roof covering. The roof slopes at each side from a central ridge. Traditionally, the rafters rest against a central ridge board at the apex, while at the eaves they are notched into a wall plate and tied together with ceiling joists. The rafters are supported with purlins, which are in turn stiffened with cross-braces. This type of roof is constructed on site and is normally fairly easy to adapt if you decide you would like to have an attic conversion in the future.

The modern roof is often constructed with prefabricated trussed rafters, in which case there is no ridge board or purlins. Diagonal bracing timbers are nailed to the undersides of the rafters and plywood sheathing is fixed to their upper surface. This type is often of much lower pitch than the traditional one. Because of this – and its prefabricated method of construction – it is not suitable for conversion into additional attic space.

Three types of covering are commonly found on older pitched roofs – slates, plain tiles and shingles of various types.

Because of their age, slate roofs are often unlined, the slates being nailed directly to the roof sheathing. You will find some lined with felt underlayment beneath the slates.

If a slate roof has been replaced in the last 20 years or so, it is likely that the roof may have been lined with felt. This makes the attic space warmer, drier and cleaner. An examination of the attic area will tell you whether felt is present or not.

To make the roof waterproof, alternate rows of slates are staggered and each row overlaps the one below by about half its length. At any

■ Roofs come in a wide range of styles. The simplest are the flat roof (1) and the shed roof (2), usually found only on outbuildings and small single-storey buildings. Small additions and porches may have a lean-to roof (3), which may be hipped at each end to improve its looks (4).

House roofs are most commonly either gabled (5) or hipped (6), but other more elaborate styles are also found. These include the gambrel roof (7), the hipped mansard roof (8), the hipped gable roof (9) and the square hipped roof (10).

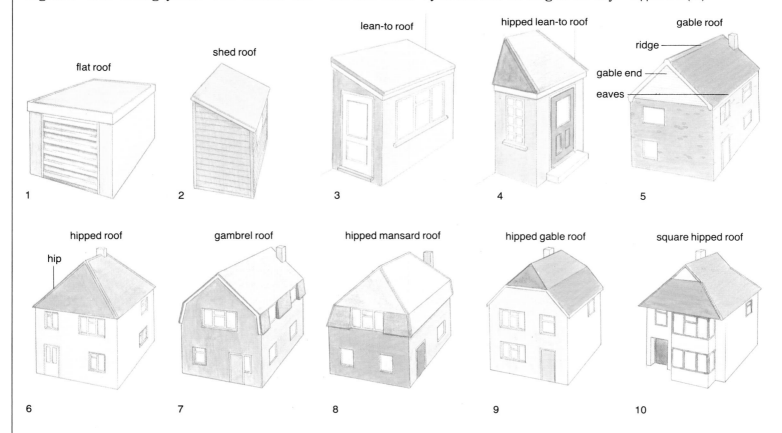

flat roof

shed roof

lean-to roof

hipped lean-to roof

gable roof

ridge

gable end

eaves

1 2 3 4 5

hipped roof

hip

gambrel roof

hipped mansard roof

hipped gable roof

square hipped roof

6 7 8 9 10

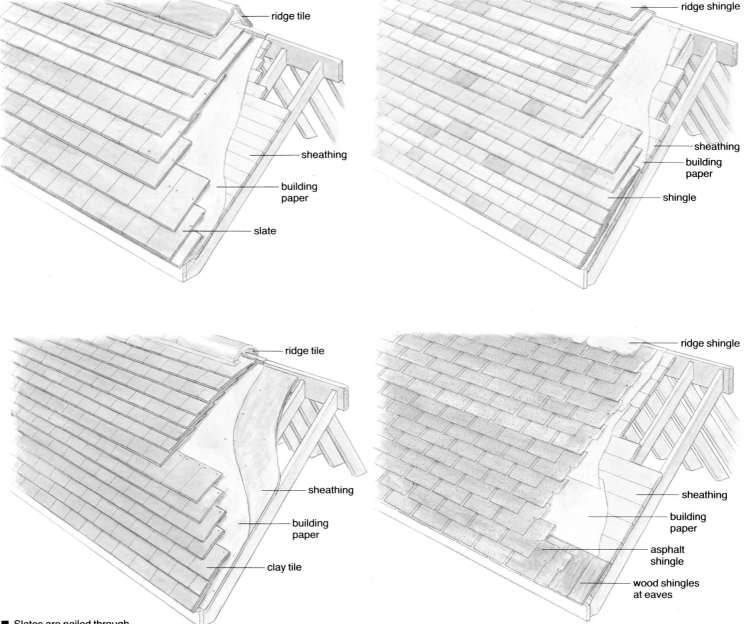

ridge tile

sheathing

building paper

slate

ridge shingle

sheathing

building paper

shingle

ridge tile

sheathing

building paper

clay tile

ridge shingle

sheathing

building paper

asphalt shingle

wood shingles at eaves

■ Slates are nailed through the head or centre line to open boards or continuous sheathing laid across the rafters. Each overlaps just over half the length of the slate beneath it.

Shingles are split timber rectangles used like slates, again nailed to open boards or to solid sheathing.

Plain tiles are nailed to the roof sheathing in regular courses. They may be laid in single or double lap.

Asphalt shingles are made in strips with tabs so one strip gives the appearance of three separate shingles, and are nailed directly to the roof sheathing. The eaves course is often laid over wood shingles.

particular point, there are at least two – and perhaps three – thicknesses of slate.

It is also possible for a plain-tiled roof to be unlined, in which case the attic space will be dirty and draughty. You might be lucky and find a roof that is lined with felt.

Plain tiles are hung overlapping, so that at any particular point there is a minimum of two tile thicknesses to ensure the roof is watertight. Alternate rows are staggered so that the joints between tiles do not line up.

Interlocking tiles are also used for re-roofing and sometimes replace an old slate roof. Usually made of concrete, but sometimes of clay, they are usually found on relatively

modern houses. And because these roofs tend to be newer, they are often lined with felt. The sides of the tiles, and sometimes the heads, are specially shaped so that the adjacent tiles interlock with one another along their edges to form a watertight roof surface.

Shingles and shakes may be laid over spaced or solid sheathing, with an exposure that depends on the roof slope, the shingle size and the grade of wood used. Underlayment is not normally used with shingles except where additional insulation is needed or blizzard conditions are common, but interlayment is essential with shakes because their textured surface prevents them from fitting closely together.

WORKING IN SAFETY

Because undertaking repairs or maintenance inevitably means working at a height, there will always be an element of danger. So make sure you never cut corners on any aspects of safety when working on a roof.

Always use a roof ladder or crawling boards and, if possible, provide access to the roof ladder from properly erected scaffolding or staging, rather than an ordinary ladder. The latter may, of course, be sufficient for minor repairs. It is best to put up staging if you are working at gutter level – replacing gutters or painting or replacing soffit boards or fascias.

You can buy a staging platform or tower. However, since you will need to use it only occasionally, you may prefer to rent one. The platform height should be about 5ft below the eaves if you are working on the gutters or level with the eaves if you are working on the roof.

Most staging platforms have a base size of about 4ft square and can be used freestanding with a platform height of up to 12ft. Above this height they should be fitted with stabilizer legs and should also be securely braced to the building. The best way to do this is to insert stout hooks into the wall framework and secure the ropes to these. Alternatively, tie the tower to a window frame mullion if one is nearby.

Platforms are supplied in sections and are quickly and easily erected by slotting together the lightweight frames, diagonal braces, decking boards, handrails and safety toe boards. Adjustable base plates are a must, since these allow you to get the first frames square and level, thus ensuring the tower is erected precisely vertically.

You can use a ladder to gain access to the roof for minor repairs. In this case, there must be at least three rungs above gutter level if you are going to climb on to the roof. It is best to hold the top of the ladder slightly away from the guttering to prevent damaging it. Use a ladder stay, which has rubber feet to prevent the top of the ladder from slipping sideways. With plastic or aluminum gutters, the use of a ladder stay is essential to avoid damaging them.

The top of the ladder must be securely tied to the building. Use rope passed through a large screw eye inserted into the wall framework or, where possible, anchored to a nearby chimney stack or other feature.

As already mentioned, a roof ladder or crawling boards are essential for working on the roof itself. Both can be pushed easily up the roof. When you reach the top, roll the ladder

ladder stay

ladder stabilisers

■ Always use a special roof ladder (right) for carrying out repairs to pitched roofs. Push the ladder up the roof slope, then turn it over so the hook engages over the ridge. Gain access to the roof ladder from an extension ladder to which the roof ladder should be securely roped for safety.

For work on chimneys, use interlocking platform tower components to construct a safe, sturdy working platform all round the chimney.

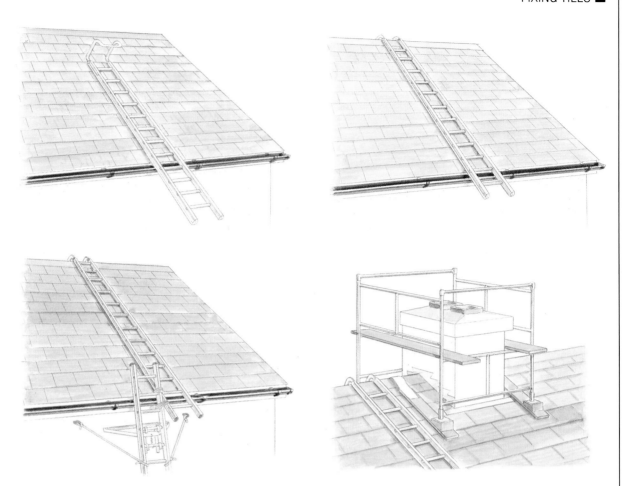

■ **Left** Extension ladders are the most popular item of access equipment for many outdoor home renovation jobs. When using one, always ensure that there is a four-rung overlap between the sections and that the ladder is set up at the correct angle, with the foot of the ladder 1m or 1ft out from the wall for every 4m or 4ft of ladder height. Use a ladder stay to hold the head of the ladder clear of overhanging eaves.

For additional safety, tie the head of the ladder to stout masonry anchors in the house walls, or to a baulk of timber inside a window opening. Fit ladder stabilisers for use on flat, solid surfaces, or set the ladder foot on sacking and weight it with a sandbag. On soft surfaces stand the ladder on a board with a batten screwed to it to stop it slipping or sinking.

over so that the large hook on the end clips over the ridge and prevents it from sliding back down the roof. It is essential that your roof ladder spans from ridge to eaves.

If you do not want to rent a roof ladder, you can get a ladder hook set to convert an ordinary ladder into a roof crawling set.

If you need to carry out minor chimney repairs and the stack is not large, it may be possible to do this from a roof ladder. If extensive work is required or the chimney is large, then you should rent a chimney scaffold set. This will form a safe working platform on all sides of the stack, regardless of the slope of the roof. Reach it via a roof ladder.

FIXING TILES

On the whole, tiles are easy to remove and replace, so it is not worth trying to patch them up if they have cracked or are broken. The only exception is for emergency repairs or if replacement tiles are not readily available.

To make temporary repairs, there is a simple method you can use. First, ease up the tiles in the row above the broken tile using small timber wedges. Cover the crack or missing

piece of tile using self-adhesive flashing strip. (This is metal-backed and normally used for flashing repairs.) If the tiles have a sandy finish, it may be necessary to paint the surface with flashing strip primer. This is supplied with the rolls of flashing strip.

Alternatively, you can use waterproof repair tape or trowel-on roofing caulk, which can be reinforced with patches of roofing felt or strips of aluminum kitchen foil.

Replacing a tile

Ease up the tiles in the row above the damaged or missing one, using small timber wedges. In most cases plain tiles will simply lift out. Sometimes, however, the tiles are held with nails, particularly in the case of interlocking ones. Here you must prise the tile up to pull the nails out. You may have to rent a slate ripper, which can be used to cut through the nails or pull them out, or to use a long hacksaw blade to reach up under the tiles.

With the adjacent tiles still wedged up, lift the new tile into place. When the tile is correctly positioned, you can remove the wedges so the other tiles above drop back into place. Check that the new tile aligns with them.

■ To replace a missing or damaged tile, drive timber wedges in to raise the tiles next to the affected area. If the damaged tile cannot be lifted out easily, release it by using a slater's ripper to cut through the nails holding it to the tiling batten. Then slide a replacement tile into place and remove the wedges.

To secure loose ridge tiles, lift the tile off and chip away any old mortar. Then bed the edges of the tile on fresh mortar and point between it and its neighbors.

FIXING SLATES

Slates are held in place with two nails driven into the boarding beneath. In time, these nails corrode (a problem known as nail sickness) and the slates slip out of place. If this happens over a wide area, it is best to replace the entire roof. But if the damage is only in patches, it is worth just replacing the slates so long as you can obtain replacements (demolition contractors and salvage firms are worth trying).

Where you have to replace several slates together, you can refix the lower ones by nailing them in to the sheathing as usual, working up the roof. It will, however, be impossible to nail in the final slates. These will have to be held in place with strips of metal, usually lead, called tingles. These are also used to hold isolated slates in place, where these have slipped out.

Nail the tingle to the sheathing between the two slates below the one being fixed. The tingle should be of sufficient length so that when the slate is pushed back into position, the protruding end of the tingle can be bent up and over the bottom edge of the slate to hold it firmly in place in line with its neighbors.

FIXING SHINGLES AND SHAKES

If individual wood shingles or shakes are cracked here and there, remove any loose splinters, butt the sides of the split tightly together and nail it to the sheathing with corrosion-resistant nails. Then fill and cover the crack with asphalt roofing cement.

If cracking is extensive it is better to replace the shingles completely. Use a chisel to split the shingle into narrow strips that can be pulled out easily, then cut through the fixing nails with a hacksaw blade. Cut a replacement shingle to fit the width available, slide it into place and nail it to the sheathing.

If the overall condition of a shingle roof is poor, you can lay a complete new layer of shingles over the existing ones. Cut back the old shingles along the eaves and up the rakes, and nail on 1 × 6in strips of pressure-treated or naturally rot-resistant siding. Strip the old ridge and hip covering and fit bevel siding strips instead with the butt edges overlapping at the peak of the roof. Then fix new shingles working from the eaves upwards, just as if you were covering a new roof. Finish off with new ridge shingles fixed with alternate overlaps.

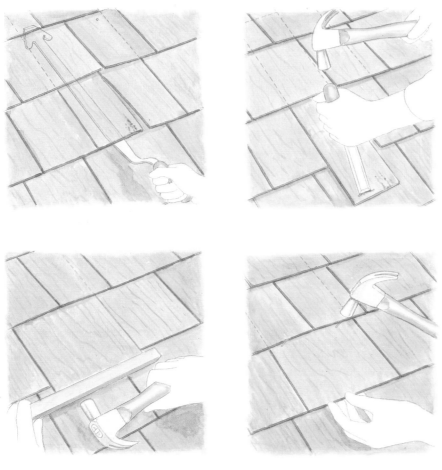

■ To release a damaged shingle, cut through the fixing nails using a hacksaw blade or a slater's ripper. Slide out the split pieces, and pull out any exposed fixing nails. Slide the new shingle into position level with its neighbors and nail it to the roof sheathing with galvanized nails.

RE-ROOFING

There comes a stage when so much patching up is needed to keep a roof watertight that more extensive repairs are required. The ultimate answer is to re-roof, although one alternative is to cover the surface with a membrane-reinforced bitumen 'skin'.

A membrane treatment can be used on pitched or flat roofs and applying one is well within the scope of the competent amateur. Basically it involves brushing liquid bitumen on to the roof, pressing reinforcing mesh fabric into the wet sealer and then applying more bitumen (see Repairing a flat roof).

This type of treatment is ideal for flat roofs, since it is easy to apply and the end result is not visible from the ground. On pitched roofs, however, being on a slope it is harder to apply and is clearly visible afterwards.

In the case of a flat roof, re-roofing is normally a straightforward, if lengthy, job that you can consider tackling yourself, particularly if the roof involved is on a garage or an extension to the house.

Replacing a pitched roof is another matter altogether. To get the work done quickly and ensure the roof is open for the shortest possible time, most people will opt to have the work done by an approved contractor.

In most cases, larger companies will guarantee both the work and the materials for a period of time, which is important. Not only does this ensure the property is protected, but it will also enhance its value.

Although the majority of new roofs are made with fiberglass shingles, apart from the expense there is no reason why the original type of roofing tiles or slates cannot be replaced. Sound secondhand tiles are still sometimes available, while to replace slates you can choose metal sheeting that looks quite realistic.

If you are re-roofing your house, you do get the opportunity to check the rafters, replace sheathing where required and ensure the attic area is draftproof and watertight. Related jobs such as repairs to chimneys and flashing can be carried out at the same time.

REPAIRING A FLAT BUILT-UP ROOF

By their very nature, flat roofs tend to present more problems than pitched ones. Although they should have been built with a slight fall to enable water to run off, pools of water tend to form on the surface. The wide variation in temperature to which a flat roof is subjected will often separate the covering layers and crack them. Inevitably leaks will occur.

You can reduce any expansion and contraction by topping the roof with a layer of white solar-reflective gravel. In time, however, this tends to be washed away.

Where the gravel is sparse or missing altogether, coat the roof with bitumen roofing compound and scatter fresh gravel over the surface, pressing it into the bitumen with a light wooden roller. This should give the roof a few years' extra life.

When you are up on the roof, check whether you can find any other existing or imminent problems. Obviously, if you notice a leak inside, you will not wait for a general inspection before carrying out any necessary repairs.

With a water leak, remember that the point at which you notice the stain inside the roof may be some distance from the problem area. Because it is common for the felt layers to separate, water trickling through the top layer may travel some distance under the felt before appearing on the ceiling below.

When you inspect a flat roof, there are some general signs of potential problems to watch out for. If the top layer of felt has started to wrinkle or looks mottled, these are sure signs that the

■ To repair small splits and blisters in felted roofs, open up the top layer of the felt with two knife cuts at right angles. Peel back the tongues and spread some bituminous mastic over the repair. Then fix the tongues back down securely with galvanised clout nails and cover the repair with a felt patch, bedded on more mastic and rolled down with a wallpaper seam roller or similar tool.

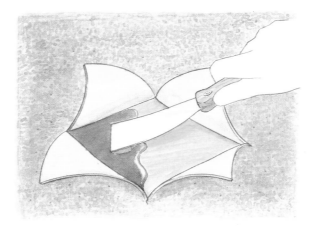

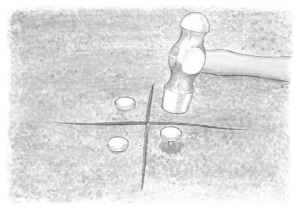

covering is reaching the end of its useful life. Watch out too for any sign of springiness in the roof decking; this indicates that the decking has begun to rot. Also check the upstands where the roof meets an abutment, like the wall of an adjacent building or a parapet wall.

You should also make sure that rainwater outlets, gutters and downspouts are clear of debris and loose gravel, so that any water will run away as quickly as possible.

This initial inspection should give you a good picture of what needs to be done and how to proceed. You will probably have the option of carrying out a patch repair to the damaged area,

applying an all-over treatment to the surface or stripping off and replacing the roof.

Patch repairs are obviously the easiest to carry out and are the answer if the area of damage is limited and the majority of the roof is in good condition. If, however, the covering is starting to deteriorate in a number of places and you do not want to go through the expense of replacing the entire covering, you should consider an all-over treatment.

Such a treatment is well within the capabilities of the competent person who does not mind ruining a set of old clothes; bitumen is a very messy material to handle! And it should give the roof several extra years of life. But it is a warning that you will eventually need a new roof covering. So it is a good time to start saving up for the cost this will involve.

If you decide on re-roofing, this is a job for the specialist. It involves applying three layers of roofing felt stuck together with hot bitumen to form a strong durable covering – hence the name 'built-up roofing'. The pour-and-roll technique using hot bitumen is a skilled and potentially dangerous job and not recommended for the amateur.

The only exception, if you are determined to do the work yourself, is to use 'torching' felt, which is backed with bitumen coating. A powerful gas blowlamp is required to heat and melt the bitumen as the felt is unrolled on to the roof surface. It is still not an easy process, but it is safer than working at heights with buckets of hot bitumen.

If the problem demands only a patch repair over a hole, it is best to use metal-backed self-adhesive flashing strip, although a piece of roofing felt coated with cold mastic would be a suitable alternative.

Scrape any gravel away from the damaged area, then apply the liquid bitumen primer supplied with the flashing strip. When this has dried, peel the backing paper away from the flashing strip, which should be cut large enough to allow plenty of overlap, and press it in place, rolling it down with a wooden wallpaper seam roller. You can use the same material when repairing an upstand.

Your problem may just be blistering on the surface. In this case make a star-shaped cut through the blister using a sharp trimming knife. Then peel back the edges of the blister to expose the underfelt. Coat the area with bitumen roofing compound and fold the flaps back in place, pressing them down with the roller. Finally apply a patch of flashing strip over the repair.

If you decide to apply an all-over surface

treatment, there are various materials you can use. The principle is to apply an initial layer of liquid proofing to the roof surface, which you can reinforce with a non-rotting fabric mesh, and then another layer, allowing it to solidify and form a tough, waterproof yet flexible sheet.

First remove the old gravel and any moss or algae from the surface. It is a good idea to apply a suitable fungicide to kill any remaining traces of growth. Then apply the first coat of liquid proofing, using a soft broom.

If you are using reinforcing mesh, unroll it into the wet waterproofing and stipple it into the surface using a wet brush. Overlap the edges of adjacent strips by about 2in.

When the first coat has dried, apply a second one all over the roof and then a third. You can give this last coat extra protection with a covering of white reflective gravel, which you should apply while it is still tacky.

SINGLE-PLY ROOFS

Flat roofs may also be covered in single-ply roofing – applied either as a liquid coating or as a sheet. Flexible sheet materials such as neoprene, PVC, CSPE or EPDM are installed in one of three ways. In the fully-adhered system, the sheet is fully bonded to the roof surface – either a smooth concrete or wood deck – with adhesive, and in addition is mechanically fas-

tened at the roof edges. In the fully-fastened system the sheet is laid loose and is then secured to the deck all over with nailed fastening plates. In the ballasted system the sheet is loose-laid with perimeter fixings, and is held down across its surface with roof pavers or a bed of gravel. You can make localized repairs with liquid waterproofers; leave bigger repairs to a roofing specialist.

REPAIRING FLASHINGS

Flashings, which can be of lead or other corrosion-resistant metal, are used widely to waterproof the join between the roof and adjacent brickwork, such as a chimney flue, or to waterproof the house wall round door and window openings.

Metal flashings give excellent weather resistance, but after a time even they can corrode, tear or lift away from the wall, allowing water to trickle down behind them.

If flashing has simply lifted away from the roof, tap it back in place with a piece of wood. If it has pulled away at the top, where it is tucked under a clapboard joint in the wall, the job of repairing it will involve more work. Carefully raise the upper clapboard and insert the flashing well under the bottom edge; nail it in a hidden location and replace the clapboard.

If metal flashing is corroded or torn, the best

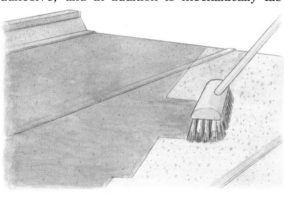

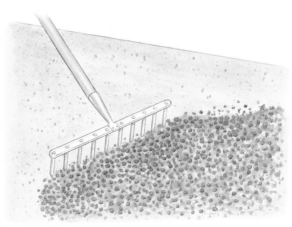

■ Where large-scale pinholing of a felt or other flat roof appears to be letting in water but the roof is in otherwise reasonably sound condition, brush on a coat of liquid waterproofer and unroll special reinforcing mesh over it. Then brush on a generous second layer of waterproofer, allow it to dry and apply a third coat before covering it with a protective layer of gravel, raked out while the top coat is still tacky.

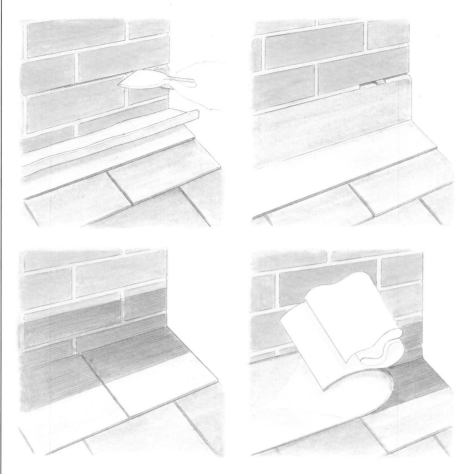

■ Where metal flashings have pulled away from a roof/wall junction, rake out the old mortar along the chase into which the flashing fitted. Then reposition the flashing, wedging it into the chase, and repoint with fresh mortar.

If the flashing is porous or is missing altogether, fit a length of self-adhesive flashing tape. Brush on the special primer first and leave it to become tacky. Then cut the flashing tape to length, peel off the release paper and bed the tape in place along the junction. Tamp it down with a block of wood and a hammer to ensure that it forms a good bond.

solution is to cover it with metal-backed self-adhesive metal repair strip. Clean the existing flashing with a wire brush, then apply the primer, which is supplied with the strip, to the affected area and leave it to dry. It will turn from brown to black. Remove the backing paper from the repair strip and smooth it into place using a soft rag. Press it firmly in place with a small wooden roller.

If the flashing is badly corroded or very loose, you should remove it completely and fit self-adhesive flashing strip in its place.

Apart from the stepped flashing at the sides of the chimney stack and the apron flashing along the front, the flashing at the back of a chimney, which is formed into a back gutter, is also prone to corrosion and water leaks. Here you can make an effective repair with several overlapping strips of flashing material well pressed down.

The same technique can be used to repair the metal-lined valley gutters which you should find between adjoining pitched roof slopes. In such a case, apply the flashing strip from the bottom of the valley upwards, tucking the edges of the flashing under the tiles.

Mortar flashings frequently crack and pull away from the brickwork, allowing water to run down behind. If the flashing is basically sound, fill any cracks by injecting a generous bead of flexible caulk into them using a proprietary caulking gun.

If the mortar flashing is in poor condition, carefully chip it away and replace it with the self-adhesive strip, pressing it down on to the affected surface, which you will first need to clean and treat with primer.

REPAIRING CHIMNEYS

Never attempt any repairs to chimneys unless the stack is small and easy to reach from a roof ladder or you have rented proper scaffolding (see Working in safety).

Because chimney stacks are in a very exposed position, it is common for the pointing between the bricks to crumble away. This can lead to dampness and make the stack unstable. Damaged joints will need to be repointed.

First rake out the old mortar to a depth of about ¾in and lightly wet the joints. A garden sprayer is ideal for this. Then press fresh mortar in place and smooth it off at a slight downward angle. The mortar should consist of one part cement to five parts sharp sand, with a little PVA adhesive added to improve its adhesion and workability.

Another vulnerable spot is the mortar bed in which the flue caps are set. If there are cracks but the caps themselves are still held firmly in place, you can fill them by injecting flexible caulk into the cracks.

If, however, the mortar is loose, you will have to chip it away – with care – and replace it with new mortar. Use one part cement to four parts sharp sand, again with a little PVA adhesive. Spread the mortar around the caps, building it up around the base and smoothing it so it slopes down to the edges of the stack. This will allow any rainwater to drain off easily.

Cracked flue caps can sometimes be repaired with caulk; otherwise they will have to be replaced. If you have an old house, you may be able to get suitable caps from a demolition contractor or architectural salvage yard. To fit the new cap, chip away the old mortar and replace it with new mortar, as described above.

If the flues are no longer used, it is good practice to cap them off to prevent rain getting in. The best way of doing this is to remove the flue caps, then to make the flues rainproof by laying patio pavers over the flues.

Metal flashings and flue flanges can also be a source of damp problems around chimney stacks. Work on these is covered under the section on Repairing flashings.

Chimney stack repairs

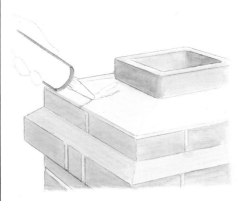

■ Repair minor cracks in the mortar cap around the flue lining using exterior-quality silicone caulk.

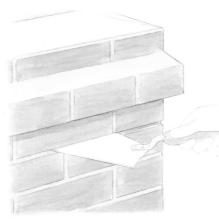

■ Rake out any defective pointing on the sides of the chimney and remake the joints with fresh mortar, left flush.

■ If stepped flashings are pulling away from their chases, wedge them back in place and repoint the chases with fresh mortar.

■ If the flue lining is badly cracked, chop away the old mortar cap to release the top section of the lining.

■ Replace the lining with a short section of the same type and cross-section, set in place within the chimney brickwork.

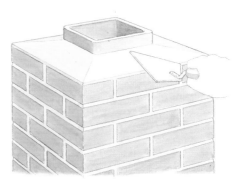

■ Shape the new mortar cap so its surface forms a gentle downward slope away from the flue lining towards the edges.

Once repairs to the chimney stack have been completed, it is a good idea to paint the brickwork and the mortar bedding with silicone water-repellent sealer to prevent rain penetration and help protect against frost damage. The sealer dries colorless and does not affect the appearance of the stack.

REPAIRING GUTTERING

It is important to keep guttering systems in good condition, since leaking or overflowing gutters will cause damp walls, stained interior decorations and possibly rotting of the fascias, soffit boards and rafter ends.

When checking or repairing the guttering, use a ladder fitted with a stay, which will hold the top clear of the gutter. If you are replacing

any of the system, you should use a scaffold tower (see Working in safety).

The best time to check gutters and downspouts is when it is raining. Then you can see clearly if there are any leaking joints or whether the system is blocked anywhere and therefore overflowing down the house walls.

Make sure the inside of the guttering is free of debris. Clean the inside of metal gutters with a wire brush and paint the surface with black bituminous paint.

Direct a garden hose into the guttering and check that it drains freely and does not collect in pools. If there are drainage problems, these can only be corrected by realigning the gutters. This is not an easy job and it is better to discard the existing system and fit new aluminum guttering (see below), or reproduction cast iron

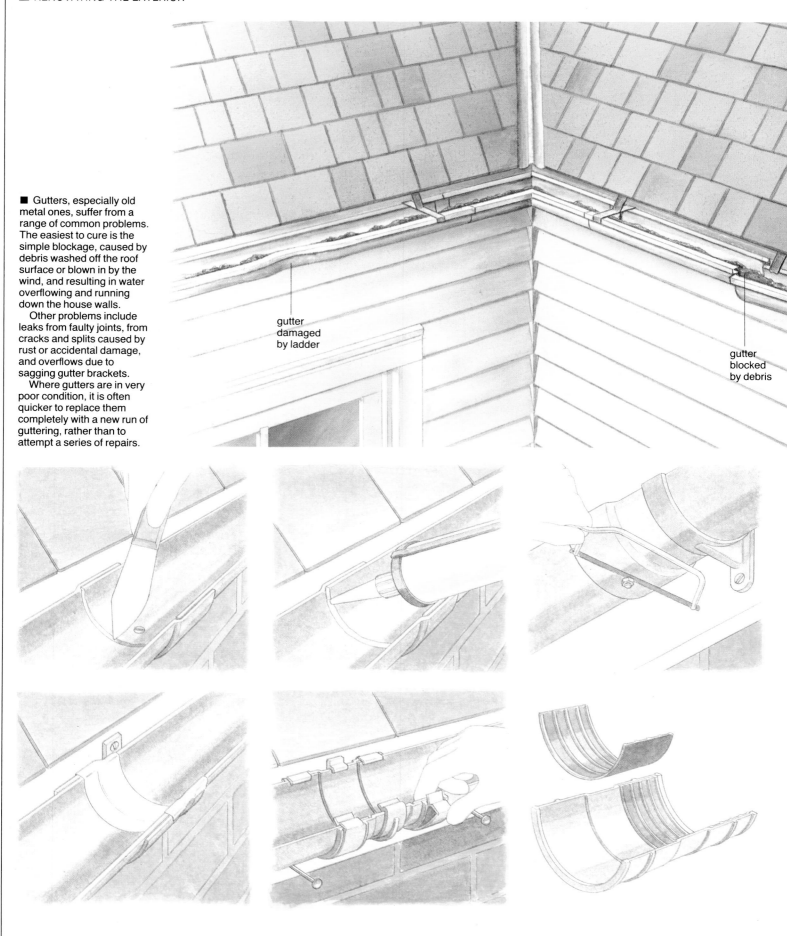

■ Gutters, especially old metal ones, suffer from a range of common problems. The easiest to cure is the simple blockage, caused by debris washed off the roof surface or blown in by the wind, and resulting in water overflowing and running down the house walls.

Other problems include leaks from faulty joints, from cracks and splits caused by rust or accidental damage, and overflows due to sagging gutter brackets.

Where gutters are in very poor condition, it is often quicker to replace them completely with a new run of guttering, rather than to attempt a series of repairs.

gutter damaged by ladder

gutter blocked by debris

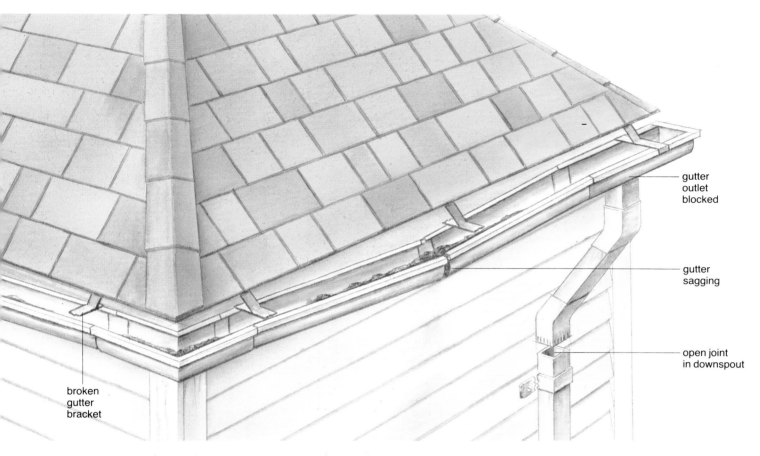

gutter
outlet
blocked

gutter
sagging

open joint
in downspout

broken
gutter
bracket

■ To repair a leaking but otherwise sound joint, scrape out any old sealing compound and re-seal the joint with caulk.

If this fails to work, undo the joint by hacksawing through the nut underneath. Then separate the joint sections, reassemble them on a generous bed of caulk and remake the joint with a new nut and bolt. As a stop-gap measure, try sealing the joint by bedding a piece of self-adhesive flashing tape over it.

If a plastic gutter joint leaks, dismantle the joint by removing the clips and fit a new sealing gasket.

gutters if you are restoring a period house.

If joints in aluminum guttering are leaking, the only satisfactory solution is to dismantle them and remake the seals between sections. The best method is to saw – from the underside – through the rivet holding the sections together to ease the joint apart. Then clean it out, pack it with non-setting caulk and refix it with a new bolt and nut.

There is an easier repair that may sometimes work. First scrape out the joint on each side. When it is thoroughly dry, inject a bead of non-setting exterior caulk into the crack. Finally, make sure of the repair by sticking a patch of self-adhesive flashing strip inside the gutter to form a complete seal.

Any gutters or downspouts that are cracked or split should be replaced with new sections. However, you can make a temporary repair by covering the affected area with a patch of self-adhesive flashing strip applied over a coating of primer. Metal gutters and downspouts can also be repaired with glass fiber paste, as used for car body repairs.

You can also use self-adhesive metal repair tape to effect a temporary repair to badly corroded cast-iron and steel gutters and downspouts. However these can be dangerous if they fall off the building, so it is better to

replace them with new aluminum guttering or with the lightweight plastic type. There are now several brands available in grey, white, brown or black plastic and they have the advantage of being easy to fix and virtually maintenance-free as well as matching the color of your existing outdoor woodwork.

Guttering is available in different sizes – usually 4 or 5in wide; these sizes will cope with a roof area of up to 750 and 1400 sq ft respectively. A 3in wide downspout is suitable for draining rainwater off a roof area of up to 1000sq ft; use a larger size for bigger roofs.

Plastic gutters are fixed by being clipped into brackets screwed to the fascia board. In theory, they will drain if fixed level. In practice, however, it is best to fit them with a slight fall of about 1in per 16ft.

When fitting a downspout, always work from the outlet. Start by fitting a leader to bring the downspout back to the face of the wall. Working downwards from the leader elbow, fit the downspout into the required number of bracket clips to hold it firmly against the wall.

If you are replacing damaged plastic gutter or downspout sections, note that the various systems are not interchangeable, so it is best to stick to what you have. Most have the maker's name molded into the plastic.

External Walls

The vast majority of houses built since the 1920s are of wood-frame construction. Older homes have walls about 6in thick, consisting of a series of 2 × 4in studs spaced at 16 or 24in centers. The exterior is usually finished with sheathing consisting of ½in thick boards laid diagonally, to which a decorative exterior finish such as shingles of clapboards are nailed.

Alternative exterior finishes include brick or stone veneer and, on less grand houses, asbestos shingles. Removal of the latter is strictly controlled by the asbestos abatement regulations at both state and federal level, so specialist demolition and disposal contractors may have to be employed to deal with them.

On the interior, the typical wall finish will be either lath and plaster (late 19th and early 20th century houses) or, in more recent houses, ½in sheetrock (drywall) nailed up with taped joints.

More modern homes may have the wall thickness increased to 8in by the use of 2 × 6in studs at 24in centers. The main reason for this is to allow the fitting of a full 6in of foil-backed fiberglass insulation batting in the cavity, and so to reduce heat losses through the house walls. The exterior sheathing is CDX plywood, ⅜in thick on studs at 16in centers or ½in thick if they are at 24in centers. Sheetrock (drywall) is the standard internal wall finish.

Most wood-framed homes are built using the platform framing technique. Each floor is a platform, resting on the sill plate at first floor level and on the top plate of the first floor walls for the second floor above. The subfloor – diagonally-laid boards in older homes, plywood sheathing in newer ones – extends to the edge of each floor platform.

Some two-storey homes were also built using the balloon framing technique, which is seldom used nowadays. The studs, usually 2 × 6in wood at 16in centers, run the full height of the building (to a maximum of 20ft) and the second-floor joists lap the studs and rest on a continuous ribbon let into the studs to provide additional support. The one advantage of balloon framing is that there is less vertical movement in the wall than with platform framing, which is a bonus if brick veneer or stucco finishes are used.

In some houses built before 1920, the outer walls are usually constructed of solid brick. These can be identified by having headers (brick ends looking like half-bricks) as well as

■ Natural stone walls often have brickwork at corners and round openings.

■ Exposed brickwork is a common exterior wall finish on many old town houses, and is found in a wide range of colors and textures.

rotten siding

split siding

rotten window casing

stretchers in the face of the wall. This type of wall is usually 9in thick, although 13½in brickwork is also found. Check the thickness of the walls at the door and window openings, making allowance for the thickness of any plaster. One significant point to remember about walls in older houses is that they may not include a damp-proof course.

Older houses may have exterior walls built from regular stone (ashlar) blocks backed with

■ Paint is often used to give old brickwork a facelift, but is virtually impossible to remove successfully once it has been applied.

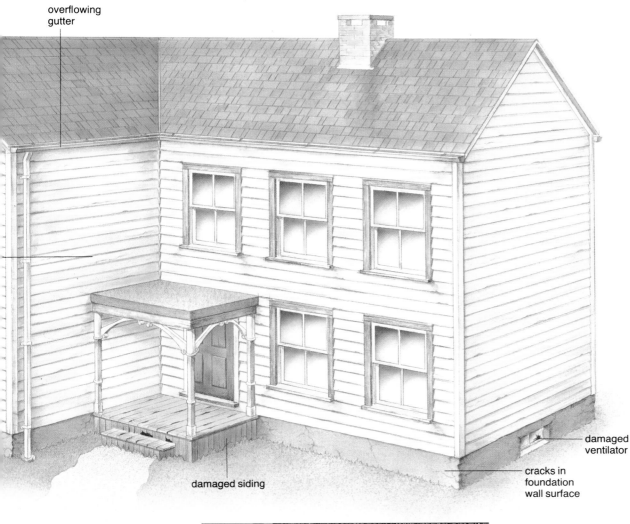

overflowing
gutter

damaged
ventilator

cracks in
foundation
wall surface

damaged siding

■ Shaped shingles provide
a highly decorative wall
finish, especially when
teamed with elaborately
carved eaves boards.

■ Bevel siding is widely
used on many wood-framed
buildings, and also as extra
weatherproofing on solid
masonry walls.

■ Gravel bedded in mortar
became popular as a finish
for masonry walls in the
1920s and 1930s.

■ Tile hanging is another
form of weatherproofing for
both wood-framed and solid
masonry walls.

bricks. Often there is a projecting plinth at
ground level and such walls may have a
damp-proof course.

Some houses with masonry walls are built in
cavity wall construction, which can be identified
by the formation of the brickwork. Except at
corners, only stretchers (lengthwise bricks)
show on the surface of the wall. Cavity walls are
about 11in thick and consist of a 4½in thick
facing brick outer wall, a 2in wide cavity and an

inner wall of 4½in thick bricks or blocks.

In more recent houses, the inner leaf may have been constructed with load-bearing building blocks, probably of lightweight insulating material, and the cavity between the inner and outer leaves may well be filled with insulation.

The inner and outer leaves are always linked together with metal ties, of which there are various types. These are built into the mortar joints at regular intervals.

Modern stone-faced houses are also built on the cavity wall principle. The facing blocks may be of natural or reconstituted stones and these are linked by metal ties to an inner leaf of stud framing or load-bearing blocks.

With some walls, good quality brickwork is left exposed. In other cases it is covered with a mixture of cement and sand mortar called stucco. This can either be left smooth or given a surface texture.

FINDING FAULTS

Most of the defects that develop in walls are noticeable simply because they make the wall look shabby – mold growth, cracks and so on – or because damp patches form inside, ruining decorations.

Provided that remedial action is taken quickly, most faults are rarely serious. At the other end of the scale, however, you may have major problems that can involve thousands of dollars of treatment.

Thankfully faults on this scale are rare and are almost always caused not by neglect but by natural causes. Narrow cracks in walls are usually superficial, even though they can sometimes extend quite a long way. They tend to stay as thin cracks and eventually stop growing. A bad crack will be extensive both in length and depth. It can split bricks in half or cause the wall to bulge. It may also appear inside the house.

You can make a fairly accurate diagnosis of the problem by asking yourself a few basic questions. If the problem proves to be serious, you are going to have to call in an architect or engineer. But running through a checklist can give you a fair picture of what is going on.

First of all, the crack itself. Have you noticed it getting wider and/or longer over a period of time? A good way to check this is to apply some filler or mortar mix into the gap. If this cracks or falls out after a while, then you know there is still movement occurring.

If you have established that the crack is getting worse, what could have caused this to happen? The weather is the first thing to consider. If there has been an abnormally dry

spell, this could have caused the subsoil – especially clay – to shrink. This in turn could have caused movement below the house foundations. In exceptionally dry weather, the ground could have dried out and shrunk, causing the foundations to follow suit.

Are there any large trees close to the affected wall? Roots can create problems by pushing against the foundations or footings. Equally, has a large tree near the house been felled recently? If it has, then it could be that roots extending below the foundations have withered and died. Where previously they 'supported' the foundations, there may now be a hollow and the foundations have sunk into it.

A less likely cause, but still a possibility, is where there has been recent mining or building work close by, which has resulted in the subsoil or foundations moving. A more obscure reason could be a hidden building failure, such as the roof structure becoming unstable and forcing walls outwards.

If the wall is unstable for any reason, the foundations will probably have to be excavated and underpinned (strengthened) and the affected part of the house may have to be rebuilt. Such repair work emphasizes the need to be well insured, since similar structural alterations can cost a lot of money.

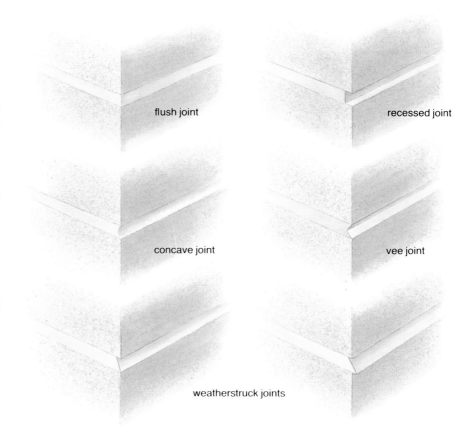

■ Various pointing styles are used to finish off the mortar joints between bricks. Flush pointing, as its name implies, is trowelled flush with the face of the bricks, while concave pointing is tooled with a round bar before the mortar hardens. Recessed pointing is raked out to a depth of about ¼in, while V-jointed pointing is profiled with the tip of the pointing trowel. Weather-struck joints have the face of the pointing angled with the trowel to throw water clear of the wall surface.

flush joint

recessed joint

concave joint

vee joint

weatherstruck joints

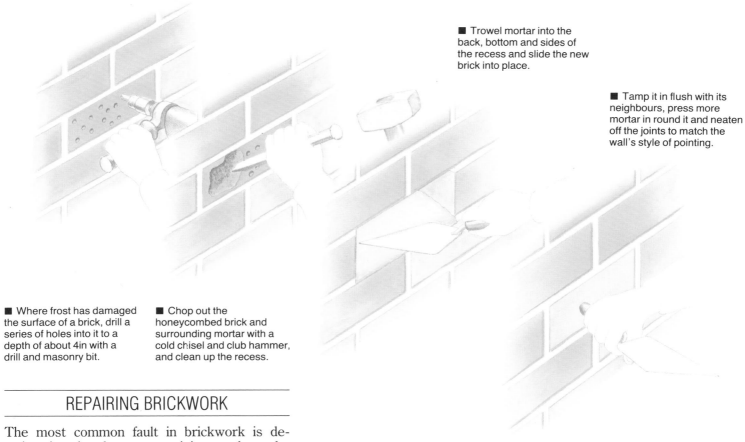

■ Trowel mortar into the back, bottom and sides of the recess and slide the new brick into place.

■ Tamp it in flush with its neighbours, press more mortar in round it and neaten off the joints to match the wall's style of pointing.

■ Where frost has damaged the surface of a brick, drill a series of holes into it to a depth of about 4in with a drill and masonry bit.

■ Chop out the honeycombed brick and surrounding mortar with a cold chisel and club hammer, and clean up the recess.

REPAIRING BRICKWORK

The most common fault in brickwork is deterioration in the mortar joints, when the mortar often flakes, cracks and crumbles. Old age and excessive weathering are common causes, especially if the initial mortar mix used was too weak.

Cracks in the mortar joints allow rainwater to penetrate. In winter this can freeze, causing the crack to widen and the mortar to decay, weakening other joints as a result.

Repointing joints
To repoint damaged joints, you must first rake out the old mortar and then insert a new mix. This is normally made up of one part cement, one part hydrated powder lime and six parts soft sand. The lime makes the mix more workable, but you can substitute it with a few drops of a proprietary liquid plasticizer.

If you make the mix stronger by increasing the proportion of cement, the mortar is liable to shrink and crack as it dries. It will also impede the drying out of the wall when wet.

If you are only repointing a few joints, then you can buy bags of mortar ready-mix to which you simply add water. Tip out the entire contents and mix thoroughly together, then put back into the bag what you do not need. The ingredients tend to separate and otherwise you may well get too much or too little cement.

TREATING OR REPLACING BRICKS

Old age and frost damage can cause brickwork to become porous, eventually allowing dampness to pass through to the inside of the house. One solution is to patch up damaged bricks with mortar, color-matched to the surrounding ones. This is, however, difficult to do well. And if you have any cracks or gaps between the patching mortar and the brick, water can be sucked in by

■ Weathering, pollution and frost damage can eventually cause serious damage to exposed brickwork and its pointing. Repointing or replacing affected bricks is essential to keep the wall surface weatherproof.

■ To weatherproof exterior brickwork that is porous but otherwise in good condition, brush on a silicone water-repellent sealer.

capillary action, causing further problems.

A better solution is to cut out the offending brick and replace it. Apply ready mixed brick-laying mortar, worked to a stiff consistency, to the top of the brick below, and on the sides and frog (the V-shaped indentation) of the new brick. Push it firmly in place, using a stick to compact the mortar inside the joint.

If some bricks are frost-damaged, the rest are probably porous and will need protection. The easiest method is to apply a silicone water-repellent sealer to the wall surface with a brush, spray or roller.

FILLING CRACKED STUCCO

You often find hairline crazing in a stuccoed wall. Such a superficial situation is easily overcome with a coat of good exterior wall paint. Small cracks must be filled, but any repair will be obvious until the wall is painted.

When treating cracks, you must first under-cut them to ensure the filler is well anchored and will not fall out later. Then dust out the crack and dampen it with water.

To fill the crack you can use either an exterior grade filler or mortar mix. The former is convenient but only economical for small areas. Dry mortar mix can be obtained in small quantities or you can make your own using one part cement, one part hydrated powder lime and six parts sand. You can of course use a proprietary liquid plasticizer in place of the lime.

■ Cracks often occur in stucco at natural breaks – in line with the corners of door and window frames, for example.

■ To repair cracks in stucco, first chip away all loose material along the line of the crack, under-cutting it to provide a better key for the repair mortar. Brush out all loose material, then spray water along the crack to stop it absorbing moisture too quickly from the repair mortar and causing it to crack. Finally, force mortar into the crack and trowel off the surplus level with the surrounding wall surface.

PATCHING STUCCO

If stucco is coming away from the wall, the cause may be dampness, a fault in the mortar mix or defective blockwork joints. This is often evidenced by bulges, where it has lost contact with the wall surface behind.

Tap suspect areas lightly with a hammer. If there is a fault, the stucco will fall away and you must clean off the affected area with a bolster chisel and club hammer until you reach an area that adheres firmly to the wall.

A stucco mix consists of one part Portland cement, one part lime and six parts sand. The lime makes the mortar mix more flexible and easier to use. But it must be applied quickly, since after mixing you only have about 15 or 20 minutes before it becomes too firm to work. Do not add water to a setting mix since this will only weaken it.

If you do not intend painting the stucco later, take care that the ingredients of each batch mixed up are uniform. Any difference will cause the wall to look patchy when the mortar dries.

For normal house work, you should apply two coats of stucco. The first should be a thick coat and the second, top coat a finishing skim about ¼in thick.

Plastering on stucco is a skill that requires

■ Where stucco has broken away from an external corner, repair it in two stages using a batten pinned to the wall as a guide. Pin it in place with masonry nails, repair one side of the corner, then reposition the batten and apply stucco to the other face of the wall.

■ To patch an area of loose or missing stucco, first cut away all loose material with a cold chisel and hammer. Then wet the wall surface and trowel on a rough first coat of fresh mortar. Rule off any high spots with a batten drawn upwards in a sawing motion across the repair, fill low spots and rule off again. Finally, use a float to give the repair a smooth finish.

confidence. If you try to 'dab' the mix on to the wall, it will just fall off again. The idea is to apply it with a sweeping motion. Always work from the bottom of the patch upwards with the first coat. When that has been applied and is starting to set, scratch its suface to form a key for the second coat to grip.

Allow 24 hours before applying the final coat, starting at the top this time and working from left to right with the same flowing movement.

When you have completed the patch, level the new material off with the surrounding wall surface. Then leave this till it is almost dry before drawing a steel float, dampened with water, across it to give a smooth, flat finish.

REPLACING VENTILATORS

Broken ventilators can cause additional problems, since they will provide access for vermin under the ground floor, where they may multiply and find their way into other parts of the house. You will need to remove the old ventilator and replace it with one of the same style and size.

With a solid wall, it is unlikely that the opening will be lined. In more modern houses, the cavity between the inner and outer skins of the brickwork should be sealed to prevent dissipation of air into the cavity. You can do this with clay or plastic ducts. Replacement ventilators, which are made from a variety of materials, must fit flush with the surface of the wall and be bedded in with cement mortar.

Remember to keep ventilators clear. They must never be blocked up, since their purpose is to ventilate the crawl spaces beneath wood floors and prevent them from getting damp and being attacked by rot.

REPAIRING SHINGLES

Wood shingles on walls sometimes warp badly and can also develop cracks, splits, or holes where dry knots have fallen out as time goes by. If these are left untended, water penetration can result.

To correct warping, drill a hole through each bottom corner of the shingle and drive in small screws to pull the shingle back into line with its neighbors. Countersink the screw heads and cover them with wood filler.

Where shingles have split, cut a piece of building paper wide enough to fit between the in-place nails and slip it underneath the split shingle. Then butt the two halves of the split tightly together and nail both halves to the wall with galvanized nails.

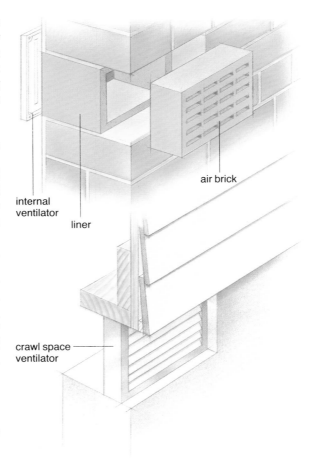

air brick

internal ventilator

liner

crawl space ventilator

A badly split shingle is best replaced with a new one. Use a hammer and chisel to split the shingle into narrow pieces which can be easily removed. Then prise out the fixing nails with a claw hammer if you can reach them; sever them with a hacksaw blade if you cannot. Patch any tears in the building paper beneath with asphalt adhesive, then slip the replacement shingle into position, aligning it with its neighbors, and secure it with galvanized shingle nails.

REPAIRING CLADDING

Unless clapboarding was properly treated with preservative before being installed and has been kept well painted since, it is more than likely to rot. And once this has set in, it can travel quickly from board to board and to the sheathing behind.

Other problems include boards warping or becoming distorted through inadequate fixings or by having been butted up tightly, leaving no room for natural expansion.

If existing rot is in its infancy, any decayed wood can be dug out and the cavity filled with exterior grade woodfiller. If the damage is more extensive, you should remove the affected

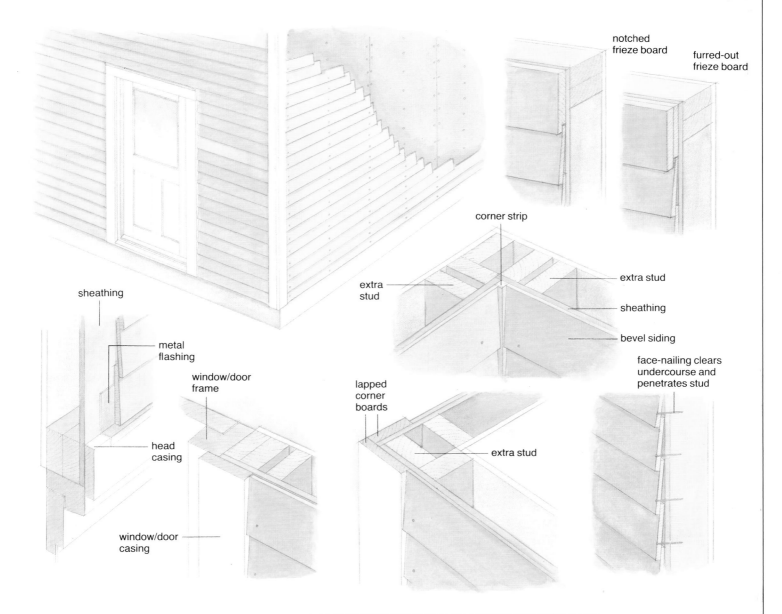

notched
frieze board

furred-out
frieze board

corner strip

extra
stud

extra stud

sheathing

bevel siding

face-nailing clears
undercourse and
penetrates stud

sheathing

metal
flashing

window/door
frame

head
casing

lapped
corner
boards

extra stud

window/door
casing

boards and discard them. If the rot is widespread, you may even have to take off all the boards – and some of the sheathing too.

You might get away with refixing one or two boards without tampering with the remainder. But it is probably going to be far easier to refix the boards by working back to the sheathing.

Sometimes you can pull warped boards back into place by refixing them to the sheathing with rustproof screws. If the boards are badly distorted, however, you will have to remove and replace them, using rustproof nails to fix them firmly in position.

If fitted correctly, vinyl siding should require no more than the occasional cleaning with warm water and detergent plus an algicide. Problems such as cracking, which indicates that the siding was fixed too tightly in the first place, mean it will have to be replaced.

■ Bevel siding is fixed direct to the sheathing over the wall studs of wood-framed buildings, and can be secured to vertical wooden battens fixed to the face of solid masonry walls (usually over a waterproof lining of building paper, and often over insulation as well). Extra battens form a neat junction at internal and external corners, and round window and door openings.

Wall Insulation and Damp-proofing

Masonry walls are built in one of two ways – either as a solid wall of bricks or as a cavity wall comprising two withes of masonry with a 2in gap between them.

Many houses built more than 60 years ago had solid walls although some, of course, used stone as opposed to brick. And it was the thickness of the material used that prevented dampness penetrating through to the inside of the house.

In a prolonged rainy spell moisture would seep into the wall, but the bricks would be sufficiently dense to restrict its progress to a minimum. When the rain stopped, the wall would dry out naturally and any dampness would gradually disappear.

Unfortunately, through the years bricks can age and become more porous, mortar joints decay and the bricks themselves can be damaged by frost. So the system breaks down. The walls no longer keep out the moisture and very soon you have damp walls, which in turn lead to ruined decorations and possibly mold growth.

The theory behind the cavity wall design is that the wall is bound to remain waterproof since even if moisture seeps through the thickness of the outer skin, it cannot penetrate

any further since there is an air space between that and the inner brick skin. So the inside wall stays dry.

By and large the theory works, although occasionally shoddy workmanship at the building stage can cause it to fail. Problems arise when excess mortar is dropped into the cavity, where it lands and sets on the metal wall ties used to hold the two withes together. This creates a bridge for the moisture to cross and reach the inner wall.

Dampness caused by moisture forcing itself through a wall is known as penetrating dampness. Generally the position of the wet patch inside the house will be directly behind the problem area, so locating the trouble and effecting repairs are relatively straightforward.

Far more serious is rising dampness, since this can be fed continuously from moisture in the ground. It can climb right up a wall and eventually soak into structural timbers, setting off a wet or dry rot attack.

To prevent rising dampness, most houses have an in-built damp-proof flashing. This is a continuous strip of impervious material set into the external brickwork a few courses above ground level.

■ Keeping heat in and dampness out have been the main tasks facing the outer envelope of every house through the ages. Modern building techniques still draw on the solutions tried and tested over time, including materials like wall shingles and stucco.

In a modern house with solid concrete ground floors, a vapor barrier is laid under the concrete slab to link up with the wall flashing. Thus there is a complete damp barrier across the house. However, with poor building practice or accidental damage, a flashing or vapor barrier can fail.

A house with suspended timber ground floors (that is with floorboards or plywood sheets laid on joists) does not normally have a damp problem since the floor is raised up from the ground and is continually aired via ventilators set around the house walls. These ventilators must be kept clear or the airflow will be impeded and the wood could eventually rot.

People are often tempted to block up ventilators to cut down on drafts around the floor. Never do this. If you have draft problems, the solution is to seal any gaps in the floor.

COPING WITH PENETRATING DAMPNESS

Where a masonry wall is in good condition but suffers from dampness, there are two ways of keeping it dry. A coat of good quality exterior wall paint will be effective and this can be applied over bricks, blocks or stucco.

Should you not want to use paint, but retain the 'natural' look of the wall, the answer is to apply a coat of silicone water-repellent sealer. This is a colorless liquid that you brush on and leave to soak into the wall, thus forming a chemical barrier against moisture penetration.

The liquid does not seal the surface, but rather acts like a microporous paint, preventing rainwater penetrating but allowing moisture vapor inside the wall to escape.

Remember to lay polythene sheeting over any path or patio likely to be splashed when you are applying the sealer. Should any fall on these surfaces, you will get a strange patchy effect whenever it rains.

You should only apply the sealer to dry surfaces – never when the wall is wet. And it should not be used before stuccoing or painting, as it contains silicone resins that prevent good adhesion of subsequent decorations.

Before you apply it carry out any essential repairs, such as replacing damaged pointing and missing or damaged bricks and blocks.

COPING WITH RISING DAMPNESS

Inside the house rising dampness will show itself in several ways. The most obvious signs will be with the decorations. Paint will blister and flake off, paper will start to peel from the wall, and plaster will begin to crumble.

■ Rising dampness in masonry walls can result from a failed dampproof course (above) or from water splashing above the damp course round blocked drains (left). The result is damp patches on the inside walls (right), which ruin the decorations and weaken the plaster, and which can also lead to outbreaks of rot in floors and behind baseboards (below).

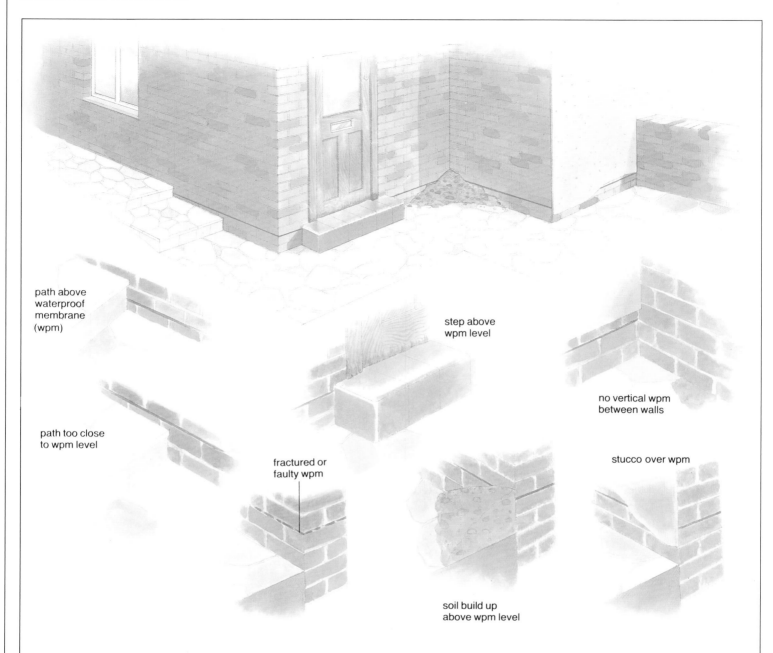

path above
waterproof
membrane
(wpm)

path too close
to wpm level

fractured or
faulty wpm

step above
wpm level

no vertical wpm
between walls

stucco over wpm

soil build up
above wpm level

Curing rising dampness

Rising dampness occurs when moisture from the ground on which the house stands is soaked up into its masonry walls. The dampness can rise to a height of 3ft or so above the baseboard level, causing unsightly staining of the plaster and the decorations and also an unpleasant smell in the affected rooms. It can also cause rot in floor timbers, door frames and baseboards.

The dampness can be caused by a failure in the dampproof course that is built into solid walls – a particularly common fault in older properties where slates or engineering bricks were used to form the damp course. It can also result from the damp course being bridged in some way – by an adjoining wall, by garden soil being banked up against the wall, or by steps, paths or other outdoor features being built alongside the wall. The latter need not be above the damp course level to cause rising dampness; heavy rain can splash back off these surfaces to soak the wall above. Even a coat of stucco on the exterior wall can suck moisture up above the damp course if it extends down over it.

If you have rising dampness, check whether any of the above-mentioned problems are present. Remove any you find and see whether the wall shows signs of drying out. Only if the problem persists should you call in a professional firm of dampproofing specialists for their advice on the best solution to the problem.

■ Common causes of rising dampness include cracks in old damp courses, paths and steps built against the wall above (or close to) the level of the damp course, adjoining garden or outbuilding walls built against the house wall without a vertical damp course, stucco covering the damp course or garden soil built up against the house wall above it.

At the highest point of the rising dampness there will be an ugly tide-mark. Along this mark a mat of fine, furry salt crystals called efflorescence will form, looking like thin cotton wool. Where the wall is very damp, green and black mold will begin to grow and this will, of course, further affect the decorations.

It is not only rising dampness, however, that causes these faults. You should also check for such things as leaking gutters and downspouts, internal plumbing leaks, drainage faults and even damaged window and door sills. All can produce the same effect.

Although you can buy a moisture meter to test for dampness, you may prefer to call in a specialist to identify the cause and possibly to treat the problem.

First, however, have a good look round the house to see if something has been done inadvertently to create the condition. A pile of earth or a rock garden built against the wall above the flashing level will, for example, serve as a bridge for moisture from the ground to rise up the wall unchecked.

The same is true of a path or patio that has been near to the flashing level. You should always allow a gap of around 6in or one block course between the top of a path and the flashing. Internal plaster or external stucco taken down over a flashing would also allow moisture to creep past unchecked.

In all these cases, the affected area is usually isolated. Once a repair has been carried out, the wall should dry and remain so.

In the absence of any obvious signs such as those mentioned, a new flashing may well be required. For this you will probably need to call in a professional.

There are several methods available. One is to cut out the existing ineffective flashing and insert a new layer – a job best left to professional contractors.

Alternatively, you can install your own damp-proofing by injecting a chemical into the wall. The method is fairly simple. You drill holes into the wall and force the chemical in through hose nozzles connected to a special machine that pumps the liquid to the hoses.

The pump and injection equipment can be hired and sufficient drums of the chemical injection fluid bought to complete the job. Your supplier will provide details of how to use the pump and how much chemical you will need. The length of the wall and porosity of the bricks are the determining factors.

There are also specialist contractors who can inject water barrier chemicals into the ground adjacent to and under the foundation walls.

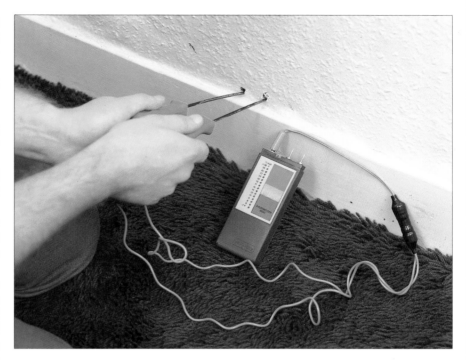

But even when a dampness problem has been cured, it can take several months for walls to dry out. During this time, as moisture finds its way to the surface it carries with it alkaline salts which it has absorbed from within the building materials, causing efflorescence.

Occurring on both internal and external surfaces, efflorescence will cause paint, wallpaper and other decorations to fall away. The usual practice is not to decorate until offending areas have dried out completely.

■ A battery-powered damp meter will reveal the presence of rising damp in walls, since wet masonry conducts electricity.

■ Once a new damp course has been injected, the old salt-infested plaster has to be hacked off and replaced.

Injecting a dampproof course

The most widely-used method of installing a new dampproof course in a masonry wall is to drill a series of holes into the masonry at regular intervals and then to pump in special waterproofing chemicals under pressure. These soak right through the wall and penetrate up to two courses of brickwork above and below the injection site. The chemical then cures to form a waterproof barrier that prevents moisture from rising up the wall. The injection process can also be used on internal solid partition walls built up off the house foundations.

As part of the dampproofing treatment, it is usually essential to hack off all interior plastering to a height of about 3ft on the affected walls, to get rid of mineral salts carried into the plaster by the rising dampness. This is then replaced with specially formulated plaster that will prevent salts in the masonry from being

brought to the wall surface as the wall dries out.

You may prefer to employ a specialist firm to install a new dpc, but this is a highly labor-intensive job and since you can rent the same pressure injection equipment that a specialist uses, there is no reason why you should not do so and inject a new chemical dpc yourself. You buy the special chemicals when you hire the equipment, on a sale-or-return basis.

Exactly how you proceed depends on whether you are dealing with solid or cavity walls. The former are usually about 9in thick, while the latter generally measure around 11in overall. The injection is carried out in two stages, working wherever possible from outside the house, so the depth of the holes you drill in the masonry depends on the wall thickness. For both types of wall the first hole is drilled to about 3in deep, and the first stage of the injection is carried out. Then the same holes are drilled deeper – to

about 6in in solid walls, and to around 8in in cavity walls – and the second stage is completed using longer nozzles. It is worth renting a professional-quality power drill to make the injection holes. This avoids the risk of overloading and burning out your own drill. Check that you have enough chemical – you may need up to 5 pints per yard of wall if the bricks are very porous. Once the new dpc has been injected, you can fill the injection holes with mortar colored with pigment.

Check the drying-out period with the manufacturers of both the chemical fluid and the plaster. Some recommend allowing as much as one month of drying-out time for every 1in of wall thickness.

If you need to complete the work sooner, you can use a special wall sealer. Several branded products are available. This can be applied to any interior surface where damp has been present, then painted or papered over within a few hours. It does not provide a solution to dampness. It just enables you to redecorate after the repair work has been completed.

Of course, sealing the wall from the inside will make rooms habitable but will not solve the problem. If the wall is allowed to remain damp, it is possible that permanent structural damage or rot will occur. So you will need to address this problem as well.

Using caulking sealants

Damp patches on the walls around a window frame indicate that rain is seeping through the gap between the frame and the wall. These gaps are sealed when the windows are installed, but often the old caulking material used to fill the gaps fails and falls out.

The problem with using a normal external filler or mortar mix to fill these gaps is that both set rigid. Throughout the year the gap opens and closes due to natural seasonal movement of the structure. Since the filling material is rigid, it eventually cracks and falls out.

In this situation you must use a caulking sealant, which will remain flexible. There are caulking compounds available for different situations and you need to buy one specifically for dealing with window frames. They are supplied in a cartridge and used with a special applicator gun, which you have to buy separately. Colors include white, gray and brown and the caulk can be painted over if desired.

First you must prepare the affected area, brushing down the gap and surround to remove

dirt and debris. Then apply the caulking as a continuous bead along the length of the gap. Smooth it off with a wet finger to give the bead a neat concave surface, and wipe off any excess with a damp cloth. At external corners on siding or round window or door casings, force the caulk as far into any open joints as possible before finishing off the surface as already described.

Using expanding foam fillers

Wherever pipes, cables or flues penetrate walls or roofs, there is a potential damp problem lurking. An ideal quick solution for sealing such areas is available with expanding foam fillers. Supplied in an aerosol, these fillers are simply sprayed on, then left to expand and fill any shape of hole. They will stick to virtually any surface and can be cut or shaped with a knife or hacksaw when dry.

Filler foams are ideal for sealing irregular gaps in awkward places, the kind of areas that would otherwise be inadequately plugged or left exposed to allow damp to gain a hold.

Most filler foams need some additional protection, however, when used outdoors. After such fillings have thoroughly dried, you can apply a layer of conventional filler or a mortar mix over the top.

■ Efflorescence (far left) is a powdery surface deposit caused by moisture in the wall carrying soluble mineral salts to the wall surface and evaporating to leave the crystalline salts behind. Brush it off if it occurs; wetting it will redissolve the salts and drive them back into the wall.

■ Expanding foam fillers are ideal for filling irregular gaps. Trim them to shape once they have hardened, and protect them with a layer of exterior filler or mortar.

■ Caulking is used to seal a wide range of small gaps on house exteriors – round window frames, for example, or on bevel siding. The surface quickly skins over, allowing it to be painted if necessary, but the body of the material stays flexible and so copes with any structural movement that may occur.

INSULATING WALLS

Insulating the cavity of masonry walls by pumping in a special insulant is a well-established practice. The insulating material completely fills the cavity and, together with trapped air, serves as a barrier to heat loss through the walls.

You have a choice of materials, all of which will remain stable for the life of the building, providing it is not altered structurally. Each material will prevent water passing across the cavity or from below the flashing level. Equally, the fire resistance of the wall is unaffected and rot, fungi and vermin are resisted.

Injecting insulation is not, however, a do-it-yourself job and you must contact a local specialist company with the right equipment and trained operatives to do the work.

Initially the house will be surveyed to ensure it is structurally sound and suitable for this kind of insulation process. The work involves pumping the material into the cavity through a series of holes drilled in the house walls at strategic positions. When the job is completed, the holes are filled in. Normally such insulation work takes a day – sometimes two; it all depends on how large the house is.

■ External wall insulation is used to improve the heat retention performance of solid walls where internal insulation is not feasible. The insulation is clipped to the wall surface, covered with special mesh and then rendered over to create a durable exterior wall surface. It is a job for specialist contractors.

■ Cavity wall insulation is pumped into the wall cavity via holes drilled in the outer leaf of the wall by trained operatives using specialist equipment; it is not a do-it-yourself job. Once the cavities are filled, the injection holes are plugged with matching mortar.

Treating solid walls

Normally solid walls are insulated from the inside using one of a variety of methods (see Insulation). There are, however, ways of doing the job effectively externally.

Certainly exterior insulation is worth considering if the house walls are in a relatively poor state – with patches of missing stucco or damaged bricks, for example. It is also a sound option where fixing internal insulation would cause an undue amount of upheaval.

Any method involving external insulation must be left to professional specialists, from whom you should be prepared for a fairly high quote compared to the price of interior work. The alternative is to fix clapboarding – a job that can be tackled on a do-it-yourself basis and should work out much less expensive.

Should you want to have this work done, then you can choose to have a layer – from 1 to 3in thick – of polystyrene, polyurethane or foamed fiberglass fixed to the wall, reinforced with metal laths and then covered with stucco.

Alternatively mineral fibre slabs covered with a protective wire lathing or reinforced with fibrous mesh can be used. These are then covered with clapboarding or stucco.

Using clapboarding

Fixing clapboarding to all or part of a house serves a dual role of decorating and insulating at the same time. Although it can cover whole walls, it is also popularly used to highlight features such as porches, bay walls, gable ends or dormers. And sometimes just one storey of the house – upper or lower – is clad.

You should remember, however, that clapboarding is not intended to cover up unsound walls. On the contrary, it can only be fixed to stable sheathing, stucco or blockwork. Any area chosen for such treatment must also be dry, so existing damp problems have to be solved first. If the sheathing to which the cladding is fixed has started to rot or is prone to do so, the clapboarding itself will eventually be affected as well.

Houses have been weatherproofed with clapboarding for many years. In those days, however, the wood was really part of the house structure, whereas now it is usually decorative.

Today cedar or redwood is almost always used because of the prohibitive cost of hardwoods, quite apart from the environmental considerations involving the destruction of invaluable trees. They are widely available in a range of attractive different profiles.

■ Clapboarding has a long architectural history, especially in areas where wood-framed construction is the norm.

Vertical siding (below) is an alternative to plain bevel siding, offering good weatherproofing thanks to the positive overlap of the boards and battens.

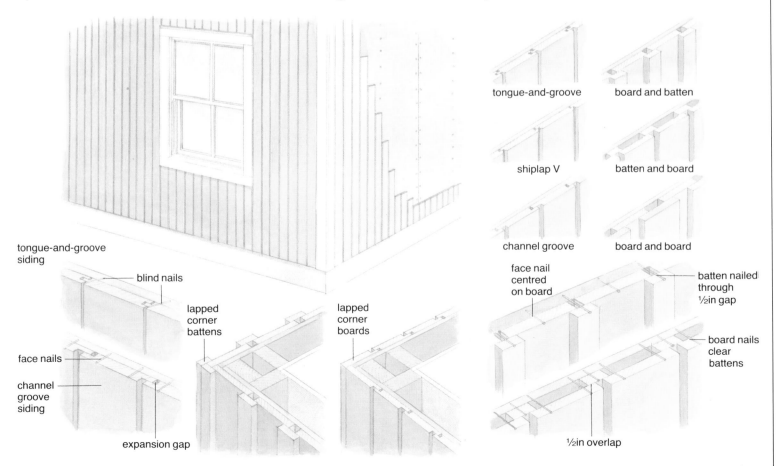

tongue-and-groove
siding

blind nails

face nails

channel
groove
siding

expansion gap

lapped
corner
battens

lapped
corner
boards

tongue-and-groove

shiplap V

channel groove

face nail
centred
on board

board and batten

batten and board

board and board

batten nailed
through
½in gap

board nails
clear
battens

½in overlap

The simplest is feather-edge clapboarding, wedge-shaped planks similar to those used for fencing. These are fixed horizontally, with their thicker bottom edge overlapping the thinner top edge of the boards below. This type is, however, prone to warping which can leave open gaps in the boards. They therefore tend to be used more on garden outbuildings or small feature areas of the house.

Shiplap clapboarding involves boards with a profiled cross-section with a rebate machined along one edge. These are the most widely used, having a more positive overlap between boards and resulting in a more weatherproof finish to the wall surface.

Tongued-and-grooved boards are also frequently used. Here the tongues of one board interlock with the grooves in the next, so warping is less of a problem and weather resistance is improved. Boards may be fixed vertically or even diagonally with little loss of performance. Additional detailing can be provided if boards with a machined V-joint are used as an alternative to plain boards.

Lastly, cedar rustic siding (normally 8 × 1in in cross-section) is sometimes used in a vertical format to create a more informal appearance.

Using vinyl siding

Maintenance problems with wooden clapboarding have been the main reason why unplasticised polyvinyl chloride (upvc) versions have emerged in recent years.

Upvc scores over wood because it does not rot, split or warp, cannot suffer from insect attack and does not need painting. All it requires is an annual clean down with detergent and the occasional, more frequent wash. In all other respects it is like wood, and can be cut and nailed or screwed in much the same way.

It is manufactured in profiles that resemble traditional clapboarding and matching fascias, bargeboards, soffits and window trims are also available. Although mainly used in white, other colors are produced. Lengths are commonly 12 to 15ft and widths usually between 4 and 6in – much as for wooden siding.

Special sections are available for joining lengths – edge-on or at corners – and edging strips are used to hold it in place.

The material expands more than wood, so extra care should be taken to fix it following the manufacturer's instructions. You must allow enough space for the boards to expand or contract as temperatures fluctuate. Even so,

■ Wall shingles are a popular alternative to wooden siding, and can be chosen to match the style and color of the house roof where this is also covered in shingles. A wide range of profiles is available.

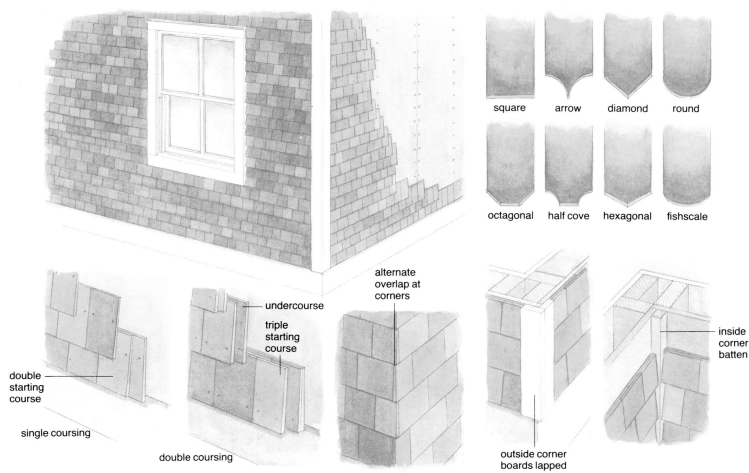

square   arrow   diamond   round

octagonal   half cove   hexagonal   fishscale

double starting course

single coursing

undercourse

triple starting course

double coursing

alternate overlap at corners

outside corner boards lapped

inside corner batten

■ The use of decorative shingles and ornate wooden trim painted in bright colors can make the exterior of the house look anything but ordinary. Decorative inserts relieve the visual tedium of large areas of plain shingles.

■ Stone cladding – slips of reconstituted stone that are bonded to an existing masonry surface – is best used to highlight a feature, rather than to cover whole walls. Very careful fixing is essential if premature failure of the bond is to be avoided.

vinyl siding may creak as it expands and contracts with changes in temperature.

Some boards are hollow-backed, while others contain internal stiffening ribs or a solid cellular core. Fixing is done using special clips or by direct nailing.

Where joins between lengths have to be made, these can be randomly spaced and hidden with special clip-on joint covers or aligned and covered with a continuous center-joint trim.

Vinyl siding can be painted using ordinary gloss paint. Simply wash down the surface thoroughly to remove dirt and grease, then lightly abrade it with fine wet-and-dry abrasive paper to provide a good key for the paint.

Increasing the insulation value

Although clapboarding itself provides additional weatherproofing and insulation, you can increase this by incorporating a lining of insulating material between the sheathing on the house wall and the clapboarding.

The simplest way is to use slabs of rigid polystyrene insulation board fitted between wall battens. Alternatively, use mineral wool or fiberglass insulation. Remember to leave a gap at least ½in wide between the outer face of the insulation and the inner face of the clapboarding to allow air to circulate.

Cladding with stone

Should you wish to make a feature of something like a bay window or porch and you would like a stone effect rather than wood, you can buy stone or brick tiles to use as cladding. These are stuck to the wall with a special mortar adhesive. A variety of types, sizes, shapes and thicknesses is available and you will need to follow the manufacturer's instructions carefully as to the correct fixing methods, especially with the heavier tiles. Some may need additional mechanical support. Most stone cladding is reconstituted, although some such as slate is of course a natural material.

External Doors and Windows

Whatever the type or age of a property, you will need to examine the external doors and windows carefully to see if they need to be repaired – or, at worst, replaced. In the latter case, you have the opportunity of enlarging, moving or adding extra doors and windows and this work is best combined with any plans you may have for repairing or rebuilding walls.

When you fit replacements, you should certainly consider the option of installing double glazing, which will save on energy, reduce heating costs and make the house a more comfortable place to live in.

BASIC TYPES OF DOOR

The chances are that external doors will be made from wood, although you may come across some of aluminum or even plastic. These are usually found in houses where doors have recently been replaced.

Anodised aluminum is widely used for front doors in a modern glass-panelled style. These are usually double-glazed with obscured, tempered safety glass and are supplied ready-hung in an aluminum subframe. Normally this is screwed into the existing door frame, although it may be fixed directly to the rough opening. Aluminum is also used for sliding patio doors.

Plastic-framed front doors are sometimes found in similar styles to the aluminum ones and are also usually double-glazed with safety glass. They are often found in houses where the windows, too, have been replaced with plastic-framed versions. Neither type gives rise to any special problems as far as maintenance is concerned.

Wooden doors are found in three basic types – panelled, flush or ledged and braced. All external doors should be a minimum of 1¾in thick to improve their security.

Panelled doors may be solid or partially or fully glazed. The rails (horizontal members) and stiles (vertical members) are made from solid wood and are mortised and tenoned for strength. A wide middle rail is usually provided for a mailslot to be fitted.

Doors of this type may be made from softwood (for painting) or hardwood (mainly for staining and varnishing, but sometimes painting). On hardwood doors the four or more panels are usually sculptured (raised and fielded) for an ornamental appearance, while softwood doors normally contain flat plywood panels that may have decorative moldings fixed around the edges.

Exterior flush doors are naturally stronger in construction than interior ones but are made in

■ Nothing suits a house better than its original front door . . .or a replacement as close as possible to the original in appearance. The choice of door styles is immense, ranging from solid panelled types to glazed versions with plain, patterned or stained glass.

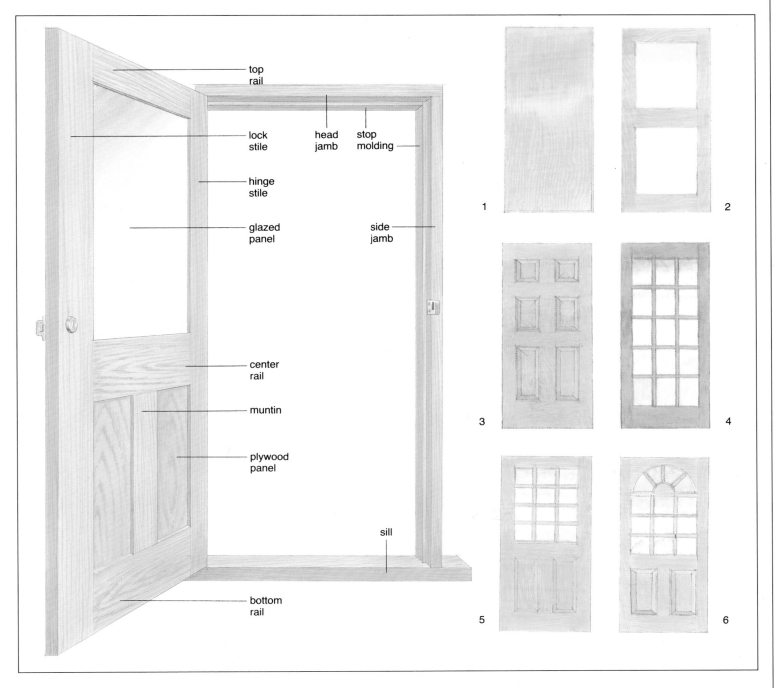

top
rail

lock
stile

head
jamb

stop
molding

hinge
stile

glazed
panel

side
jamb

center
rail

muntin

plywood
panel

sill

bottom
rail

1

2

3

4

5

6

a similar way – from a light wooden framework containing a honeycomb of packing material faced with exterior grade hardboard or plywood. Solid-core fire-resistant flush doors are also available.

The surfacing panels are usually flat, although they can be embossed by pressing to give the appearance of a panelled door, particularly after being painted. There is a wooden block set midway along one edge to take a lock and there may also be a center block to take a mailslot. Usually rubber stamp marks on the edges of a new flush door indicate the position of these blocks. You can also buy flush doors with open

panels for glazing, although most are available complete with glass.

If you have an older property such as a farmhouse, the doors may well be ledged and braced. This type is also often found on outbuildings and as side gates.

They are functional and sturdy, in most cases being made from V-jointed matchboarding nailed to wide horizontal members called ledges. To prevent the door from sagging, diagonal braces are fitted and it is most important to check that these run diagonally from low down on the hinge side of the door to high on the lock side.

■ Panelled and glazed doors have similar basic frameworks, with vertical stiles and horizontal rails linked by mortise-and-tenon or dowelled joints. Here (top left) a vertical muntin subdivides the lower part of the door into two panels; the upper part is glazed.

Some of the commonest door patterns (above) include the flush door (1); the two-panel door (2); the 15-pane glazed door (3); the six-panelled solid door (4) and half-glazed doors in a range of designs (5 and 6).

■ Doors can suffer from a range of different faults as a result of wear and tear, old age, lack of maintenance or improper hanging. Here are some cures for the most common problems, clockwise from top left.

1 Secure loose door frames by drilling a hole through the frame, then switch to a masonry drill bit and drill on into the masonry behind. Insert a long plastic frame plug, and screw the frame securely to the masonry.

2 Ease doors that bind in their frames at the top by chamfering the top edge slightly with a plane.

3 Tighten up loose corner joints by driving hardwood wedges into the mortise alongside the tenon, or by inserting glued dowels through the tenon.

4 Hinge screw heads that are not driven fully into their recesses will prevent the door from closing. Replace the screws if necessary.

5 Hinges set too deep in their recesses can also stop the door from closing. Fit packing under the hinge leaf to cure the problem.

6 If hinge screws work loose, remove them, drill out the screw holes and tap in a short piece of glued dowel. Make a new pilot hole and replace the screw.

7 If door bottoms bind slightly in solid floors, use abrasive paper to remove a little wood from the bottom edge of the door.

8 Where the door bottom binds seriously, take it off its hinges and plane wood from the bottom edge.

9 Cut out rot in the bottom of exterior door frames and replace it with new wood, scarf-jointed into place for extra strength.

10 Stop the leading edge binding against the door frame by sanding or planing down any high spots.

In superior quality houses you may find framed ledged and braced doors. Construction here is more or less the same, except for a mortised-and-tenoned outer frame which considerably strengthens the door and enables you to fit a good mortise lock.

Fitting a replacement door frame

In contrast to internal doors, an external door frame is substantial, with the jambs (side members) and head (top) mortised together and with the sill, which will probably be of hardwood, mortised and tenoned into the jambs.

If the sill is of stone or concrete, there are likely to be galvanized steel dowels in the base of the jambs which are cemented into holes in the sill. The jambs are made from solid pieces of wood and rebated (stepped) to take the door. If the frame was fixed when the house was built, it is likely to be held by metal ties screwed to the wood frame wall studs.

To remove an old frame, you will probably have to remove the nails or ties connecting it to the rough opening frame. Using a general purpose saw – or a metal-cutting blade in a trimming knife handle – cut through the metal fixings holding the frame to the wall studs.

At about the mid-point, use the general-purpose saw to cut through the jambs at a sloping angle. This will enable you to prise away one part from the wall using a wrecking bar. With one piece out of the way, you will then be able to work round the opening, removing the other pieces of the frame in turn.

Check that the new frame fits in the opening, then remove it and bed a strip of waterproofing material at the base of the opening. Reposition the frame, making sure it is central, level and plumb (vertical) – and not twisted. Either lag-bolt or nail the frame into the rough opening in the wall.

Fitting a new door

Saw off the horns of the stiles that protect the corners of the door in transit, then try the door for fit by holding it against the frame. It is certain to need trimming on one or more edges. Get someone to help you hold it in place, if necessary supporting it on wedges under the bottom edge while you mark it.

Working from the frame side, draw round the edge of the frame with a pencil on to the face of the door against the frame, allowing a $\frac{1}{16}$in gap all round after trimming.

Saw across the bottom of the door and plane along the edges until the door fits correctly in the opening. Pass the plane a couple of extra times along the leading edge of the door to ensure it will clear the frame edge as it closes even if the door should expand slightly.

External door frames usually have a metal water bar along the sill. To prevent drafts and water ingress, it is important that the door closes up against this. Therefore you must cut a rebate (or step) along the bottom edge of the door on the face (outer) side. You will need a router and suitable cutter for this. Otherwise use a circular saw to cut the rebate to the correct depth, working first along the face of the door and then making a cut at right angles to the original one in the base of the door to complete the rebate.

If you are fitting the door in an old frame, mark the hinge positions on the back of the door while it is wedged in the opening with the correct clearance all round. Remove the door and transfer the marked hinge positions on to the edge of the door.

Cut the recesses with a chisel, holding it upright and striking it with a hammer to cut the outline of the recess. Then make a series of cuts about ¼in apart across the width of the recess. Turn the chisel so it is flat in the recess and pare out the waste wood carefully to the required depth.

Get someone to hold the door on wedges in its open position and then, with the hinge flaps positioned in their recesses, initially fit just one screw in each hinge. Close the door to see how it fits in the frame, adjusting the depth of the hinge recesses if it binds. When you are satisfied that it fits correctly, insert the rest of the screws and drive them fully home.

If you are fitting the door in a new frame, wedge the door in place and mark the hinge positions on both the door and the frame. Use three hinges for an external door. The highest one should be fitted about 5in down from the top of the door, the lowest about 8in up from the bottom and the third hinge (if fitted) midway between the two.

Remove the door, mark out the hinge recesses on the door edge and frame, then cut the recesses as described above. The width of the recesses should be such that the knuckle (pivoting part) of the hinge protrudes from the edge of the door. Finally screw the hinges in position as before.

Always ensure that the screw heads are recessed into the countersinks in hinge leaves. If they stand at all proud, the door may not close properly.

In certain circumstances it may be preferable to install a completely new door and frame

Hanging a new door

■ Hanging a new door can seem a complex operation, especially if the original door was a non-standard size. Buy a door in the next largest available size so it can be cut down to fit.
1 Start by propping the door against the door frame on wedges to give the necessary floor clearance.

3 If the door is only fractionally over-size, plane it down to the marked lines (right), taking care not to split the wood as you approach the corners.

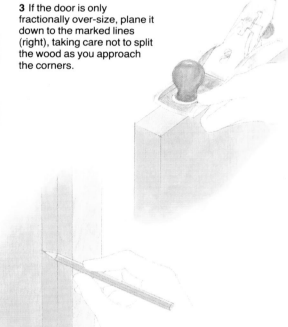

2 Run a pencil along the door face, first against the top of the frame (above) and then down the sides (right). It helps to have an extra pair of hands available for this stage of the job.

bought as a pre-hung unit. The range of styles and sizes available is quite extensive and they are simple to install, just needing a rough opening about 1in taller and wider than the new unit. This is set in place, squared off, shimmed and nailed to the frame of the opening, ready for the casing trim to be added.

Fitting door hardware

A back door needs a good quality mortise deadlock (ideally with at least five levers) and bolts top and bottom. A front door also needs a deadlocking cylinder rim latch or nightlatch so you can open it easily and quickly. Again, there should be bolts top and bottom and also a door chain and door viewer for complete security.

Locks come with fitting instructions and you must follow these carefully. Mortise locks, for example, are secure because the body of the lock is concealed within the thickness of the door. However, cutting too wide a slot for a lock can weaken the door, so buy the narrowest type available.

To fit this type you will have to mark the outline of the lock on the edge of the door and drill out the mortise slot to the depth of the lock case. Clean up the slot with a chisel and bore the door stile to take the key and spindle holes.

Rim locks screw to the surface of the door and are very easy to fit. The hardest part is drilling a large hole for the cylinder of the lock in the door stile. Use a large-diameter flat wood bit for this or drill a ring of small holes and cut out the waste with a key saw.

It is a good idea to fit bolts at the top and bottom of all external doors, but rather than fix surface-mounted barrel bolts, go for higher security mortise bolts. These comprise a cylindrical bolt enclosed in a barrel which is fitted into a hole drilled in the edge of the door.

By inserting a splined key in the edge of the door, you can wind the bolt in and out. And because it is enclosed, the bolt is difficult to tamper with and therefore provides better security than a surface-mounted bolt.

If you want to fit a door chain, you simply screw the device to the inside face of the door. This will prevent an intruder pushing in should you open the door.

If you have solid doors, you should always combine this type of security with a peephole to enable you to see who is at the door before you open it. All you have to do is drill a hole of about ½in diameter through the door at eye level and screw the two halves of the viewer together from opposite sides of the door.

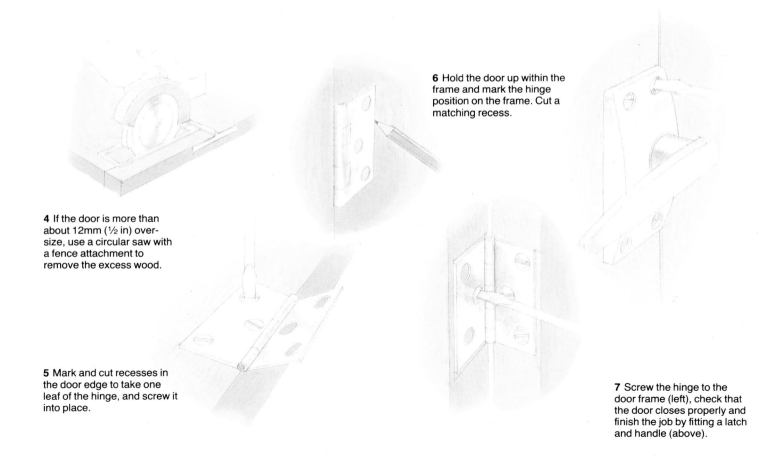

4 If the door is more than about 12mm (½ in) over-size, use a circular saw with a fence attachment to remove the excess wood.

5 Mark and cut recesses in the door edge to take one leaf of the hinge, and screw it into place.

6 Hold the door up within the frame and mark the hinge position on the frame. Cut a matching recess.

7 Screw the hinge to the door frame (left), check that the door closes properly and finish the job by fitting a latch and handle (above).

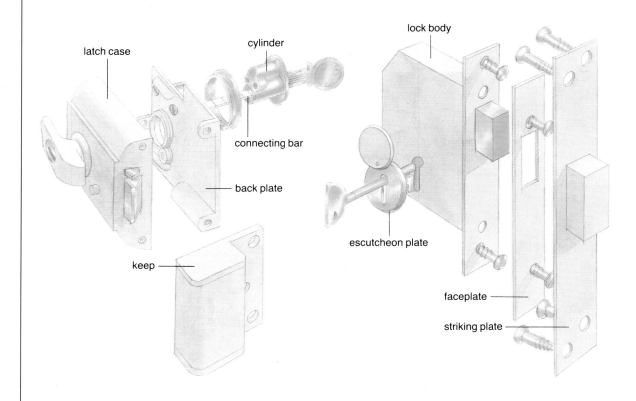

latch case

cylinder

connecting bar

back plate

keep

lock body

escutcheon plate

faceplate

striking plate

■ A cylinder or rim lock (far left) consists of a latch case that is screwed to the inner face of the door and a lock cylinder that fits in a hole drilled through the door stile. To fit one, use the template provided to mark the cylinder position and drill its hole. Screw the backplate to the door, insert the cylinder so its connecting bar passes into the backplate, and cut this to length with a hacksaw. Insert the connecting screws through the backplate to secure the cylinder, then screw the latch case to the backplate. Finally, fit the keep to the door frame.

■ A mortise lock (left) has a lock body that fits in a mortise cut in the door edge. To fit one, mark the position of the lock body on the door edge, mark out and cut the mortise and chisel out a recess in the door edge for the lock's foreplate. Mark the keyhole position on the door face, drill and cut the keyholes, then fit the lock into its mortise and check the key operation. Finally fit the striking plate to the frame.

To fit a door knocker or door pull you simply drill a hole (or holes) centrally for the fixing bolt. You fit the knocker or pull in place from the outside and then hold it secure with a fixing nut or screw on the inside.

Fitting a mailslot is more tricky. Mark out a rectangular opening on the centre of the door slightly larger than the plate flap. Drill a hole at each corner big enough for a power jigsaw blade or pad saw blade to pass through. Cut out the rectangle of wood and clean up the sides of the opening with a large chisel.

One refinement is to slope the top and bottom edges of the cut-out downwards so that mail does not lodge in the opening. Finally drill a hole at each end of the opening to take the fixing bolts and screw the mailslot in place.

BASIC TYPES OF WINDOW

Apart from the variety of styles, the first thing you will notice about windows is the range of materials from which they are made. What sort you have in your home will have a dramatic effect on the maintenance required.

In the majority of cases, the windows will be made of wood. Here the type used and the quality of their construction will have a significant influence on their likely lifespan.

Many 19th and early 20th century houses still have their original windows, providing they were properly installed and have been regularly maintained since. Wooden windows on newer houses, however, are often made from fast-grown wood and are much less durable. Even if they are correctly maintained, they are unlikely to last more than 30 or 40 years. On the other hand, you may be fortunate enough to have a house with hardwood windows, which can be expected to last 60 years or more.

There are advantages of having wooden windows – durability, as long as they are properly maintained; cheapness; a well-insulated frame; and a wide choice of finishes, using traditional paint or modern preservative wood stains.

The disadvantages include the need for regular maintenance every few years; the rapid deterioration that takes place if the windows are not painted regularly; the lack of built-in weatherstrips on older wooden windows to prevent drafts; and the variable quality of wood used in their construction.

The other material sometimes used in older houses is steel. Such windows are poor insulators and condensation on the frames and glass is a frequent problem. This condensation often leads to rusting, especially on earlier frames which were not galvanized or where the galvanizing has broken down.

This type is often drafty, can look out of keeping with traditional-style properties and needs frequent painting. On the plus side, galvanized frames tend to be unaffected by dampness, can be painted any color and are not expensive to replace if required.

In houses where improvements have been made, you may find aluminum windows and, as likely as not, these will be double-glazed. Although they may not be aesthetically suited to an older property, they do present few problems. Bear in mind, however, that the timber subframes into which they are fitted will need frequent painting.

Aluminum frames are unaffected by dampness and are usually weather-stripped to prevent draughts. But sometimes they can suffer from condensation since older types were not fitted with a thermal break.

Anodized finishes and acrylic coatings should last 50 years or more if they are washed down regularly, although their life may be considerably shortened by pollution in industrial areas.

Plastic is a comparative newcomer to the renovation scene, although the material has been used for years in Europe. With such material you can expect a life of at least 30 to 40 years for your windows.

One advantage is provided by the 'chunky' look, enabling such windows to make good replacements for wooden ones in older style properties. They offer good insulation and, because they are self-colored, they generally need no decoration. You may, however, have to freshen them up by applying a coat of paint after 10 or 15 years.

FITTING A REPLACEMENT WINDOW

If a window has deteriorated to such an extent that repair becomes impossible, then it will be best to replace it with a new frame.

Although you will have the choice of a wide range of designs, do bear in mind the style of the house and that of the windows in neighboring properties when selecting new ones to ensure they are sympathetic with the style of the building.

Removing the old frame
Always start by removing the opening frames, unscrewing them at the hinges. If the screw slots are clogged with paint, clear them by striking the handle of the screwdriver lightly with a hammer.

Next remove the fixed panes. Wearing safety spectacles and thick gloves, chip away the glazing compound and prise out the glazing

■ Windows are a house's eyes, and are often a major architectural feature in their own right. There is probably more variety found in window styles than in any other part of the house exterior except for the front door. Despite these variations, however, most still fall into one of two groups – those with hinged casements and those with sliding sashes.

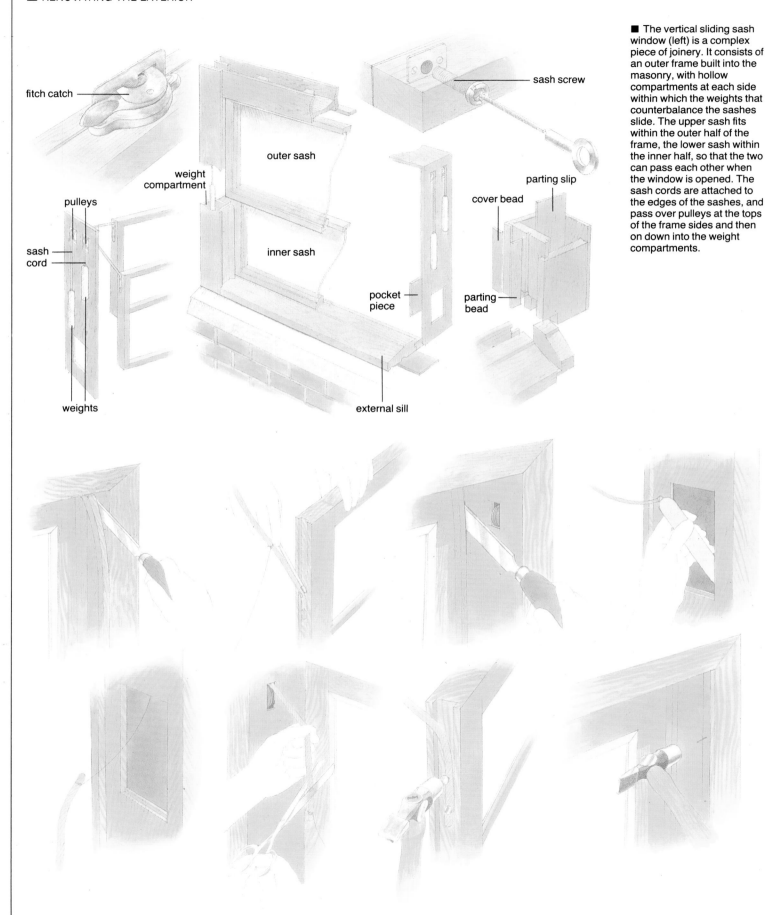

fitch catch

sash screw

outer sash

weight compartment

parting slip

cover bead

pulleys

sash cord

inner sash

pocket piece

parting bead

weights

external sill

■ The vertical sliding sash window (left) is a complex piece of joinery. It consists of an outer frame built into the masonry, with hollow compartments at each side within which the weights that counterbalance the sashes slide. The upper sash fits within the outer half of the frame, the lower sash within the inner half, so that the two can pass each other when the window is opened. The sash cords are attached to the edges of the sashes, and pass over pulleys at the tops of the frame sides and then on down into the weight compartments.

■ The casement window is simpler in construction than the sash window, consisting of a main outer frame into which fixed glass and hinged casements and top lights are fitted. The frame is screwed to masonry walls or nailed to the wall studs otherwise.

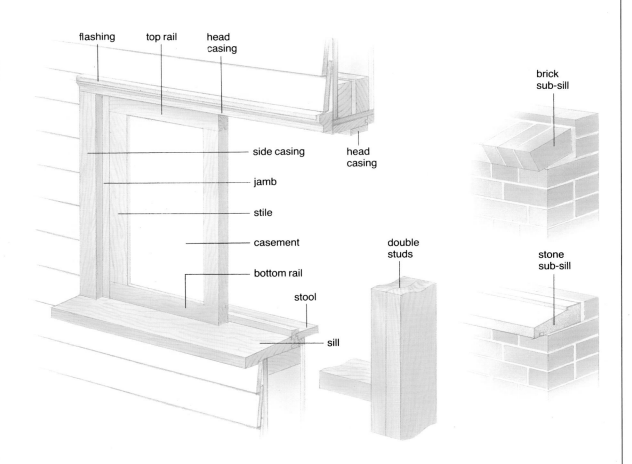

■ To replace a broken sash cord, start by prising off the parting bead at each side so you can lift out the inner sash. Tie string to its cords, and cut them from the sash. Remove the parting beads and repeat the procedure to free the outer sash. Then lever out the pocket pieces, lift out the weights and pull the cords out so they draw the strings over the pulleys.

Remove the old cords and tie the pulled-through string to the new cords. Draw them over their pulleys, tie on the weights and trim the other end of the cord roughly to length. Get a helper to offer up each sash in turn, and nail the new cords to the sash sides. Finally, replace the parting bead and then the sash bead.

points if you want to save the glass. Otherwise carefully break out the old glass.

If the window being replaced is itself a replacement, it may be possible to unscrew it and lift it out of the sub-frame in one piece.

To remove the sub-frame from the opening, use an old saw to cut through the side members. The reason for using an old saw is simply that it will not matter if the teeth hit fragments of glass, old fixing nails or hidden frame fixings.

Lever the side pieces away from the wall and then prise away the head of the frame and the sill. If you are considering altering the size of the opening, this is the time to do it. A large opening can be partially framed out to make it smaller, while a small opening can be made deeper by cutting out and lowering the sill. To make the opening wider, however, you will have to fit a new, longer header (supporting beam) at the top of the opening.

Use a broadly similar technique to remove old frames from masonry walls. Once you have levered the frame sections out, remove or cut through any old fixing screws and chop away old mortar from the sides and bottom of the opening ready for the new frame.

Fitting the new frame

If your replacement frame is a conventional pre-manufactured one, this will be supplied as a ready-made unit that is fixed in place and then glazed on site. If it is of plastic, aluminum or galvanized steel, this will usually be fitted into a subframe that must first be fixed into the wall opening. The new unit may well be supplied ready-glazed.

In the case of a conventional wooden frame, it will probably be possible to keep the original internal window frame ledge and fit the new frame against it.

The new frame will probably be supplied with horns (corner projections) for protection in transit. Cut these off and give the exterior surfaces of the frame an extra coat of wood primer or preservative stain, depending on the final finish you require.

Lift the frame into position and check it is square – that is, with equal diagonals. Wedge it in place so that it is level and plumb (vertical), making sure it is not under strain or twisted. If the frame is slightly too small for the opening, you can use packing pieces to wedge it in place in the opening.

When it is correctly fitted, mark the positions

of the wedges and the fixing nails. Most window frames need three or four nails on each side and these should be positioned so they go firmly into the sub-frame. A little wood filler will cover up the nail heads ready for subsequent painting. Fill any narrow gaps between the frame and the wall with mastic injected into the gap, using a trigger-operated applicator gun.

If you are fitting the new frame into a masonry wall, set it in place within the opening on a bed of mortar and again wedge it in place so you can check that it is level and plumb. Then mark the positions for the fixing screws through each side of the frame, making sure that they will be passing into solid masonry and not into the mortar courses for a secure fixing.

What you do next depends on whether you are using conventional screws and wallplugs or special frame plugs with extra-long fixing screws. With the former, drill clearance and countersunk holes for the screws in the frame first, then mark the fixing hole positions on the masonry through these screw holes. Lift the frame out, drill out the holes in the masonry and insert the wallplugs. Replace the frame, aligning the holes carefully, and drive in the fixing screws. With frame plugs, which have an elongated sleeve that passes through the frame

■ The commonest problems with casement windows are casements that bind in their frames, and sagging joints. Use a plane to shave the binding edges, then stain or paint the bare wood. Repair sagging joints temporarily with metal repair plates. For a more permanent repair to a mortised-and-tenoned frame, either knock the corner joints apart and re-glue them, or drive in slim hardwood wedges alongside the tenons.

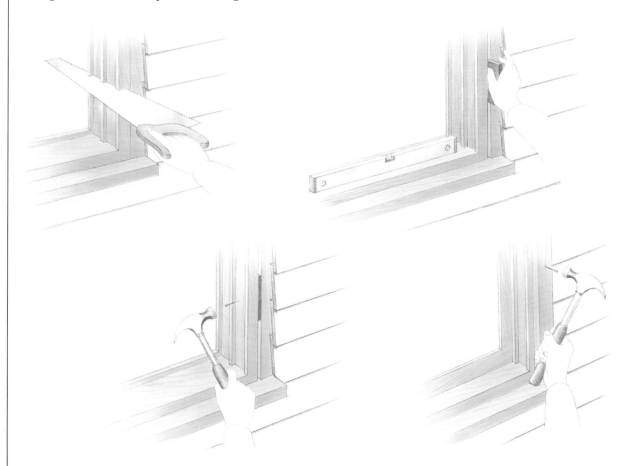

■ To replace a window frame, unscrew any opening casements or top lights, and carefully break out fixed panes of glass. Then saw through the frame at each corner and prise the frame sections away.

Next, set the new frame in place within the opening, with the top flashing over the head of the frame, and nail through the sides into the wall studs to secure the frame in place.

■ To reglaze a window, lift out the broken pieces of glass and chip out the old glazing compound. Then press some fresh compound round the rebate and press the new pane into place to compress it to a thickness of about ⅛in. Secure the pane with glazing points, press in the facing compound and finish it to a neat 45° angle all round. Finally, trim off excess compound.

into wallplugs. Then screw the new window frame securely into place within the sub-frame.

Glazing a window

Before glazing a window, you must first treat the frame with a suitable primer paint and allow this to dry.

Select your glazing compound according to the type of frame – conventional or brown for wooden frames and universal or metal for metal frames. Modern double-glazed windows have gaskets to hold the glass in position. If they are not already glazed, fitting instructions will be supplied with the frames.

Work the compound in the hands to soften it before applying a ⅛in thick band into the rebate of the frame. Press it out between the thumb and forefinger. If it is too sticky, wrap it in newspaper for 24 hours to dry out the solvents a little.

Now lift the glass into place in the rebate and carefully press it (edges only) back on to the compound. Hold the glass in place by inserting glazing points (small wedge-shaped nails) about 8in apart round the perimeter in front of the glass. Tap in the points carefully with the edge of the glazing knife or large chisel held flat over the face of the glass.

Apply a second layer of compound to the outside of the glass and smooth it off to a bevel of about 45° with a filling knife. If the knife sticks, moisten it with water.

Remove excess compound from the inside and outside of the pane with the knife and allow it to harden for about two weeks before priming and painting it.

INSULATING WINDOWS

Of the total heat lost from the average house, about 15 per cent will go through ordinary single-glazed windows, two-thirds of which can be cut by fitting double glazing. Secondary benefits from this will include a reduction in drafts and noise from outside as well as a considerable heat gain inside the house on sunny days, even in winter.

So you should, when replacing windows, seriously consider the advantages to be gained from installing one of the systems available (see Insulation, page 199). Although the initial costs will be increased, the long-term savings can be considerable. A major consideration here is that you will be removing your old window anyway, so the installation costs of a sealed unit will be effectively reduced by the price of the single thickness of glass you would have to buy otherwise.

and into the wall, drill a larger clearance hole through the frame first, then change to a masonry bit and drill on through this hole into the masonry. Then insert the frame plug fully and drive the special long fixing screws home. Finish off by covering the screw heads with filler or caulk, and seal all round the outside perimeter of the frame with more caulk for a weatherproof finish.

To install some metal and plastic window frames in masonry walls, you have to fit a wooden sub-frame within the opening first. Bed it on caulk all round and fix it with screws driven

RENOVATING THE INTERIOR

The inside of your home offers you even greater opportunities for restoration and renovation than does the exterior. Not only do you have a greater variety of features and materials to work with indoors; you also have the opportunity to ensure that both the looks and the performance of the interior suit the needs of your family and match your lifestyle.

Floors and Staircases

TYPES OF FLOOR

Two kinds of floor are to be found in houses – either a suspended wooden construction or a directly laid solid concrete slab.

Suspended wooden ground floors are found mostly in woodframe houses. Upper floors are always suspended. The term 'suspended' means that the floor hangs from the house walls. Joists sized according to span and load (typically 2 × 8in or 2 × 10in for normal residential conditions) span between loadbearing walls. Recently constructed floors may be supported on metal joist hangers. The joists are typically spaced at 16in centers, but may be as far apart as 24in.

Upper floor joists are sometimes given intermediate support by internal walls (hence the term 'supporting wall') over long spans.

The joists are covered by a sub-floor of wide boards or plywood sheathing, to which the finished floorboards are then nailed. These boards can either be square-edged or tongued-and-grooved. Square-edged boards generally develop gaps between them which allow dust to pass through. In the last 80 years these have largely been superseded by interlocking tongued-and-grooved boards. If you pass a blade down between the boards, you can establish which type is fitted.

In the most modern houses, it has become commonplace to dispense with floorboards and nail large sheets of flooring grade particle board or plywood to the joists. The sheets are either ¾ or ⅞in thick and usually measure 8 × 4ft.

Wooden floors have to be kept clear of the ground and be well ventilated to prevent wood rot developing as a consequence of the wood becoming damp. Ventilation is provided through air vents situated in foundation walls where there is no basement.

Solid ground floors are sometimes found in houses built in the 1940s and 1950s, although wooden floors are still the norm for this period.

Older solid floors can be the source of dampness simply because there is no damp-

■ In platform framing (below left), the first floor is built up off a sill plate bolted to the foundation walls. The joists rest on the sill plate, with double or triple end joists at each side and single end joists across the cut joist ends. The sub-floor is nailed to the joists, then a sole plate is nailed on and the ceiling-height wall studs are toe-nailed to it at the fixing centers. At second-floor level a double top plate bridges the tops of the studs, then come the second-floor joists, the sub-floor and the second-storey studs and top plate.

■ In balloon framing (below), the studs run to the full building height, nailed directly to the main sill plate above the foundation walls. First-floor joists rest on the sill plate alongside the studs, with vertical firestops between the studs at open joist ends. At second-floor level the joist ends rest on a ribbon let into the studs.

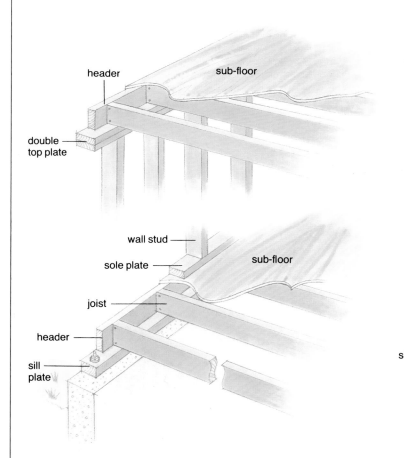

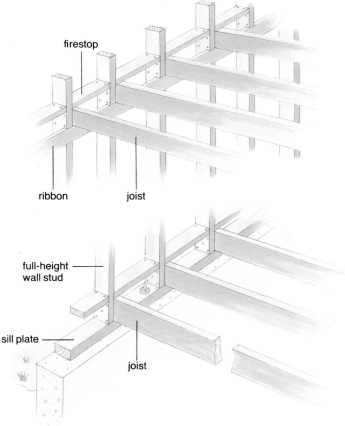

■ Solid floors are either separate reinforced concrete slabs cast on top of compacted gravel inside the foundation walls, or are cast at the same time as the foundations as a continuous slab and grade beam. A vapor barrier is laid over a gravel base course to keep dampness at bay. The slab is then covered with a thin screed of fine concrete which forms the finished floor surface.

Solid floors benefit from the inclusion of insulation; this can be added to an existing floor underneath a new floating floor surface or new floor screed (far right) or, if the floor is being completely re-laid, it can be placed beneath the new vapor barrier.

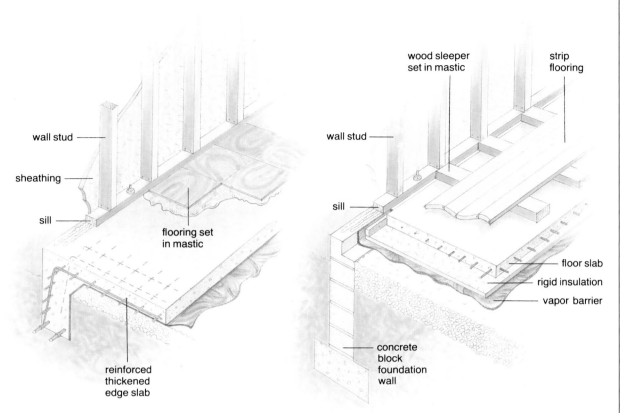

wall stud

sheathing

sill

flooring set in mastic

reinforced thickened edge slab

wood sleeper set in mastic

strip flooring

wall stud

sill

floor slab

rigid insulation

vapor barrier

concrete block foundation wall

proofing layer built into them. This is not normally the case with their modern counterparts, although they too can suffer through poor workmanship or faulty materials.

Nowadays a solid floor consists of a layer of 4 to 6in of crushed stone or gravel. This provides a solid firm foundation and a smooth base on which to lay a vapor barrier of 6-mil polyethylene over which the floor itself is laid. The concrete floor, which should be 4 to 6in thick, can be reinforced with wire mesh and may have a fine concrete levelling course laid on top ready for the flooring to be laid.

Insulation can be built into the floor by incorporating sheets of 2in thick rigid expanded polystyrene between the floor slab and the levelling course.

Should dampness become a problem in a solid floor, it can be treated by brushing on a dampproof membrane. This can be a moisture-cured plastic sealer, a black pitch epoxy type or a bitumen product. These are all available from builders' supply companies.

Normally the membrane has to be taken up the surrounding walls to link with the damp-proof layer. You must follow the manufacturer's specific instructions for each product regarding drying time, the number of coats that should be applied and so on.

Removing old floorcoverings

If you have to carry out repair work to an old boarded or solid floor, you will first of all usually have to lift the old floorcovering. In the case of carpet you simply pull it away from its fastenings and take up any underlay beneath it. Sheet vinyl floorcoverings are usually stuck down at edges and seams, and can be lifted easily; use an electric hot air gun to soften the old adhesive and scrape it off.

Tiles are the most difficult floorcovering to remove. Use a club hammer and brick bolster to dislodge ceramic tiles, and lever up vinyl or cork tiles with a wide-bladed scraper.

Lifting floorboards

The type of floorboard determines the way each board can be lifted. If you do not know what kind you have, look for a board that has been lifted before and remove it. Alternatively stick a knife blade between several boards. If it goes right down, the boards are square-edged. If it is blocked, the boards are tongued-and-grooved.

To lift a square-edged board, you can sometimes insert a bolster chisel near one end and lever the nails free from the joists below. Insert another bolster or lever on the opposite side and work them along until the nails at each joist have been released and the board is free.

■ Old boarded floors suffer from a variety of faults. Board ends may warp and lift, especially if they have been prised up before for maintenance work on services run beneath the floor surface. Shrinkage can lead to gaps between boards or along baseboards, while physical damage can cause splits and cracks. Boards may also bow upwards along their length, pulling up their fixings and causing the boards to creak when stepped on.

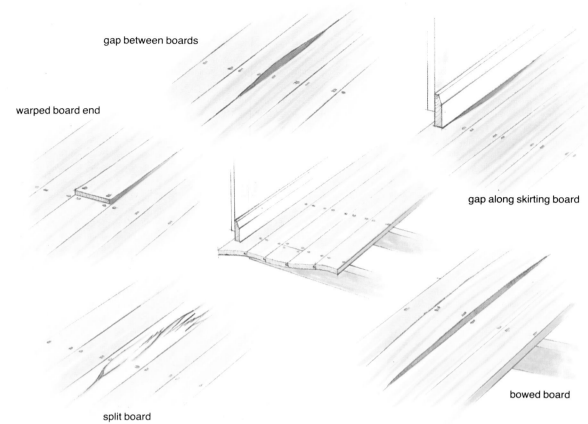

gap between boards

warped board end

gap along skirting board

split board

bowed board

■ Most homes have a wooden sub-floor – either diagonal boarding made up of square-edged boards laid at 45° to the joist line in older homes, or plywood sheathing laid with the joints staggered as shown.

Some building codes require cross-bridging or solid blocking between the joists to prevent their rotation or displacement. A separate layer of underlayment-grade plywood is also sometimes used to provide a smooth base for resilient floorcoverings.

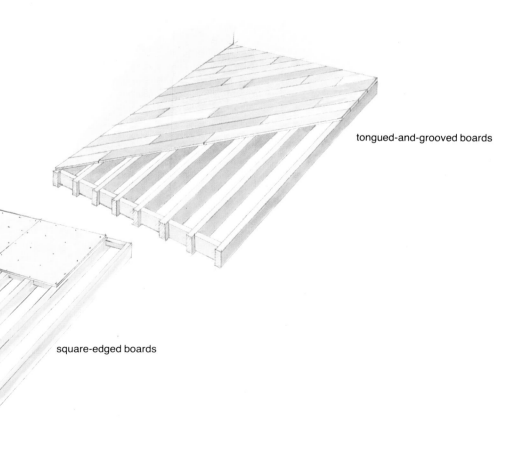

tongued-and-grooved boards

square-edged boards

■ To lift old floorboards for repair or replacement, or to gain access to services run beneath them, prise up a board end with a bolster and then lever it up along its length. If the boards are tongued-and-grooved, saw through the tongues along each side of the board first with a circular saw set to a cutting depth of about 12mm (½in). To lift just a section of board, drill a starter hole through it beside a joist and cut across the board with a padsaw. Wedge up the cut end and saw through the board at the next joist position. Fix battens to the joist sides to support the ends of the new length of board, and nail it into place.

Alternatively slide a metal bar or piece of wood under the board and press down on the end to 'spring' the nails free.

If you can't get a bolster below the board, drill a ½in diameter hole near to a joist end. The nail positions will guide you. Then cut through the board at a right-angle using a jig saw or a saber saw, taking care not to cut any cables below. You can now raise the board as described earlier.

Removing the first tongued-and-grooved board is more tricky. After that, the others are easy. First you will have to cut through the tongue along the length of the board using a circular saw or a floorboard saw. The circular saw should be set to cut to a depth of no more than ½in.

Lifting particle board flooring

To take up a damaged area of a particle board floor you need a circular saw set to cut to a depth of either ¾ or ⅞in depending on the thickness of the board. Do not go any deeper than necessary or you may cut through the tops of the joists. Make a cut along the joint between adjacent boards and lever up the board with a bolster chisel.

Measure up carefully for the replacement piece of board (of the correct thickness) and refix it, if necessary on to 2 × 1in cross timbers nailed between the joists. If there are gaps at the edges, fill them with caulk or wood filler.

Treating warped boards

If boards are warped, but the trouble is only slight, you can use an electric industrial floor sander to smooth off the surface. Remove any carpet tacks and punch all nails below the surface using a nail set and hammer so they do not tear the abrasive belt fitted to the sander.

A floor sander can be obtained from a tool rental company. Apart from levelling boards, it can also be used where you want to resurface the boards before polyurethaning them. Because sanding is very dusty work, make sure you seal off the room, cover any furniture left in and wear a face mask.

The sander will be supplied with sheets of abrasive, which you fit to the large revolving drum of the machine. Assuming that the boards are in an average state, then start sanding with a medium-grade abrasive and end with a fine grade to get a smoother finish. Only on a very uneven surface or where there is a thick coating of paint or polish should you need a coarse abrasive to start with.

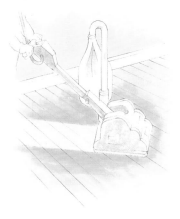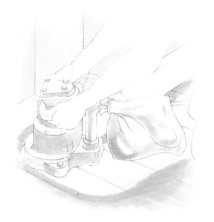

■ To restore floorboards that are sound but very dirty or marked, hire a powered floor sander. Use coarse abrasive initially and sand at 45° to the board direction. Then sand along the board direction, first with medium-grade abrasive and then with a finer grade. Finish off the edges of the room with a smaller disc or belt sander.

Since a large floor sander will not reach into the edges, you will also need a hand-held belt sander to finish off close to the baseboards.

Normally you sand a floor in the direction of the boards. If, however, they are in a poor condition, make the first pass at a 45° angle to the boards. Finish off working parallel with them. Never work at right-angles to the boards, since this will tear the surface.

Tilt the sander off the floor before switching it on. Then lower it on to the boards and work it slowly backwards and forwards over a few feet. Then move to the next section of board and repeat the process, overlapping the previous sanded area by about 3in. The machine will take off about ⅛in of wood fairly quickly.

If you switch on with the sander flat on the floor or work too slowly, you can make indentations in the floor surface. Before applying any final treatment such as polyurethane, you will have to vacuum the floor and room thoroughly to remove all dust.

Where floors are generally uneven, nail or screw the boards down firmly and then lay sheets of Masonite, secured with pins at about 9in intervals to provide a smooth surface on which to lay the new floorcovering.

Filling gaps between boards

An odd gap between boards can be filled with floor caulk. With a wider gap, glue a suitably sized wedge-shaped piece of wood and tap it into the gap. Then level it off with a plane.

Where there are lots of gaps, the quickest repair is to lay hardboard. (Masonite) as mentioned earlier. You would normally do this anyway if you were laying a new floorcovering.

Where you want to leave the boards exposed so they can be polyurethaned and rugs or a carpet square laid in strategic areas, you will have to relay them. This gives you the opportunity to refix the boards upside down to provide a fresh, clean surface although you are likely to have to do some localized sanding to remove the joist marks.

Treating sunken boards

If any of the floorboards have dropped, take them up and insert shims of Masonite or plywood where they are fixed to the joists. If they have warped downwards slightly, refix them upside down and sand them smooth. If either problem cannot be cured using these methods, then fit a replacement board of the required thickness.

■ **Right** If all the boards have shrunk to leave wide gaps, lift them all and re-lay to close up the gaps. Loose-lay four or five boards, then nail another board to the joists about 2in away and use a floorboard cramp or a pair of wedges to tighten up the first group of boards. Nail them down, remove the odd board and lay the next group. At the far side of the room, lay the last board tight against the wall and fit a cut-down strip of board in the remaining gap.

■ **Below** Before laying any new floorcovering, check that the heads of all the nails securing the boards to the joists are well punched down. Fill occasional gaps with narrow strips of timber, glued and hammered into place and planed down flush with the floor surface. Cover uneven floorboards with sheets of hardboard before putting down thin sheet floorcoverings, with narrow strips laid over pipe or cable runs to provide access for future maintenance.

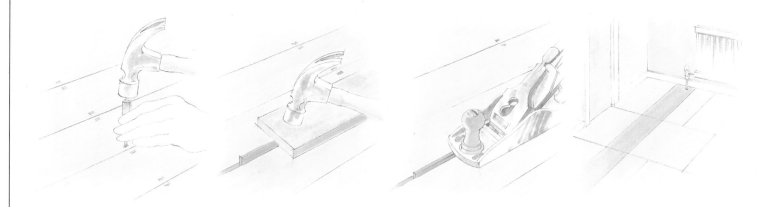

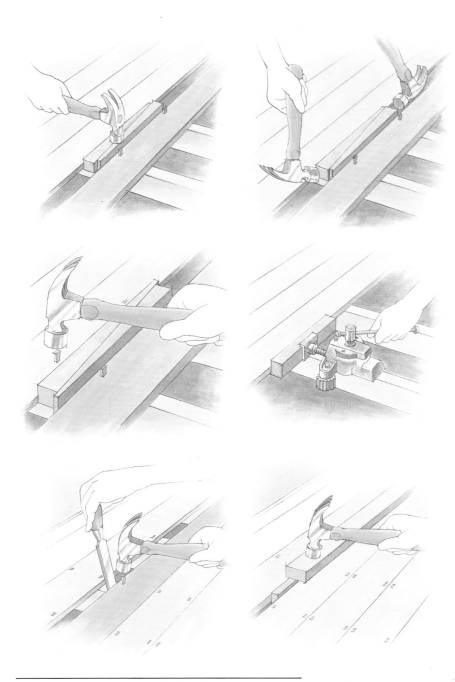

end-nailed through the header at each end. With balloon framing the joist ends lap the sides of the wall studs; they rest on the sill plate at first-floor level and on a ribbon let into the studs at second-floor level, and are nailed to the studs to secure them in position. Then add the new floor sheathing.

Relaying boards

If you are replacing boards, lay four or five in position on the joists, butting up their edges closely. Next nail a length of $1 \times 4in$ timber to the joists about 3 or 4in away. Cut two tapered wedges and hammer them into the gap between the piece of wood and the boards. This will force the boards tightly together so that they can be nailed correctly in place. Then remove the wedges.

Repeat this with the next group of boards and carry on with this procedure until the floor is complete. You will probably have to cut a narrow strip to finish off at the baseboard when you reach the far side of the room.

LEVELLING SOLID FLOORS

You can fill irregularities on a solid floor with cement mortar and then smooth it over, up to about ⅛in deep, with a self-smoothing layer. This is mixed with water to form a creamy paste, which you pour on to the floor and roughly spread out with a steel float. The screed will automatically smooth out any trowel marks before it hardens.

With irregularities up to about ⅜in deep, you can apply a ready-mixed filler to level the surface. Indentations up to 2in deep can be filled by resurfacing the floor with a conventional cement mortar layer consisting of three parts clean sand to one part cement. Before applying the mix, paint the floor surface with pva bonding agent to improve adhesion.

REPLACING FLOORS

Replacing a complete floor either of a suspended or solid construction is a rare requirement. Normally you will find any work involved should be a matter of straightforward repairs.

If joists are badly affected, new ones will have to be laid. This is not skilled work since all you have to do is replace the old joists with wood of the same dimensions that has been treated with preservative.

If you do the job yourself, make sure that the joists are properly secured and levelled. With platform framing the joists must be toe-nailed onto the wall's sill or top plate, and then

■ Use self-smoothing compound to level an uneven solid floor. Pour it on . . .

. . . .then trowel it out evenly and leave it to find its own level and harden.

■ You must call in a professional extermination contractor to treat a full-scale insect infestation; you cannot do the work yourself. The chemicals needed are unpleasant to handle and potentially dangerous to inhale, and are available only to licensed operators. A professional firm will treat the attack thoroughly and also issue a guarantee against fresh attacks.

LOOKING OUT FOR TERMITES AND ROT

Timber floors in a house have two natural enemies – termites and rot. Both will attack where the right conditions exist. It is a classical case of prevention being better than cure, since the upheaval and cost of remedying either can by considerable.

Termites pose the biggest threat to wood in buildings, especially when it is close to or in contact with the ground and is therefore damp and attractive to eat. They may build tunnels of earth against the house walls to reach timber above ground level, and in areas prone to termite infestation a continuous sheet metal shield is often incorporated in the wall between the foundations and the wall's sill to protect the woodwork from attack. Once an attack starts, the inside of the wood may be completely eaten away leaving the outside surface intact; the affected wood will then simply collapse at the slightest provocation.

Check your home for termites at least twice a year, looking outside for the tell-tale earth tunnels mentioned earlier. Also check crawl spaces, cracks in walls and all joints between wood and concrete or masonry. Indoors, probe all exposed woodwork with a sharp penknife; if

it penetrates easily by more than about ½in, you probably have termite damage.

Dealing with termite attacks
Under the floorboards the wood will probably be covered with dust and dirt. This must be removed to enable you to carry out a thorough inspection and treatment. Where there is severe damage to the joists, you will have to have them strengthened or replaced, so expert advice will be essential.

When it comes to treating affected areas, you must employ a professional company – only they have access to the insecticides needed, and must have a special license to carry out the treatment work.

Although it is possible to brush on the insecticide, it is easier, quicker and more efficient to use a sprayer. The spray pressure is important. If it is too fine, then the timber will not be sufficiently drenched. If it is too coarse, the timber will be over-soaked and the treatment will prove costly.

Most fluids should be applied at the rate of about 200sq ft per gallon. All timber surfaces are sprayed thoroughly to flood areas where the insects are likely to lay their eggs, such as in crevices, end grain and open joints.

Although the treatment can be carried out at any time of the year, the best period is in the summer when windows and doors can be left open. Treatment fluid leaves a pungent odor which is very strong for the first couple of days and will still be evident several weeks later.

The firm carrying out the work will wear special protective clothing, masks and goggles. Keep children and pets well away from the area while work is proceeding.

Fire is a potential hazard, so ensure there are

■ Infestation can spread to roof frames too, and here spraying is the only effective way of tackling the problem. Since ventilation is generally poor in attic areas, it is essential that special masks are worn; again you must leave the treatment work to professional contractors.

no naked flames near the work area. Isolate any electrical circuits nearby and, if light is needed, a portable flameproof handlamp connected to a socket outside the treatment area must be used. Do not let anyone smoke in the area for 24 hours afterwards.

When tackling floor joists, every third or fourth board is removed and a sprayer with a hand-lance extension is used to apply the insecticide under the fixed boards and on to both sides of hidden joists.

With baseboards and panelling, spraying just the exposed surfaces is usually sufficient. However, in severe cases of attack, facing timbers will have to be removed to allow access to the rear and any unpainted studding timbers.

ROTTING WOOD

Wood rot is usually categorised as either 'wet' or 'dry', which is confusing since dampness causes them both. They are both fungi and there are various species of each type. Wet rot confines itself to damp wood, whereas dry rot can spread itself from wet to dry material.

Obviously the best way to discourage rot is to guard against dampness. Make regular checks to ensure that there are no areas of damage to the house which could let in moisture to soak the wood.

Recognising wet rot

Wet rot is the name given to the cellar fungus *Coniophora cerebella*. This is found in floors and also causes decay on fence posts, wooden sheds, window sills and other outdoor wood.

It occurs much more frequently than dry rot and requires substantially wetter conditions in which to flourish. Mercifully it does not produce well-developed conducting strands, so it will not penetrate brick walls. Bathrooms, kitchens and basements are typical places to find it. Once cured an attack of wet rot is unlikely to start again, provided the damp is eliminated.

Cellar fungus is evident where wood is stained dark brown or black and starts to soften. Yellow or brown streaks or patches can also be found in decayed wood. There may be cracks along the grain and fine cracks across the grain. The wood often feels damp to the touch.

Attack is often internal, showing little or no sign on the surface. Where surface growth is present, this consists of thin dark brown – almost black – strands.

Curing wet rot

First locate the source of the dampness and cure it. Then allow the wood to dry out, since this will make the fungus inactive. Cut back infected wood to sound material and replace it with new treated wood. Smaller areas can be repaired with a wood filler. Finally treat all surrounding areas of wood with preservative.

Recognizing dry rot

The dry rot fungus *Merulius lacrymans* flourishes under conditions of bad ventilation and high humidity. It is more efficient at destroying wood than any other fungus and, once established, can even spread to wood that would normally be too dry to be attacked.

Early on, dry rot is a fluffy white growth, which soon resembles thick cotton wool. The wood later appears to be coated with grey matted strands, behind which the fungus forms thicker strands capable of transporting moisture from one part of the wood to another. This creates the ideal conditions for the spread of the fungus to new sites.

Dry rot fungus is extremely dangerous, since its strands will pass through walls in search of new wood to attack. Even if the strands are cut off from the fungus and isolated from the wood, they can remain for three of four years and then attack any new wood nearby that is inadequately seasoned and dry. Then the whole process starts all over again.

Once it has matured, the fungus produces what are called fruit bodies. These have brick-red centres with white edges tinged with lilac. They are sometimes several feet square and can give off as much as 2,000 spores a minute from each square foot for several days.

A damp, musty, 'mushroom' smell, which at times becomes quite offensive, indicates dry rot. So investigate further. The surface of the wood can take on a warped appearance and paint may start to flake off. Unpainted wood splits both along its length and across the grain into large cubes up to 2in wide.

Since attacks usually start at ground level and may work their way up the building, lift floorboards and look behind baseboards for signs of the strands. You may even first notice the condition by the 'cotton wool' material seeping out under the baseboard.

Where only a fruit body is visible, remember that a great deal of wood must already have been consumed before that could have been produced.

If you are not confident of being able to eradicate the problem completely yourself, you must call in a specialist company. But make sure they are prepared to give you a reasonable guarantee against further outbreaks. Long guarantees from unknown or newly formed companies may be useless.

Curing dry rot
Remove all affected wood and burn it immediately. Examine any surrounding plaster to determine the full extent of the attack and make sure you cut back the problem area to about 3ft beyond the farthest sign of trouble. Use a propane torch to kill surface spores and strands on nearby masonry and the subfloor.

Having sterilized all surfaces, paint any masonry, the subfloor and all wood within about

6ft of the attack with dry rot fluid. Apply the recommended number of coats.

To eradicate completely the fungus that may be within the wall, drill into the masonry at several points using a large diameter drill bit, then have the holes well drenched with an acidic fungicidal chemical applied by a pressure sprayer.

To be on the safe side, it is wise to treat any furniture close to the area – or destroy it, if the rot has spread to it. Pay particular attention to electrical outlets, too. Dry rot can infest even these and it has a detrimental effect on pvc-sheathed cables. Replace all electrical outlets and cables in the danger zone.

Make sure you locate and cure the cause of the dampness that enables the fungi to flourish and ensure that, when the floors are hollow,

■ Dry rot not only looks and smells disgusting: it can also wreak havoc with concealed framing if the attack is not caught in time, leaving affected wood dried out and so brittle it can simply crumble away.

■ Treating a serious outbreak of dry rot can involve major structural work. All infected wood must first of all be cut away, as must any plaster behind which the fungus strands may have travelled.

■ Once all the infected wood and plaster has been removed, all neighboring wood and masonry must then be treated with special chemicals, before new wood is fitted and the walls are replastered.

there is adequate ventilation. Clear air vents and check that crawl spaces are well ventilated to allow a through passage of air.

Any new wood used must be pressure-impregnated with preservative. Treat any fresh surfaces exposed as a result of cutting or drilling by brushing on a liberal coat of wood preservative.

It also helps just to coat the joists ends with a bituminous waterproofing compound. An alternative is to locate the joist ends in galvanized steel joist hangers.

Once you have cured an attack of wet or dry rot, check regularly that the conditions which caused it do not recur. Make sure that areas such as crawl spaces are kept well ventilated, and watch out for signs of dampness anywhere which could affect the house structure.

■ Staircases are more than just a means of access to upper storeys. They are a focal point of both the entrance hall and the landing, and their design and decoration are often a major feature of the home.

TYPES OF STAIRCASE

Staircases come in a variety of styles, depending on the age of the property and the amount of space available. But the straight flight is the most common.

Where space is restricted, the staircase may have either a quarter-turn (through 90°) or a half-turn (180°). At each turn, there may be a small landing. To save even more space, the staircase may have been built with tapering treads, called winders, rather than landings. Spiral stairs may have been installed where space was really restricted.

A traditional staircase incorporates what are known as closed-riser stairs, with vertically fitted boards between the treads. Open-riser stairs have spaces between the treads.

Either type of wooden staircase may have closed or cut (also called open) stringers. These are the sloping boards at each side of the staircase that support the treads and risers. Most stairs are made with closed stringers, which have straight parallel edges with both the treads and risers fixed into grooves in the inside faces of the stringers.

Cut stringers are formed into a series of steps and the treads are supported on the flat tops of them. Being weaker, these stringers are made from thicker wood.

REPAIRING STAIRCASES

If you attend to minor defects promptly, staircases will generally give little trouble during their long life, unless they are affected by any movement of the house.

In residential work you do not normally need building code permission to make minor repairs to staircases. However, any change affecting the size or angle of the staircase itself may be subject to building code control and will require approval by the local building inspector.

If, for example, you want to replace a traditional staircase with an open-plan one or a spiral design, you must get approval since it may impose added stress that the building structure is unable to cope with, and may also violate safety codes.

If there is a closet under a staircase, the access it provides to the underside of the steps will make any repair work that much easier. A plastered or boarded underside, on the other hand, will make life more difficult since these should not be disturbed unless absolutely essential. Repairs should therefore be made from above the staircase.

■ Domestic stairs come in one of three common configurations — straight runs, L-shaped stairs that turn through 90° and half-landing stairs turning through 180°.

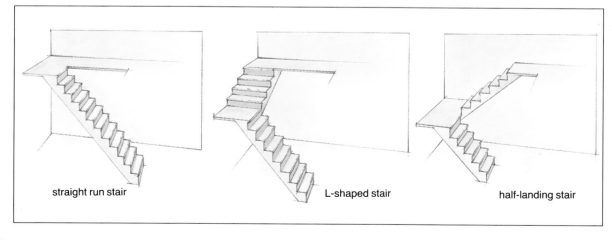

straight run stair

L-shaped stair

half-landing stair

■ The staircase is one of the most complex wooden structures in the home. Two parallel boards called stringers fixed to the newel posts link the first and second floors. The treads and risers are housed into the stringers or, in the case of an open or cut outer stringer, are fixed to cut-outs in the upper edge of the stringer. A handrail links the newel posts, and balusters are fitted between it and the stringer to guard the flight.

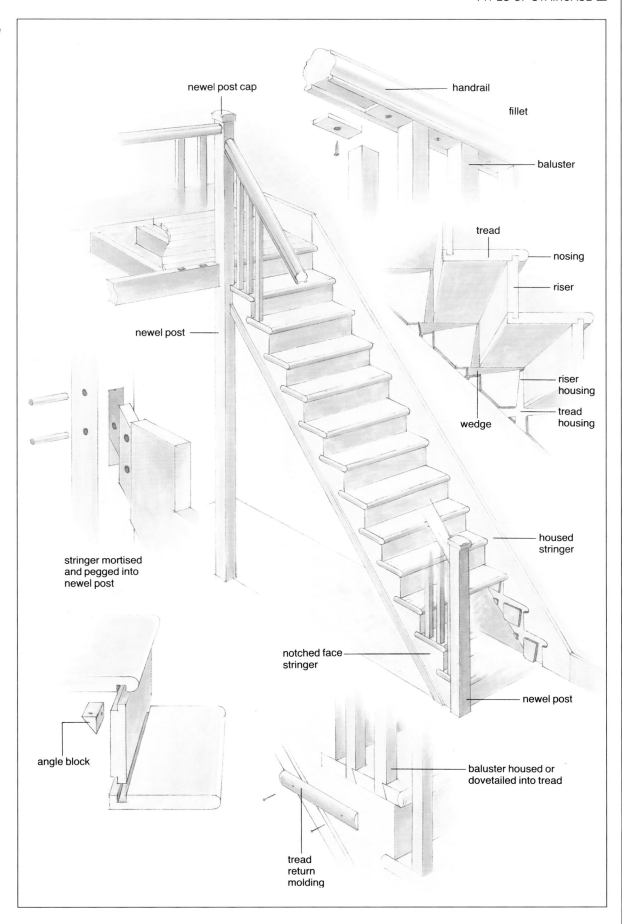

newel post cap

handrail

fillet

baluster

tread

nosing

riser

riser housing

tread housing

wedge

newel post

stringer mortised and pegged into newel post

housed stringer

notched face stringer

newel post

angle block

baluster housed or dovetailed into tread

tread return molding

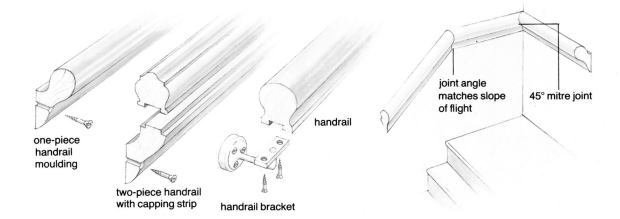

■ An inner handrail may be secured directly to the wall beside the flight, or may be mounted clear of the wall on handrail brackets. The rail follows any change of slope or direction taken by the flight itself.

one-piece handrail moulding

two-piece handrail with capping strip

handrail bracket

handrail

joint angle matches slope of flight

45° mitre joint

Replacing balusters

Balusters on cut-stringer staircases fit into mortises or slots in the ends of the treads. On a closed-stringer staircase, they rest in a groove in the stringer capping and have short lengths of timbers set between them as spacers. Their top ends are either toe-nailed to the handrail or set in a groove in its underside.

Replacing a missing baluster normally means having to dismantle the balustrade. However, it is possible to replace the odd one by splicing a new baluster into two at an angle in a convenient position, fitting new top and bottom pieces

into the rail and stringer and then carefully remarrying the mating halves with glue and countersunk screws.

If you have to replace several balusters, then make sure that identical ones are available before completely dismantling the staircase. Square-section balusters are easy to match; but turned balusters may have to be specially made. If you give an undamaged baluster to a skilled carpenter, he will be able to make replicas but it will be expensive.

If the balusters on a cut-stringer staircase have worked loose, drive small glued timber

■ A variety of carpentry techniques and specialist fittings are used to assemble the balustrade. The handrail itself may be secured to the newel post with brackets, and lengths of rail are often joined with concealed handrail bolts. The balusters may be simply skew-nailed into place, or may be set in mortises in the handrail and housings in the treads.

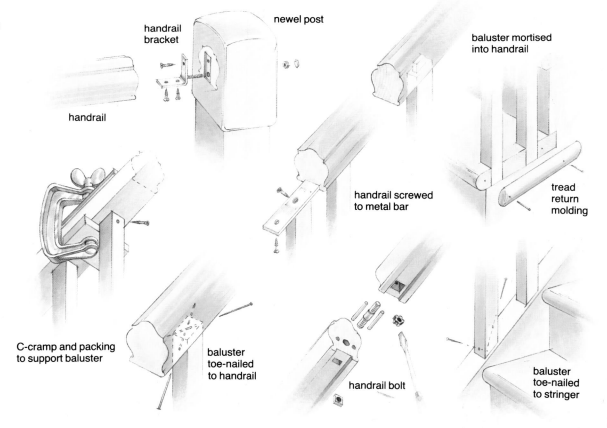

handrail bracket

newel post

baluster mortised into handrail

handrail

handrail screwed to metal bar

tread return molding

C-cramp and packing to support baluster

baluster toe-nailed to handrail

handrail bolt

baluster toe-nailed to stringer

wedges into any gaps in the tread mortise. Then, to secure them completely, drive in two nails or fine screws at an angle to lock the end of the baluster to the tread. With closed-stringer flights, toe-nail the baluster to the string.

With either type, do the same at the point where the baluster meets the handrail. Finish off by concealing the repair using wood filler.

Repairing handrails

Handrails with balusters usually have their ends tenoned into the newel posts. If an end becomes loose, simply secure it by driving a screw or dowel peg in through the side of the newel post into the handrail tenon.

Where a handrail is damaged, cut out the offending section and replace it with a new matching piece, if available. Saw at a sloping angle to the line of the rail to give a greater contact area for the new piece to form a scarf-joint. Glue and screw the piece into place. On the underside of the rail, screw on a metal plate as reinforcement. Then refix the baluster tops, as previously described.

If a matching section of handrail is not available, then you can either have a piece specially machined or else replace the complete rail with a different one.

Refixing a wall-mounted handrail

Wider staircases and those having a wall either side should have a handrail fixed to a wall to provide any necessary support for those who need it while using the stairs.

The only fault likely here is if the screw fixings become loose. Sometimes the handrail is supported on brackets which are screwed to the wall. Depending on its type, you might be able to detach a single bracket for refixing or, possibly, you will have to remove and replace the complete handrail.

Either way, you need to refix the screws after plugging the old holes with filler and drilling new ones. Insert wall plugs and screws the same size as the old ones to make the bracket secure.

If the rail is screwed directly to the wall, it may be possible to replace the existing (loose) screw with a thicker one – even though this may mean drilling a new hole through the rail. If this does not work, then take the rail down and make a repair as previously described.

To ensure all the screw holes line up again, replace the rail while you mark off the position of the new hole. Remove the rail, drill and plug the hole and then replace and refix the rail. This is the only way you can be sure the holes will line up. Where you are fitting a new handrail or

replacing an old one, the important thing to remember is that it must run parallel with the string throughout its length.

Mark the position for the rail on the wall at the top of the stairs, then screw it to the wall. Repeat this at the bottom. When you are satisfied with its position, mark the intermediate holes and then remove the rail while you drill and plug the wall. If you are using brackets, fix these to the rail first.

Curing creaking treads

The problem of creaking treads is caused by the staircase shrinking, which allows adjacent parts to rub together when someone uses the stairs. If the underside of the staircase is accessible via a closet, the first things to look for are the wedges securing the ends of the treads and risers into their grooves in the stringers.

If these are loose, tap them in firmly with a mallet. If they will not tap in then remove them, coat them with woodworking glue and hammer them back into place. It is rare to find one missing, but if you do it is very easy to cut and fit a replacement.

If that does not cure the problem, fix the back of each creaky tread to the bottom of the riser above it using two screws, placed one-third and two-thirds of the way across. The screws will

■ If the staircase creaks and the underside of the flight is accessible, check that all the wedges holding the treads and risers in their housings are secure. Then glue and screw wooden blocks into the internal angles between treads and risers, and drive screws through the rear edge of each riser into the tread to lock the two together.

If there is no access beneath the staircase, use recessed repair brackets to secure the rear edges of the treads to the risers, and drive screws down through the fronts of the treads into the top edges of the risers beneath.

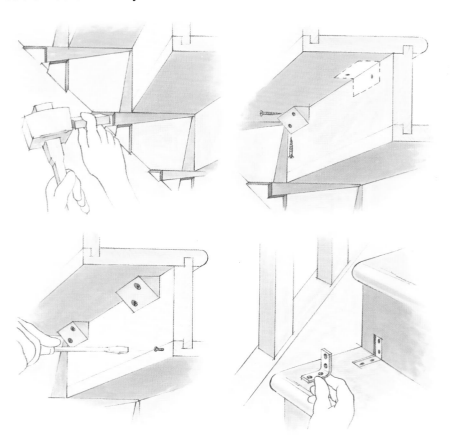

need to be 2in long. To avoid splitting the wood, first drill pilot holes up through the rear edge of the tread into the center of the riser.

Finally, secure the joint between the front of each creaky tread and the top edge of the riser beneath it by gluing and screwing wooden blocks into the angle between them. Use two blocks to each tread.

If there is no access, tackle the problem from above. Screw the front of each creaky tread to the top edge of the riser beneath by driving screws down through the tread nosing. Use two screws and countersink the heads neatly so that they will not snag the carpet underlay or backing when this is replaced.

At the rear of each tread, prise open the joint between the tread and the riser above, using a chisel, and squirt in woodworking glue right along the gap. If possible, do the job last thing at night, when the stairs are less likely to be used until the glue has set.

Treating worn treads

The tread nosings can wear and in time split. Such splits can also be caused by resting heavy furniture on the tread edge during moves.

Using a chisel, coping saw or saber saw, cut back the split or damaged nosing flush with the face of the riser beneath and plane the exposed

edged flat. Round off the edge of a piece of wood that matches the tread thickness, saw it to the required width and glue and screw it to the front edge of the tread. Fix the screws about 3in apart. Plane the strip down as necessary to get a good fit.

If, particularly in older houses, you find the treads and risers have parted from the stringers, the cause may be wall movement. In newer houses, it may be the result of wall ties disintegrating. Sometimes it is evidence of a general overall deterioration in the staircase's condition.

If it is simply settlement, which has finally come to rest, and the movement has wrenched the stringer no more than about ¾in from the treads and risers, you can effect a do-it-yourself repair. But make sure that all movement has stopped first.

Make some wedges sufficient to hold the stringer away from the wall. These can be of $1 \times \frac{1}{2}$in timber and roughly 12in long. Hack off the wall plaster above the stringer and drive the wedges as far as possible between it and the wall. Saw off any protruding wood.

Make sure that the treads and risers are securely locked back into the stringer. Doubly secure the wedges by screws through the stringer, countersunk and concealed with filler and paint. You can then replaster the wall and tack a molding in place to conceal the gap. If this gap widens again, get professional advice.

Fitting new treads and risers

If a tread or riser is cracked or rotten or has pulled away from a stringer, it may be possible to replace it. Balusters that slot into the treads will have to be removed. You will also need to ascertain whether the treads are tongued and grooved to the risers or are simply nailed or screwed in place.

Making a new riser or tread should not be a problem provided you take the necessary measurements carefully and accurately. Any replacements can be fixed with small wedges and glue or by using screws.

Any balusters you have temporarily eased out of the way to enable you to remove the old riser and tread can be slid into a prepared slot in the new ones and covered with a molding.

REFURBISHING A STAIRCASE

If the staircase itself is in good condition, you can give it a complete facelift by replacing both handrail and balusters. Alternatively, you can leave the handrail in position and just fit new balusters between it and the stringer.

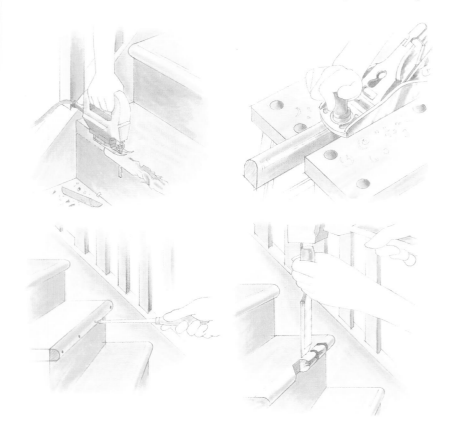

■ To repair damaged tread nosings, first cut away the wood flush with the face of the riser beneath. Then cut a new nosing to match the tread thickness and width, and plane its edge to a semicircular profile. Check its fit, then glue and screw it into position. If the damage is small in scale, saw and chisel it out and fit a smaller patch instead.

All the components you need for a new balustrade are available from lumber yards or builders' supply companies. When calculating the number of balusters to buy, remember that they must usually be set at no more than 9in centers to comply with building codes.

Remove the old balusters or other infilling. With wooden balusters, the simplest method is to saw through them and prise each end away from the tread or stringer and the handrail. It is then simply a question of cutting each new baluster to length, using a sliding bevel to give the correct angle at its upper end (and also at the lower end on flights with closed stringers).

■ Kits of replacement stair parts are now widely available, allowing the complete balustrade to be replaced. Strip out the old handrail and balusters, cut off the newel posts at stringer level and join on the new posts. Then fit the new handrail, and secure the new balusters in place with spacer fillets between them.

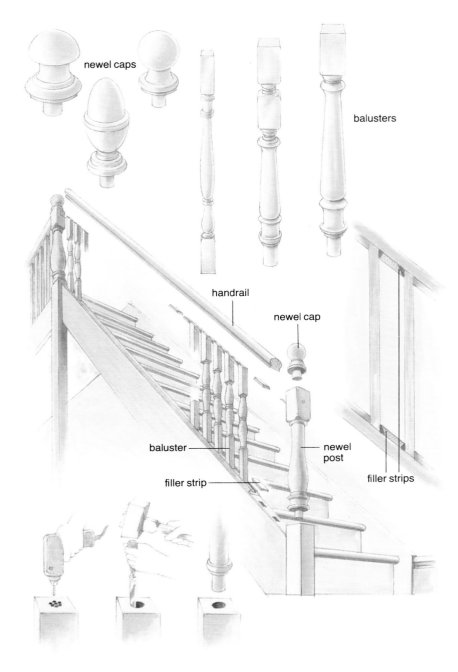

newel caps

balusters

handrail

newel cap

baluster

newel post

filler strip

filler strips

Set the first baluster in position, check that it is vertical and toe-nail it to the stringer or tread and handrail. Then fit spacers top and bottom before offering up the next baluster. Continue working in this way along the handrail until the new balustrade is completed.

If you want to replace the handrail and newel posts for a complete refurbishment of the staircase, then you can buy kits of parts that simply bolt together.

If you want to refurbish an old staircase to give it a new look, then you can infill the balustrade with wrought ironwork or laminated or toughened glass. Custom-made wrought iron panels can be ordered from specialist fabricators in a wide range of designs. The panels are positioned in the frame formed by the newels, the stringer and the handrail and are then screwed into place through pre-drilled holes in the panel edges.

Glass must be either of the reinforced or tempered variety. Ordinary float glass can be highly dangerous if accidentally broken. Your local glass dealer will cut laminated glass to size for you. But he will have to order tempered glass in the panel shapes you want, since it cannot be cut once annealed. Make a paper or card template of each panel to ensure it is accurately cut for a perfect fit.

First create a rebate using slim wooden battens glued and pinned to the staircase woodwork. Then position the glass panel in the rebate and add further battens or molding to hold it securely in place. It is a good idea to bed the glass in glazing compound or caulk to prevent it from rattling through vibration as people walk up and down the stairs.

FITTING A NEW STAIRCASE

It is rare to have to replace a staircase completely, but you might need to install one to provide access to a new attic room, for example. Prefabricated standard staircases or spiral kits are available and, if they are suitable, will be much less expensive than having one custom-made by a carpenter – which, incidentally, is not a task for an amateur. Skilled joinery is required to calculate, cut and fit a staircase together exactly and to ensure that its design and construction meet all the requirements of local building codes.

It is worth remembering that although you may like the idea of a spiral staircase, it is not always easy for older people and children to negotiate one safely. It is also very awkward to move larger items of furniture up or down this type of staircase.

Working on the Walls

Interior walls obviously have an important part to play in the building of your home and you should therefore understand their purpose and construction before attempting to repair, modify, remove or build them.

By referring to your plan of proposed alterations, you can identify which walls if any need to be removed or repaired. But before starting work, you must know how they are built and what type they are. That way there will be no danger of the wall – and perhaps the floors above or even the roof – crumbling around you.

IDENTIFYING TYPES OF WALL

Some walls are structural or loadbearing, while others are non-loadbearing partitions, and it is essential to know the difference between the two before attempting to alter or modify them in any way. Basically a structural wall is holding your house up and a partition wall is acting just as a divider between rooms.

In many rooms, one or two walls will be the inside face of external ones, which are of course always loadbearing. The remaining walls of the room could be either structural or a partition.

A non-loadbearing wall acts merely as a divider between rooms and supports no load from the structure itself. The wall may be of single room height or it could extend upwards from the first to second floor level. The crucial point is that it supports only its own weight.

You can identify a non-loadbearing wall by looking at the floor and ceiling joists. These run parallel to the wall and the ends of the joists will not be built into it. Upstairs you can tell which way the ceiling joists run by looking in the attic. You can sometimes see which way floor joists run by looking at the floorboards, which usually run at right angles to the joists.

Non-loadbearing walls are usually built of lighter materials than loadbearing ones and they are frequently constructed on top of floorboards with no special foundations.

Loadbearing walls support part of the structure of the house – usually floor and ceiling joists or roof timbers, which rest on the wall or are built into it. The floor and ceiling joists will be at right angles to the wall and the floorboards will usually run parallel with the wall.

■ **Right** Internal walls may be loadbearing – supporting parts of the house structure higher up the building – or non-loadbearing. You can remove the latter without affecting the house structure, but the former must be replaced by loadbearing beams.

It is generally possible to identify the type of wall involved by examining the direction of the floor joists in the room above.

The first dividing wall (top right) carries no load and stops at ceiling level, so can safely be removed.

The second also stops at ceiling level, but this time supports the joists of the floor above, so a beam must be provided if it is removed.

The third wall is not supporting any floor joists, but the ground-floor section supports its continuation upstairs, and this may in turn support the roof structure, so again a beam is needed.

The fourth wall is clearly loadbearing in all respects.

■ Knocking two rooms into one is a very popular home renovation project. Before tackling the job, however, it is essential to identify exactly what function the dividing wall has as far as supporting the house structure is concerned.

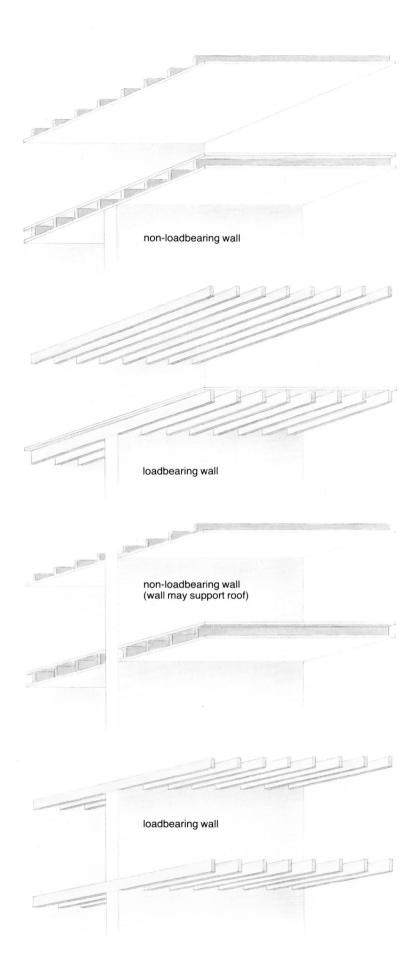

non-loadbearing wall

loadbearing wall

non-loadbearing wall
(wall may support roof)

loadbearing wall

The real significance of knowing whether a wall is loadbearing or not comes when you are considering making a hole in it, perhaps for a window or door, or you are considering removing it to join two rooms into one.

The wall above any opening must be supported with a special beam called a header, which is fitted into the wall before the opening is made. How the wall is supported while this is done and the size of the header required will depend on whether or not the wall is a loadbearing one.

Cutting a hole up to about 3ft wide in a non-loadbearing wall should present no real problems. However, if you are dealing with a loadbearing wall or making larger holes or a hole close to the corner of a building or close to a floor supported by the wall, then it will be necessary to get expert advice. So check with an architect or engineer before you decide whether to continue with the job and equally whether to tackle it yourself. You may prefer at that stage to call in an experienced contractor.

In either case, remember that you will need building code approval for the work from the local authority.

Using headers
Before deciding what type of header to fit above a proposed opening in a wall, you need to know what load it will have to support. This is a job for an expert, so take advice from an architect, an engineer, an experienced contractor or the building inspector at your town or city hall.

Headers have to rest on the wall at each side of the opening and it is important that there is sufficient 'bearing' to support the ends. For openings up to 5ft wide, the bearing should be about 5in deep. For wider spans, the bearing should be 8in deep. For heavy loads, bed the ends of the header on steel plates to help spread the load.

In masonry walls of comparatively recent construction, galvanized steel beams of various types are widely used to bridge door and window openings, and these are your best choice if you need to enlarge an opening or form one as part of alterations to the building. Older homes may have reinforced concrete lintels or even stout wooden beams (often hidden behind stone external lintels or brick soldier arches) doing the same job.

Structural steel beams must in certain circumstances be protected from the effects of fire. In walls the masonry and plaster provides adequate protection, but an exposed beam must either be encased in concrete or clad in multiple layers of gypsum board.

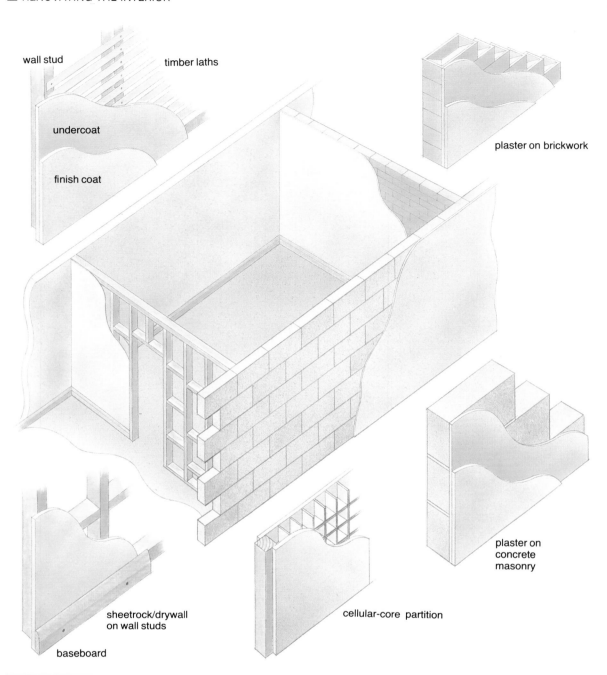

wall stud

timber laths

undercoat

finish coat

plaster on brickwork

sheetrock/drywall
on wall studs

baseboard

cellular-core partition

plaster on
concrete
masonry

■ Internal walls in older
homes may be of solid brick
or blockwork, plastered on
each face with a two-coat
layer of plaster. Alternatively,
they may be built up as
timber frame partitions clad
on each side with lath-and-
plaster in older homes or
sheetrock (drywall) in newer
homes. Cellular-core
partitions are another
possibility in newly-built or
recently-renovated buildings.

TYPES OF INTERNAL WALL

Depending on the type and age of the property, there are several basic types of internal wall construction you are likely to come across in your house. Recognising each type may in some cases help you determine whether the wall is loadbearing or not.

Stud partitions
Stud partition walls are made with a timber framework covered with sheetrock (drywall). Normally they are non-loadbearing, but can be structural. In this case, diagonal braces are fitted between the studs, or the wall thickness is increased for extra strength.

With a loadbearing stud partition, the main timbers are 2×4in in size. This type of wall is easy to build and makes an ideal new partition.

Lath and plaster stud partition
This type of wall is often found in older houses. The timber framework is as for a modern stud partition, but the wall has a lath and plaster finish. In the same way, it can be either non-loadbearing or structural.

You will often find that the plaster is loose and in poor condition. Although messy, it is an easy job to hack off the old plaster and laths and nail up sheetrock (drywall) in their place.

Plaster-covered single brick

Bricks were often used to make partition walls in older houses. These may be loadbearing or non-loadbearing. They sound solid when tapped and usually produce a reddish dust when drilled.

Steel stud partitions

Although used more commonly in commercial buildings, steel stud partitions are becoming more popular and may be found in residential work that has been recently renovated. The basic framing technique is essentially the same as for wood studding, and the surface finish is again sheetrock (drywall) fixed to the steel studs with self-tapping screws. Steel stud walls are more difficult to adapt to interior change than wood-framed ones, but have far greater loadbearing capacity and are generally faster and more economical to install.

Cellular-core wallboard partition

These walls form non-loadbearing partitions. They are made from sheetrock (drywall) panels that have a hollow cellular cardboard core. Adjoining panels are linked with timber studs wedged into the core.

Such walls are thin – only about 2½in thick. Although they are obviously hollow, as you will discover when drilling them, they will not necessarily sound so when tapped.

PROBLEMS WITH INTERNAL WALLS

Internal walls can be prone to a number of problems, depending on the type of construction and their overall condition. In some cases, these can be local to the wall itself or caused through another source, which you must first trace and cure.

Damp patches

It is important to ascertain whether any dampness you find is due to penetrating or rising dampness in the wall, indicating a structural fault, or whether the problem is condensation caused by a build-up of moisture-laden air in the room saturating the wall.

A simple test to distinguish between penetrating dampness and condensation can be carried out using cooking foil. Dry out the damp patch with a heater and stick a sheet of foil over the area, sealing the edges with adhesive tape. Then leave it for a few days.

If moisture droplets accumulate on the surface of the foil, the problem is due to condensation and steps should be taken to reduce the amount of moisture in the air. If the underside of the foil becomes damp or the damp patch reappears on the wall under the foil, then the problem is due to penetrating dampness coming through the wall.

Damp patches on internal walls usually indicate problems elsewhere. If the dampness is on the inside of an external wall, look for faults on the outside. Damp patches on a chimney breast wall can often be traced to water penetrating the flue at or above roof level.

If the damp patch is on a partition wall, it may be caused by rising dampness due to a faulty dpm, if the wall is loadbearing with conventional foundations. In this case, a new dpm may be required, which can be installed as for an external wall.

If the wall is simply an internal partition one, it is likely that the damp patch will have been caused by a problem in the plumbing. This could be a leaking water pipe within the wall or possibly a leaking waste pipe nearby. Equally a poor seal around a bath, shower tray or lavatory could be the culprit, if the damp patch is within the vicinity of these fittings or in a room that backs on to them.

If the problem is condensation, the cure is to reduce the amount of water vapor released into the air and to increase ventilation and heating levels. Fit extractor fans in kitchens and bathrooms, where most water vapor is generated. Depending on the circumstances, other action to be considered includes making sure clothes driers are fitted with vent kits, installing a stove hood, buying a portable dehumidifier and improving wall and window insulation.

■ Penetrating damp often shows up around window and door openings, or at the edges of ceilings next to external walls. Tracing how the water is getting in can be a difficult task.

Mold growth

Black mold spots on internal walls form as a result of damp or condensation problems. So if you cure these faults, the mold should not return. After curing the fault, remove the black mold by scrubbing the wall with a strong fungicide solution as used in the preparation for exterior painting.

Small cracks and holes

Small cracks and holes in the surface of internal walls are the result of such things as natural movement, knocks, drying plaster, passing traffic and slamming doors.

Use the edge of a filling knife to enlarge the crack or hole and remove all loose plaster. Brush or blow out the dust, then fill the space with a ready-mixed filler or a powder filler to which you add water. Draw the blade of the knife over the top of the repair to leave a smooth surface.

If the crack or hole is quite deep, apply the filler in two parts, allowing the first application to dry before putting on the second.

Cracks between baseboards and walls tend to reopen if conventional fillers are used. In this situation use a flexible caulk, which can be applied using a caulking gun and smoothed off with a damp finger. Caulk is available in white, brown and various other colors which help it to blend in with existing decorations.

Large cracks and holes

These can be repaired using proprietary fillers, building them up in layers as described above. For particularly large cracks and holes, however, these will prove expensive to use.

On solid walls, a cheaper option is to use conventional plaster. Chip away all loose material and brush out the dust. Then with an old brush or hand-held sprayer, wet the area and apply an undercoat or browning plaster to within about ⅛in below the wall surface.

As soon as the undercoat has set, apply the top coat of finishing plaster, which you smooth on using a steel float (also called a plasterer's trowel). Allow this to become firm, then spray the surface with water and polish it flat and smooth using the steel float.

If the hole is in a lath and plaster wall, cut the plaster away to expose the laths. If these are broken, fold a piece of expanded steel mesh over the sound laths at the top and bottom of the hole and then replaster as described above.

Where the holes in sheetrock (drywall) walls are small, the use of an ordinary filler should do

■ To repair cracks in wall plaster, first strip off any old wallcoverings. Then use a filling knife to rake out the crack along its length, undercutting the crack edges slightly so the filler can bond well. Brush out all loose material, and spray water along the crack to cut down the absorbency of the surrounding plaster; if the filler dries out too quickly it may crack.

Mix up some plaster filler to a firm consistency and fill the crack slightly proud of the surrounding plaster. When it has hardened, sand it down flush for an almost invisible repair.

■ To repair small holes in sheetrock (drywall), take a small offcut a little taller and narrower than the hole and thread some knotted string through it. Spread some filler onto each end of the patch, insert it through the hole and use the string to pull it against the inner face of the sheetrock. Fill the hole with more filler, then cut off the string. When the filler has hardened, skim over the repair with a little more filler for a flush finish.

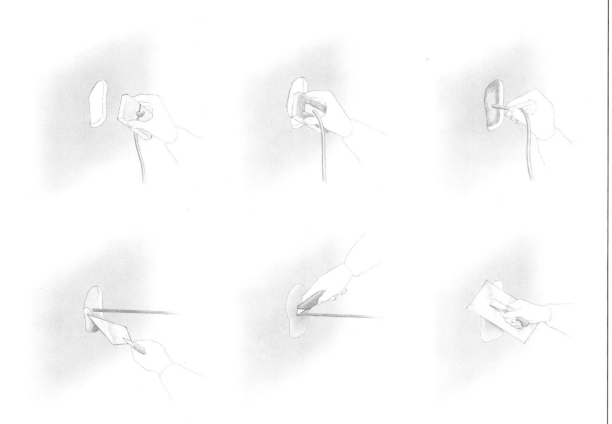

the job. But larger holes will have to be patched. Use a utility knife to cut back the damaged board to leave a clean outline. Then prepare an offcut of sheetrock slightly wider than the hole and use this to fill behind the hole.

To help you position this offcut,, make two holes in it and feed some string through them, leaving the two end lengths hanging so you can use them to hold the offcut while you position it.

Apply some fresh plaster or filler around the edges on the face of the offcut. Then, keeping hold of the string, pass the offcut through the hole and pull it up behind. Leave it like this until the plaster has set. Pull out the string or cut it off, then fill the hole in the normal way.

In the case of a large hole, it may be better to fill the majority of it with a scrap of sheetrock over the previously fixed offcut using wet plaster. When dry, you simply have to tape the joints, fill the remaining cracks around the edge of the repair and possibly finish off with a skim coat of plaster over the whole surface.

If the hole is very large – more than about 6in across – then it will be better to cut out a rectangle of sheetrock to expose the timber studs at each side of the damaged area. You can then fix a new section of sheetrock to the studs on each side with galvanized fixing nails. Use joint filler to repair the crack around the patch

and reinforce the joint with fiberglass jointing tape, which can be concealed with a skim coat of plaster applied to the surface.

Loose plaster

If a plastered wall sounds hollow when you tap it – and often there will be a surface bulge as well – the plaster has come away from the surface behind it. This is a common problem in older houses, especially on lath and plaster walls.

With lath and plaster, the first stage is to hack off the loose plaster to uncover the extent of the damage. Once one area is affected, it is likely that much of the wall will be in a similar condition. This is because the nibs that hook over the laths drop off with age and the plaster then becomes loose.

If this has happened over more than half the wall surface, then it will be best to hack off all the old plaster and the laths as well. You can then nail new sheetrock on to the now-exposed timber wall studs.

This will provide a good opportunity to upgrade lighting and power circuits or heating pipework and enable you to install wall insulation within the timber framework.

If you decide to replaster patches of lath and plaster wall, first remove any damaged laths and nail new ones to the studs. Brush the edges

■ To patch larger holes in lath-and-plaster (right), cut back the plaster and the broken laths to the adjacent studs or joists. Do the same round a large hole in sheetrock. Then nail or screw supporting battens into place as shown, nail in a matching sheetrock patch and skim over the repair with plaster or filler.

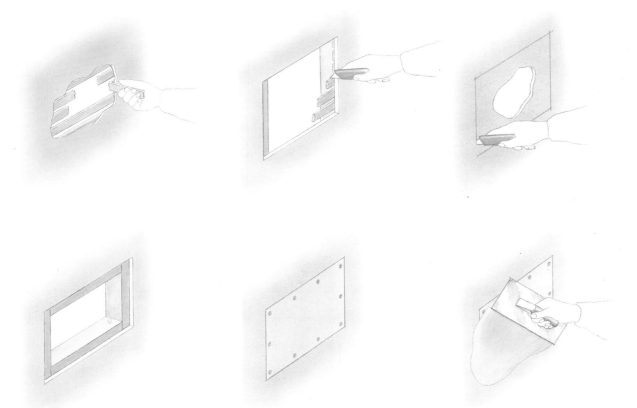

■ To patch areas of loose plaster (below), cut back the area until sound plaster is reached. Then apply new plaster with a float, rule it off with a batten flush with the surrounding wall surface, and polish it off flush with the float.

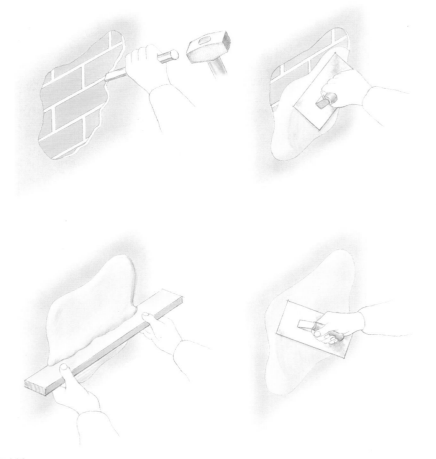

of the adjacent plaster to remove dust and debris, then dampen these edges and brush down the laths with a wet brush.

With a steel float, apply a coat of lightweight bonding plaster or metal lathing plaster, using a fairly firm pressure to ensure that the plaster pushes through the laths at the back. Allow this coat to harden, then apply a second coat to within about ⅛in of the surface. Check this is smooth and level by drawing the edge of a long length of straight wood across the area to remove excess plaster. Lightly scratch the surface of the second coat to give a good key and, when hard, apply a coat of finishing plaster.

If you find loose plaster on a solid wall, again you will have to cut back all the loose material until you reach sound plaster. Extensive re-plastering could be required. If half the wall or more is affected and you do not feel particularly confident about plastering, a sensible solution would be to hack off all the plaster and 'dry-line' the wall with sheetrock.

To replaster a large area, brush down the brick or blockwork to remove any remaining dust or debris, then dampen the wall. Use a lightweight browning plaster as the undercoat and mix this with water to make it smooth and easy to apply.

Starting at the bottom of the wall, load the steel float and apply the plaster firmly to the wall with an upward stroke. Continue this way, building up the thickness to just below the surface level of the sound surrounding plaster.

As already mentioned, use a long length of straight wood held on edge to pull over the replastered area to check there are no high spots. The surface of this undercoat should be $\frac{1}{16}$ to $\frac{1}{8}$in below the finished surface level required, to allow for the finishing plaster.

As soon as the undercoat has hardened, you can apply the finishing coat, again using the trowel. Pull a straight-edge over the surface to ensure no high spots. Smooth the surface with a steel float and, as soon as the plaster has hardened, dampen the surface with a small hand spray. Then polish it smooth and flat with the steel float.

Pitted plaster
Small indentations and gouges over a wide area of the surface of a plastered wall are easily rectified by applying a skim coat of finishing plaster over it.

Lightly dampen the wall surface and, with a steel float, apply the plaster in as thin a layer as possible. As soon as the plaster begins to harden, lightly spray over it with water and polish the plaster smooth with a steel float.

If you cannot get the surface flat, it will help if you draw a wooden straight-edge over it while the plaster is still wet.

Corner cracks
You will find two types of corner in a room. Internal (inside) corners are created where two walls join at right angles. External (exterior) ones are formed where the corner projects into the room, such as on the outside of a chimney breast or in a door opening.

Internal corners usually give very few problems and you can normally repair any cracks you find with joint compound. Sometimes cracks tend to reopen after they have been repaired. If this occurs, you should be able to prevent it from happening again by raking out the crack, applying joint compound and running joint tape into the wet compound. You then have to apply more compound on the joint tape and feather it out with a wide filling knife. Finally wipe it over with a damp sponge to leave a smooth finish.

You can also use joint compound to repair a slightly damaged external corner. With more extensive damage, you will have to build up the

■ To replaster corners and reveals, hack off all the old plaster. Then nail a timber batten to one face of the corner, projecting beyond it by the required plaster thickness, and plaster that face of the corner. When the plaster has hardened, remove the batten carefully and reposition it on the other side of the corner. Plaster the second face, remove the batten and round off the corner with fine abrasive paper.

corner with one-coat or two-coat (undercoat and finishing) plaster.

Repair the corner one side at a time. Using masonry nails, fix a length of wood to one side of the corner so that its edge is level with the plaster surface on the other side. Apply undercoat plaster to this side, using the wood to give you an edge to work against.

Allow this side to set, then move the wood to cover the repaired section and fill the other side of the corner in the same way. When that plaster has set, again remove the wood and, if necessary, rub the corner smooth.

If the area is particularly prone to damage, such as with a doorway, it is best to reinforce the corner at its susceptible point using a strip of metal corner beading.

Trim back the plaster to accommodate the beading, then apply blobs of undercoat plaster to the wall. Press the beading in place on the wet plaster, checking with a level that it is vertical and that the rounded edge of the beading is level with the wall surface on each side of the corner. Allow the plaster to dry and secure the beading in place, then apply more undercoat and a skim coat of finishing plaster to complete the repair.

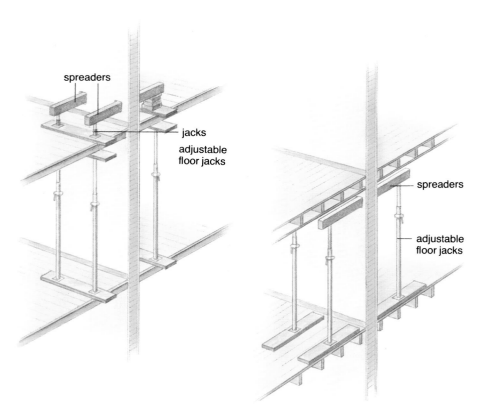

REMOVING A WALL

If you want to gain extra space, it may be possible to remove a dividing wall and so join two rooms into one. Remember that you must obtain building code approval before doing this. You will have to supply structural calculations to show that the header you must install above the opening will support the load.

If the wall is non-loadbearing, it will only have to support the weight of the wall above the opening. If it is loadbearing, a substantial header will be required to support the other parts of the building above it.

Basically the job involves cutting holes in the wall above the proposed header position so that the wall can be temporarily supported on wooden beams held up with adjustable steel jacks, which you can rent. With a loadbearing wall, two sets of jacks will be needed. One set supports the wall as described above, while the other set is placed under the ceiling to support the upper floor joists, which run at right angles to the wall.

If the room has a high ceiling, the holes for the supports can be made through the wall just under the ceiling above the planned position of the new header.

If the room has a low ceiling, some floorboards may have to be removed in the room

above the opening to allow the jacks to pass through and support the temporary support beams, which are positioned to support the wall in the upstairs room. This allows the header to be positioned immediately below the floor joists to give maximum headroom.

With the wall and floor well supported, the wall can be removed and the wall studs built up at each side of the room to support the header. When this has been completed, the header can be lifted into place on them.

The next stage is to make good the wall above the header by framing up around the supports. When the new framing studding is in place, the temporary supports can be removed, then new sheetrock can be added and taped or skim-coated with plaster.

BUILDING A PARTITION WALL

If you want to divide a large room, the easiest way is to build a stud partition wall. This involves making a framework of 2 × 4in timber studs, clad on both sides with sheetrock.

The first stage is to screw a length of wood called the base plate to the floor at the wall position. Mark plumb lines up the side walls to ascertain the corresponding position on the ceiling and then fix another length of wood (the header plate) to the ceiling. The screws holding

■ Before starting to remove part of a loadbearing wall so a supporting header can be inserted, take the weight of the wall above on wooden spreaders and adjustable jacks. If the wall is to be removed right up to ceiling level, pass the supports through the wall at second-floor level, supporting them on two sets of jacks as shown (above left). If the header will be installed below ceiling level, the supports can be passed through the wall lower down (above right).

the header plate should go into the ceiling joists, which you can find by probing through the ceiling surface with a thin screwdriver.

Next nail the end studs to the side walls of the room between the header and base plates. Decide on the door position, remove a section of the base plate and fix double studs at each side, using rebated housing joints in the header plate for a secure fixing. Allow for the thickness of the timber lining that will frame the door.

Fix further studs at 16in centers by toe-nailing them to the header and base plates. Three studs should support each 4ft wide sheetrock board.

Next nail the horizontal spacers in place between the studs at about 4ft centers. In tall rooms extra spacers may be needed to coincide with the top edge of the sheetrock boards where single lengths will not reach the ceiling. You will need a spacer at the top of the door frame and you can fix additional spacers as required to form windows in the wall. This may be necessary to allow more light into one room from the adjoining one.

At this stage you should run any utilities, such as plumbing lines or electrical wiring, within the framework of the wall and get them inspected and approved.

Cover the wall with sheetrock, fixing the boards with nails or screws at 6in intervals. After putting up the sheetrock on one side, you can fit insulation into the cavity before you clad the other side to reduce sound transmission.

Cover up all nail or screw heads and joints with filler. While this is still wet, press joint tape into the filler and smooth off. Apply further filler as a wide band over the tape and feather off the edges using a damp sponge.

BLOCKING A DOORWAY

Remove the door and lining or frame by sawing through and prising off the lengths of wood. With a stud partition wall, the best way to block the opening is to fix an additional wooden frame in the gap and clad both sides with sheetrock. You can then skim over the surface with finishing plaster to bring the surface level with the adjacent walls.

With a brick or block wall, you can use the same method, but it is better to block the opening with a similar material to that used for the wall construction. In this case there will be less chance of differential movement causing cracking that would later highlight the alteration you have carried out.

■ An internal partition wall consists of a head and sole plate with evenly-spaced vertical studs nailed in place between them. The studs themselves may have horizontal braces between them to prevent them from bowing. If the head plate runs parallel to and between the joists above, fit blocking between the joists to which the head plate can be secured. Fix side studs to the side walls, and add extra studs at corners as shown. Finish door and top light openings with linings. Run in any services such as electrical and plumbing lines before completing the fixing of the sheetrock cladding.

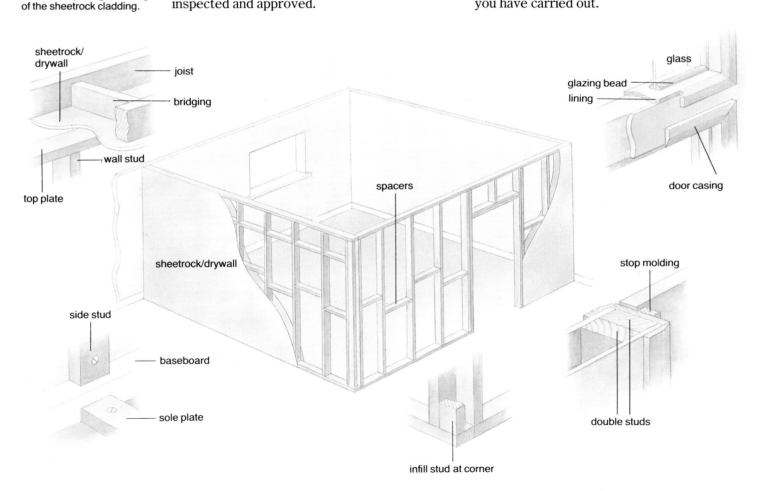

sheetrock/drywall

joist

bridging

glass

glazing bead

lining

wall stud

top plate

spacers

door casing

sheetrock/drywall

side stud

baseboard

stop molding

sole plate

double studs

infill stud at corner

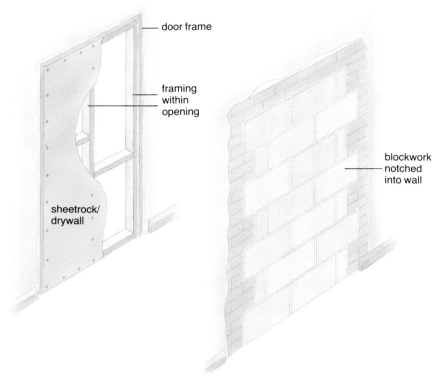

door frame

framing
within
opening

sheetrock/
drywall

blockwork
notched
into wall

■ Block off an unwanted doorway with a wooden framework fixed to the door frame and covered on both sides with sheetrock, or remove the frame and fill the opening with blockwork.

Remove the door frame and chop out half bricks or blocks at approximately 12in intervals so that the bricks or blocks being used to fill the opening will key into the walls at either side. When you have bricked up the opening and the mortar has set, apply an undercoat of browning plaster and then skim over with finishing plaster, levelling if off flush with the original walls on either side.

WORKING ON THE CEILINGS

While ceilings may not suffer a lot of wear and tear, things can go wrong with them. So it pays to check them over from time to time. It is surprizing how long a crack or stain can otherwise go undetected!

In upstairs rooms look out for damp patches caused by roof problems and also for signs of stress – possibly through too much junk being stored in the attic.

If an old lath-and-plaster ceiling is badly cracked and sagging, carefully probe it and pull away the loose parts. You may find that the plaster has come away from its backing. In this case you will have the messy job of pulling away all the old laths too so that a new sheetrock ceiling can be fixed in its place.

Normally any repairs and alterations to a ceiling are straightforward to carry out. The only real difficulty is in getting to the ceiling in

safety so you can work in relative comfort.

For small localized repairs, a stepladder will provide suitable access. Ideally this should have a platform and handrail for safety. For larger repair work you should work from the base section of wheeled scaffold or staging or stand on a builders' staging board between two pairs of stepladders.

You should be able to stand upright with your head about 3in below the ceiling to avoid undue neck strain. Remember to wear safety goggles if you are drilling, scraping out cracks or cleaning off old finishes.

Some ceiling alterations can have a noticeable effect on the appearance of a room and significantly reduce the heating costs.

A lowered ceiling, for example, will reduce the volume of air in the room and thus create a smaller space to be heated. Cladding the ceiling in wood or fixing insulating sheetrock in place of the standard type will significantly cut down on the amount of heat lost through it, and will also reduce condensation.

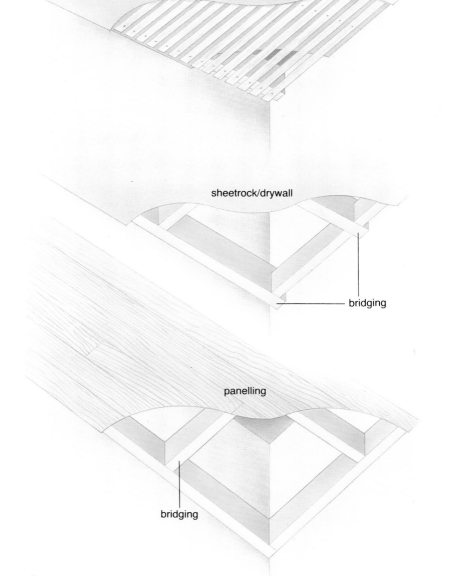

lath-and-plaster

sheetrock/drywall

bridging

panelling

bridging

■ Ceilings are often ornamented with decorative plaster coving and center pieces, both of which may need as much renovation as the ceiling itself.

■ Older ceilings are formed by nailing slim wooden laths across the joists at about ⅜in spacings, and then plastering their undersides. Plaster is forced up between the laths and forms a key that holds the plaster surface in place. If the key fails, areas of plaster may crack or even collapse.

More modern homes have ceilings of sheetrock (drywall), which is nailed directly to the joists.

Sometimes ceilings are formed with plain-edged or tongued-and-grooved softwood and hardwood boards, either nailed directly to the joists or fixed beneath an existing ceiling.

Replacing a ceiling or fixing a lowered one also gives you the opportunity to improve the standard of lighting in a room. You could, for example, fix recessed can-lights, spotlights or track lighting instead of the single center light.

TYPES OF CEILING CONSTRUCTION

There are four basic types of ceiling construction, depending on the style and age of the property. Check which one is used in your house since it can affect the type of problem the ceiling has and therefore the repair work that might be required.

Sheetrock (drywall) ceilings
Sheetrock (drywall) is widely used to dry-line ceilings in modern houses and may be found in older houses where original lath-and-plaster ceilings have been replaced.

The sheetrock is nailed or screwed directly to the ceiling joists and is either finished with a skim coat of plaster or the joints are sealed with filler and joint tape.

Lath and plaster ceilings
Lath and plaster is the traditional way of finishing ceilings. Timber laths are nailed to the ceiling joists with narrow gaps between them.

■ Suspended ceilings are a perfect cover-up for old plaster ceilings in poor condition. They may be tailor-made from timber (above), or bought as a kit in a form that can also permit concealed lighting effects to be used (right).

These are then covered with two or three layers of rough browning plaster and a skim coat of finishing plaster to achieve a flat surface.

Boarded ceilings

Where this type of ceiling exists, often it was put up to replace an earlier plastered ceiling. Matching tongued-and-grooved boards can look attractive when stained or varnished, and form a well-insulated ceiling too.

Ceilings of fiberboard, fire-resistant building board and plywood sheets, with wooden trim pinned to the surface to hide the joins between boards, are occasionally found in older or unrestored properties.

Suspended ceilings

These ceilings can be conventionally constructed, fitted to a wooden framework to lower the height. In many cases, however, proprietary suspended ceilings comprise a light metal framework forming a grid, which is hung from the original ceiling by wires. Translucent plastic or fiberboard panels are fitted into the grid framework and often there is a lighting arrangement above the ceiling to create a concealed illumination effect.

FITTING A NEW CEILING

A new sheetrock (drywall) ceiling can be fitted directly under the existing one. But you will probably have to screw the new sheets in place. By hammering in nails, you could well shake down the original material. It is much better to pull down the old ceiling and replace it completely with new sheetrock (drywall) nailed directly to the ceiling joists.

Pulling down an old ceiling is messy, but not difficult. Wear old clothes, a hat, dust mask and safety goggles. Open all the windows in the room and tape round the door to prevent dust from drifting to other parts of the house.

Take down the old ceiling using a hammer and cold chisel or a wrecking bar, which is a small crowbar. This usually has a nail-puller at one end and this is ideal for removing nails from the joists. If this proves difficult, drive the nails into the joists instead.

If you are replacing the ceiling using sheetrock nailed to the undersides of the joists, use tapered-edge board in the smallest sizes available. Sheetrock is heavy and awkward to lift.

Start in one corner and fix the first sheet so its length is at right angles to the direction of the joists. It will probably be necessary to trim the board so its end falls midway across a joist. Fix it in place with galvanized large-head nails

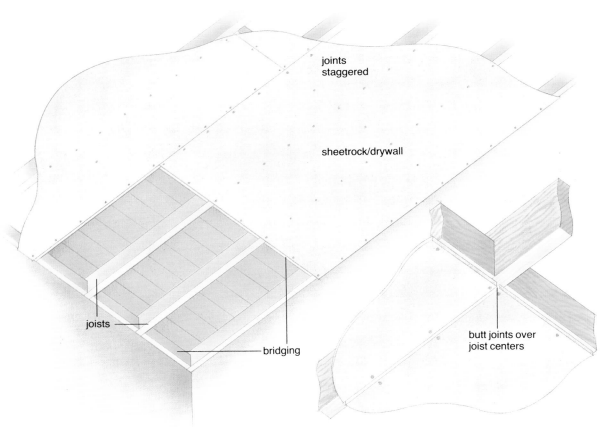

joints
staggered

sheetrock/drywall

joists

bridging

butt joints over
joist centers

■ Sheetrock (drywall) is fixed directly to the undersides of the joists with galvanized nails or screws. Adjacent boards are butt-jointed along the centre line of each joist, and board positions are staggered in adjacent rows. The joints are taped over and filled ready for decorating.

■ Cast plaster ceiling centerpieces are a common feature in older homes. If they cannot be restored, modern replicas can be used to replace them.

with the cream-coloured face of the board downwards. Insert the nails about 6in apart and drive them in so their head just dimples the surface of the board but does not tear it.

Cut subsequent sheets so that the joints between the ends of the sheets do not line up. You should butt the long paper-covered edges together, but keep the short cut edges at the ends about ⅛in apart. Fill nail heads and finish the joints with filler and joint tape.

FITTING A CENTERPIECE

If an ornate centerpiece is damaged, it may be possible to repair it. You can try using a rubber molding, which is normally sold in craft shops, to copy a section of the undamaged molding. This forms a mold into which you pour plaster of Paris. When the new piece is set, you glue it into the missing section using pva adhesive. Some trimming may be necessary to get it to fit in the gap exactly.

Modern ceiling centers, made from rigid polyurethane or fibrous plaster, are easy to fit. Turn off the lighting circuit at the mains, disconnect the wiring and fit the center direct to the ceiling, remembering to thread through the wires first. Spread construction adhesive over

the back of the center and press it into position on the ceiling. Support it with flexible props until the adhesive sets. Then reconnect the light fitting and restore the power.

Heavy ceiling centers should be further fixed with zinc-plated screws driven into the ceiling joist; the heads can then be covered with filler.

FITTING COVING

Plaster or rigid plastic coving round the wall and ceiling join provides a neat finish to the room as well as sealing off those awkward and unsightly cracks that always appear.

First pencil a guide line, the width of the coving, around the top of the walls and the perimeter of the ceiling. Cut lengths of coving as required to fit, mitering the corners at 45 degrees to ensure a neat, snug fit. Use a miter box for this or the template that is sometimes supplied. All types of coving can be cut with a fine tooth saw. Remove burrs from rough edges with fine abrasive paper.

Spread construction adhesive on the edges and press the coving in place so it is aligned with the pencil guide lines. The adhesive should hold the coving. If, however, the wall is uneven, you can temporarily hold it in place with partly-driven nails until the adhesive has set. These can be pulled out later and the holes filled.

Remove excess adhesive with a damp cloth while it is still wet. You can also use the adhesive for making good any gaps between the coving and the walls or ceiling and between adjacent lengths. If using expanded polystyrene coving, you can smooth over the surface using a fine surface filler, which should be rubbed down lightly when dry. Use only water-based paints to decorate polystyrene coving.

LOWERING A CEILING

This alters the proportions of a room and makes any with a high ceiling much more economical to heat. The lowered section can be all over or just part of the ceiling.

It is best to make up a sturdy wooden framework and cover it on the underside with sheetrock. Screw 2 × 2in square battens around the room at the desired new height. Across the shortest width, span these with 2 × 3in joists fixed at 16in centers to form the framework. If the span is more than 9ft wide, fix 2 × 2in wooden hangers centrally between the framework and the joists above to prevent the ceiling from sagging. Cover the underside of the framework with sheetrock (drywall) fixed as described earlier.

■ To fit new coving, cut a miter joint on one end of the first length, butter adhesive onto its rear surfaces and press it into place in one corner of the room. Fit a second length at the other end of this wall, then fit square-ended lengths (cut to size if necessary) in between. Work along the other walls in the same way, mitering any external corners as shown. Finally wipe off any excess adhesive along the lengths and at joints.

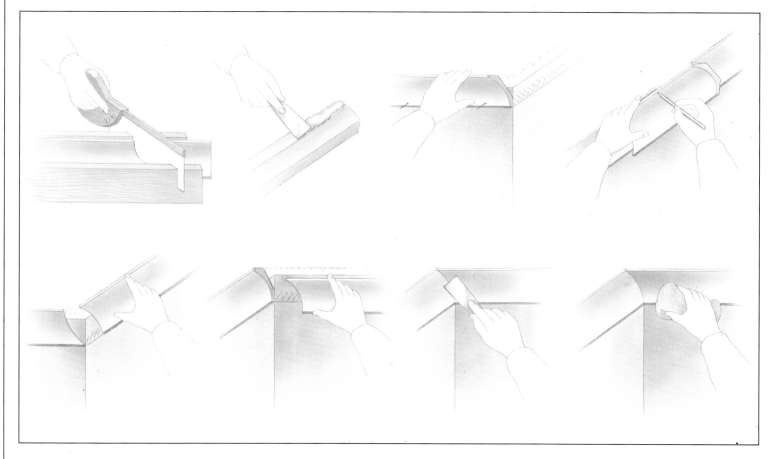

■ Suspended ceilings come in kit form. They consist of a series of bearers and cross-pieces that interlock to form a grid into which the ceiling tiles fit. The grid perimeter is fixed to the walls all round the room, and the centre is suspended from wires attached to the ceiling to prevent it from sagging.

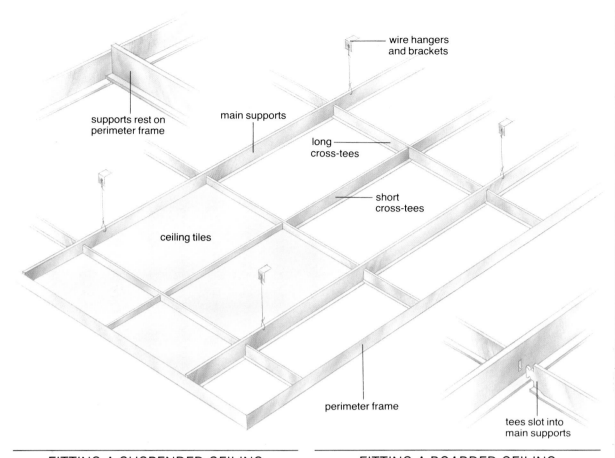

supports rest on perimeter frame

main supports

wire hangers and brackets

long cross-tees

short cross-tees

ceiling tiles

perimeter frame

tees slot into main supports

FITTING A SUSPENDED CEILING

A proprietary lightweight suspended ceiling provides an attractive surface, while at the same time hiding unsightly pipework, cracks, sags and stains in a ceiling. By incorporating lighting above translucent panels, it is also easy to create an illuminated ceiling.

Decide on the height of ceiling required and, with a level, mark a line around the perimeter of the room for the support channel. Screw the lightweight perimeter channel to the wall, mitering it at the corners for a neat join.

Next calculate the size of the border tiles so that they will create a balanced appearance all round the perimeter of the room.

Fit the main bearers along the length of the room, so they rest on the wall channel at each end and are supported every 4ft or so with wires fixed between hooks in the ceiling and the bearers. Form a grid into which the individual ceiling tiles will rest by cutting the cross pieces to fit between the main bearers, and set them in place using a tile as a spacer.

Fit whole ceiling tiles by placing them into the grid from above and finally cut the border tiles to size and fit them into the perimeter of the grid all round the new ceiling.

FITTING A BOARDED CEILING

A good way to hide a cracked ceiling is to fit tongued-and-grooved boards. You can either pin the boards to bearers screwed to the ceiling surface or remove the ceiling and fit the boards direct to the ceiling joists. Allow the boards to 'condition', which will reduce shrinkage, by storing them in the room for a few days first.

By probing or using an electronic joist and stud detector, locate the joist positions and mark these on the ceiling. They are usually at 16in centers. Nail 2 × 1in bearers to the surface of the ceiling, fixing them about 2ft apart and at right angles to the run of the joists.

Starting at one side of the room, fix the boards to the bearers using special metal fixing clips or by secret nailing through the tongues into the bearers. If the boards will not span the room width in one length, cut them so that butt joints will coincide with the bearer positions.

Around the edges of the ceiling, leave a small gap to allow for natural expansion of the timbers and cover this gap with scotia or quadrant molding to create a neat finish.

If you plan to fit a boarded ceiling, check with your building inspector that it satisfies the fire resistance requirements of local building codes.

Fireplaces and Chimneys

Although central heating is regarded as a necessity for modern living, many people still want a 'real' fire as a focal point in their living rooms, even when this is gas burning with a log or coal effect. As a result, probably more fireplaces are being opened up than sealed, as was at one time fashionable.

When you come to plan your rooms, possibly to make alterations or additions, it is most important to give consideration to the position and use of any existing fireplace, whether you are going to retain or replace it or maybe seal it up. And if you do not have a fireplace but would like to install one, you must decide where it can go, bearing in mind the practical requirements of siting a new chimney.

RESTORING OLD FIREPLACES

If you are lucky, you may have one or two original fireplaces in the house which are worth restoring. It is amazing how many 'improvements' in the past involved daubing a thick layer of paint over what was once a perfectly respectable fire surround or even covering it up with a layer of fiberboard.

In the first instance, therefore, it is worth looking behind such treatments to see exactly what kind of fire surrounds you have, so that a decision can be made on whether to restore or replace them.

If the covering is of fiberboard or a similar material, remove this carefully to cause as little damage as possible to the surround and wall plaster. You may find fixing screws and be able to remove these. Otherwise you will have to prise the cover away from the wall. Use a wrecking bar for this and take care not to pull away chunks of plaster.

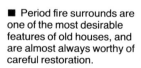

■ Period fire surrounds are one of the most desirable features of old houses, and are almost always worthy of careful restoration.

■ Surrounds may be of wood, masonry or metal and may be highly ornamented, requiring considerable skill and patience to restore them to their former glory.

Old layers of paint, whether on timber, metal or ceramic tiled parts, can be removed with paint stripper. The paste type is especially useful here since it will remove several thick layers of paint at one time.

If on examination you decide the surround is not worth keeping, you will have to remove it and fit a new one. If the surround looks interesting and can be restored, the result should be a good-looking fire in keeping with the age of the house.

Some wooden surrounds were intended to be painted and here a white satin sheen finish looks good. But if the surround has been stripped and the wood is knot-free, then all you need do to restore it is to fill in any cracks and then stain and polish it. Alternatively, you can use a polyurethane finish.

Cast iron is often used for fire surrounds. A wash with a wall and floor cleaner in hot water should take off most of the grime. You can get rid of difficult spots of tar or soot with automobile tar remover, white spirit or methylated spirit. Apply this with fine wire wool to speed up the cleaning. Fireplace and wood stove shops sell proprietary black polish for restoring the shiny finish once so popular with cast iron fire surrounds.

Ceramic tiled surrounds are also very common and you may come across some fine Victorian tile inserts. These must not be treated with any abrasive cleaner or they could be scratched. A wash with sugar soap or detergent in hot water should be sufficient.

If you find any loose tiles on this type of surround, remove and refix them with heat-resistant ceramic tile cement. White or colored tile grout can be used to fill the gaps between the tiles (see Repairing a fireplace).

Brick surrounds are difficult to clean. A stiff brush may be sufficient, but where they are heavily soiled you may have to use a proprietary brick, stone and concrete cleaner, which is available from builders' supply stores. This type is very caustic, so wear protective clothing and rubber gloves and make sure the room is well-ventilated as you work.

Stone surrounds are also difficult to clean. Since there are many different types of un-

■ Within open fireplace recesses the grate is often completely free-standing, and can look highly decorative even when not being used as a real fire.

■ The fireback and grate is often a one-piece insert set within the fire surround, and may be framed by panels of marble or decorative tiles.

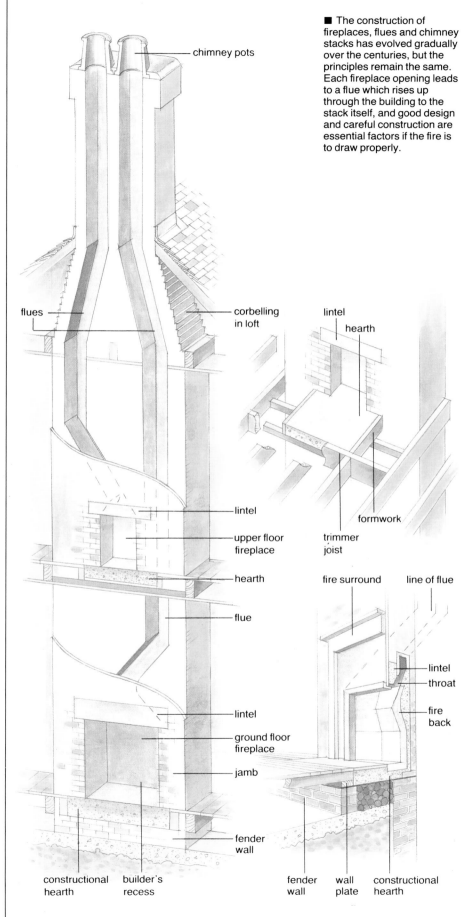

chimney pots

flues

corbelling
in loft

lintel

hearth

lintel

upper floor
fireplace

trimmer
joist

formwork

hearth

fire surround

line of flue

flue

lintel

throat

lintel

ground floor
fireplace

fire
back

jamb

fender
wall

constructional
hearth

builder's
recess

fender
wall

wall
plate

constructional
hearth

■ The construction of fireplaces, flues and chimney stacks has evolved gradually over the centuries, but the principles remain the same. Each fireplace opening leads to a flue which rises up through the building to the stack itself, and good design and careful construction are essential factors if the fire is to draw properly.

polished stone used – granite, slate and marble are just a few examples – it is impossible to make blanket recommendations.

Start by cleaning with a stiff brush. If this does not work, a wash with detergent in hot water may be successful. Only use a caustic brick and stone cleaner as a last resort.

Polished stones such as marble, slate and granite should be washed with soapy water, then sponged off. The polished surface can be maintained with a good quality wax polish.

Repairing a fireplace

If you are going to keep a fireplace, you may find you have to make certain repairs. There are a number of problems you are likely to encounter.

Loose tiles Concrete fire surrounds are often covered with ceramic tiles and over the years it is quite common for these to work loose or become cracked or chipped.

Loose tiles should be carefully eased out so as not to disturb adjacent ones, unless these are also loose and therefore need removing. With a small, sharp cold chisel, carefully remove traces of the old tile adhesive or mortar from where the tile came away from the concrete background. Never attempt to chip old adhesive off the back of the tile, since this would probably crack it. Soak it overnight in water.

Clean off the debris then spread heat-resistant tile adhesive with a notched spreader on to the back of the tile. If only one or two tiles are being replaced and they are fairly well away from the heat source, you can use ordinary tile adhesive, to which a little pva adhesive or bonding agent should be added.

Press the tile into place so it is level with adjacent ones and wipe away any surplus adhesive. You can grout the tile once the adhesive has set. You will probably need a cement-based grout to match the existing one.

Cracked and chipped tiles In an old fireplace the tiles may well be valuable. In this case it is certainly worth keeping the original ones, whether or not they are crazed, cracked or chipped. To attempt to replace them would ruin the value of the fireplace.

Damaged tiles in an attractive, but not particularly valuable, fire surround can be replaced. You will be very lucky to find a good match for the old ones. So rather than attempt to find an exact replacement, it may be better to go for harmonizing, but entirely different, tiles.

You must remove the damaged tiles bit by bit using a small cold chisel and hammer. Start in the middle of the tile and work outwards to the edges, taking care not to damage adjacent ones.

■ Removing an unsuitable fireplace is generally quite straightforward. Once the fixing lugs at each side have been located and freed, the surround and then the hearth can be prised away. Both components are likely to be very heavy, so make sure help is available to support, lift and remove them.

■ Re-bed ceramic tiles on hearths and in tiled surrounds with heat-resistant tile adhesive, making sure that the replacement tile sits flush with its neighbours.

■ Lay replacement quarry tiles on a bed of cement mortar, taking care not to smear it onto the faces of the tiles. Then seal the surface of the new tile to match its neighbours.

Once the tile is out of the way, proceed as described for loose tiles.

If a number of tiles are damaged, you should consider retiling the entire surround using heat-resistant ceramic tiles. The new ones can be stuck directly on to the existing tiles, if these are firmly fixed. Where tiles are missing, you can fill the gaps with new tiles, using a heat-resistant ceramic tile adhesive.

Cracked hearth If a crack in the hearth is due to settlement, do not disturb it. Simply fill it with wall filler. If the sections of the hearth either side of the crack are at different levels, brush the lower section with pva bonding agent or adhesive and build up the surface with filler or cement mortar. When the repair is complete, you can retile the hearth by bonding new tiles into position.

Damaged marble If cleaning does not remove stains on marble, you can try using a proprietary marble cleaning kit, available from specialist fireplace shops. There are various types you can buy. A popular cleaner includes a paste which you spread over the stained area and leave for 24 hours to absorb the stain. A special abrasive polish for marble is available to complete the repair.

If a marble surround is chipped and you still have the broken piece, use a two-part epoxy resin adhesive to glue the chip back in place.

If the broken part is missing, make a marble-colored filler by mixing some kaolin powder (china clay) with epoxy resin adhesive, if necessary coloring it with a dye. Rub it down with a carborundum stone or wet-and-dry abrasive paper when the filler has set and finish with a clear varnish or lacquer.

Damaged fireback If a fireback is cracked or chipped, it can be repaired with fire cement. Let the fireback cool, if you have been using the fire, and rake out the cracks with the edge of a wallpaper scraper or the tip of a mason's trowel. Ideally you should undercut (widen) the crack with your scraper so that the fire cement will hold better after hardening. Remove all soot with a wire brush and clean away any dust and other loose debris.

Spray the whole area, particularly inside the cracks, with water then press the fire cement into the cracks and holes, making sure the surface is smooth. The cement, incidentally, is supplied in containers ready for use. Leave it to dry for as long as possible before lighting the fire again.

Loose, damaged or missing firebricks If you are going to use the fireplace, you will need to repair or replace the fireback. In most cases it will be molded in fireclay and will be in one or two pieces. In older fireplaces, however, the fireback may be formed from several specially shaped sections.

Modern firebacks are made in one or two pieces and in standard sizes to suit modern openings. So if you have a period cast-iron or other old fireplace, it will be worth keeping the old firebricks even if they are badly cracked. They can be patched up with fire cement.

If they are very badly damaged or there are missing pieces, new firebricks can be formed in place with moldable firebrick. This is a very stiff fire cement supplied ready to use. After cleaning and dampening the opening, you simply tap balls of the fire cement into place with a hammer and mold them to the shape required for the firebrick.

Remove any loose firebricks and carefully brush them clean – as well as the backing to which they are to be refixed. Dampen this area and the back of the firebricks, trowel fire cement on to the backing and then press the firebricks in place, tapping them into position using the wooden handle of a hammer. Do not hit these bricks too hard or you will crack them.

If you have a standard opening (16 or 18in wide, measured across its mouth), it will probably be best to fit a new fireback. In many cases you can do this without removing the fire surround. But if the surround has to be moved anyway, do this first before you install the new surround to make fitting the fireback easier.

Removing a fireback is a messy job, so empty the room as far as possible and cover any remaining items with dust cloths. Wear old clothes and a dust mask and lay extra dust cloths over the hearth and the floor around the fireplace. Take away any separate parts of the fire such as the grate and then remove the fireback in pieces, using a cold chisel and hammer to break it up.

There may be a fire-resistant rope between the fireback and the back of the surround. It will probably be asbestos-based and should be left in place if it is in good condition. If the rope is crumbling, however, you will have to remove it and dispose of it as local rules require.

Wearing a dust mask and gloves, first lay plastic sheets in the opening, then spray the rope with water to dampen it. Place it in a plastic bag for disposal by the local authority. The plastic sheets should also be disposed of in a similar way.

Behind the fireback will be loose mortar and broken bricks. If this is in sound condition, it can be left. If, however, the heat has made it crumble badly, you should shovel it up and clear the recess completely of debris. This is a good

stage at which to have the flue swept.

The fireback may be supplied in one or two pieces. A one-piece fireback will be cast with a central horizontal cutting line. If you tap the back gently along this line with a bolster chisel and hammer, the two halves will separate.

Put the bottom half of the fireback in position so that it lightly compresses the fire-resistant rope at the back of the surround. If this has been removed, put a straight piece of wood across the opening to be sure that the front face of the fireback will be just behind the inside edge of the surround when it is fitted.

Mark the outline of the fireback on the hearth, remove the fireback, dampen the hearth and spread a layer of fire cement on it. Lift the fireback into place and tap it down until

■ If the existing fireback is badly cracked, the best solution is to replace it. Check the measurements across the front of the fireplace opening, and buy a matching replacement. Then break out the old fireback, remove it and clear out any rubble that was packed between it and the walls of the fireplace recess.

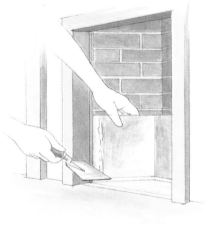

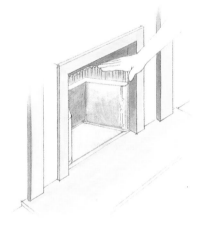

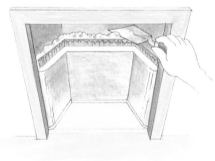

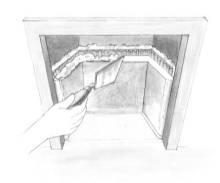

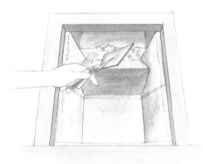

■ Position the lower fireback section within the opening on fire cement. Then place some corrugated paper behind the fireback to form an expansion gap, and fill the void behind the fireback with clean rubble and weak mortar. Next, trowel more fire cement along the top edge of the lower fireback section, position the upper section on it and neaten the fire cement joint. Finally, use more fire cement to seal the joint between the fireback and the throat leading to the flue.

it is correctly positioned and precisely level.

Now place two thicknesses of corrugated cardboard behind the fireback to provide an expansion gap between that and the infilling that has to be put into the rear cavity.

Fill in behind the fireback with vermiculite mortar – made from one part hydrated lime or cement and four parts vermiculite (as used for attic insulation). Alternatively, make up a mix of one part lime, two parts soft sand and four parts broken brick. These soft insulated fillings will allow the fireback to expand under heat without cracking. They will also absorb heat and help to

protect the wall surface behind the fireback.

Lay a bed of fire cement on the top edge of the lower section of the fireback, lift the top section into place and tap it down. Again, put two layers of corrugated cardboard behind the fireback and fill in with weak insulating mortar. Tamp down the filling with a stick and, at the top, smooth it off at an angle of about 45° to form a smooth 'throat' into the flue. Sloping mortar may also be needed at the sides to prevent the formation of any ledges, where soot could otherwise collect.

For most modern fires, the throat should be

built-up fire surround

one-piece tiled
surround

timber/cast iron
surround

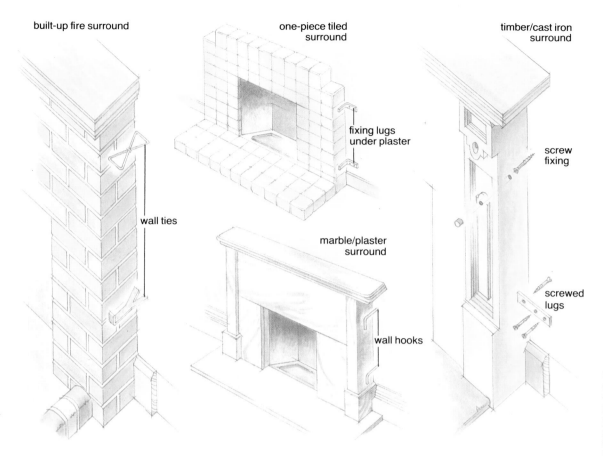

wall ties

fixing lugs
under plaster

marble/plaster
surround

wall hooks

screw
fixing

screwed
lugs

■ Fire surrounds may be
secured to the wall in a
variety of ways – by wall ties,
lugs, dowels or screws and
plugs. The fixings are
generally at either side of the
fire surround, concealed
beneath the wall plaster.

about 12in wide and 4in deep. In older houses
the throat may be much larger than this and it
will be a good idea to fit an adjustable damper
into the flue at this stage of the project to
reduce unnecessary heat losses up the flue.

If the flue is old and has not been used for
some time, it may have deteriorated to the
point where it leaks fumes and does not draw
properly. It would be sensible to have it tested
by a chimney specialist. If a new flue lining is
required, this can be fitted at this stage (see
Lining a chimney).

Removing a fireplace
If you have fireplaces in the house and decide to
remove any or all of them, you will have to take
away the surround and seal up the opening.
This is not a particularly difficult job to carry
out, but it may involve a considerable amount of
work and a lot of mess.

Fire surrounds are usually screwed or nailed
to the wall through metal lugs or wire loops
attached to the surround on each side, close to
the top. The lugs will have been plastered over,
so the first job will be to chip away the plaster to
expose them ready for removal.

When you have located the fixings, you may
be able to saw the heads off the securing

screws. It is most unlikely that you will be able
to undo the screws; however, it may be
possible to cut them off with a sharp cold chisel
and hammer or a hacksaw blade.

With someone to help steady the surround,
which will be very heavy, the hearth can be
prised from the floor. A garden shovel is ideal
for this. Have some wooden wedges handy to
slip under it to enable you to get a handhold
underneath. As you drag the hearth out of the
way, you will find the concrete constructional
hearth, which should be retained. Chip off any
bedding cement remaining on the surface.

Wooden fire surrounds could be valuable, so
think twice before removing them. They could
also be in keeping with the style of the property
and perhaps be worth more than the fireplace
you are thinking of installing.

A wooden surround may have a tiled or
cast-iron insert. The wood itself will be a hollow
box section fixed to nailers, themselves secured to the wall. The surround will probably be
fixed to the nailers by screws which go through
the box sections at the side. It may, however,
be difficult to find these screws since the heads
will be covered with filler. A portable cable and
pipe detector may help locate them. Carefully
chip away the filler, enabling you to remove the

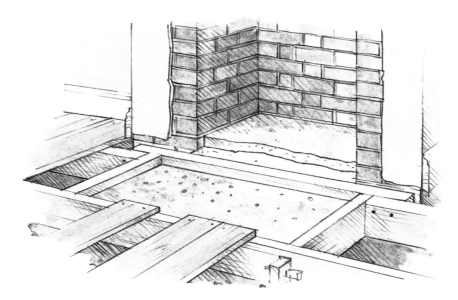

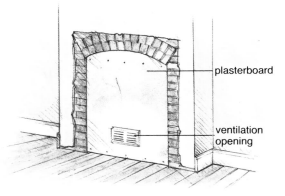

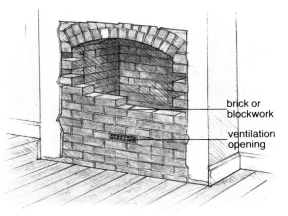

■ To decommission an unwanted fireplace, remove the fireback and lift the superimposed hearth to reveal the constructional hearth beneath. Cover this with sections of new boarding. Block off the fireplace opening either by fixing a wooden framework within it and cladding this with sheetrock (drywall), or by blocking it up. In either case, include a small ventilator near floor level to allow some air to flow up the flue and help to prevent condensation from forming.

timber framework

plasterboard

ventilation opening

brick or blockwork

ventilation opening

screws. Keep the surround in good condition, either to be refitted elsewhere in the house or for maximum resale value.

The tiled or cast-iron insert will probably be held by lugs fitted at the top and sides. These will be visible when the outer wooden surround is removed.

Cast-iron fire surrounds are definitely valuable – and fragile. So take great care when removing them. They will be held by metal lugs set in the wall plaster at each side of the surround, close to the top and just under the mantelshelf. Because the lugs can crack off, drill through the fixing screw heads to remove them. There may also be fixing lugs positioned above the mantelshelf.

Sealing a fireplace opening

There are basically two ways to seal a fireplace opening – by fitting sheetrock (drywall) over a wooden frame or by building a block wall and plastering over it in the normal way. In both cases it is important to leave an opening for ventilation. By providing a gentle flow of air through the flue, you will prevent the chimney from becoming damp. Before starting any work, make sure you have the chimney swept.

The wooden frame method is best if you are likely to want to open up the fireplace at a later date or if you are sealing the opening for use with a gas heater. In this case, the cover should be of asbestos-free insulation board, rather than with sheetrock.

Blocking-up produces a solid wall that is unlikely to crack. Of course, you could always remove the blocks later on to reopen the flue, but they will not prove as easy to dislodge in future as a framed infill.

In most cases the constructional concrete hearth can be left in place. Skimming it with a layer of mortar will bring the surface up to floorboard level. When the floorcovering is laid, the hearth will not be seen.

The only reason for removing a constructional hearth would be if the floorboards are to be left exposed in the room. Here you will have to remove the hearth and lay new joists and floorboards to match the existing floor.

If you decide to seal the opening with blocks, it is a good idea to fit stainless steel block-jointing channel to the inside edges of the wall at each side of the opening. This way you will avoid having to chip out bricks to bond the new blocks into the wall at each side.

Make sure you fit a ventilator into the new wall three or four courses up from the floor to provide ventilation into the flue. Providing the vent block is set this high, it will not get blocked if debris subsequently falls down the flue.

To make a frame for the opening on which to fix the sheetrock or insulation board, use 2 × 3in sawn wood. Cut the head (top) and sill (bottom) frame members first so they wedge into place. Then cut the side (upright) members so they wedge in place between them.

Set the framing so that the face of the board when fixed will either be level with the surrounding masonry, if the wall is to be plastered in the normal way, or so the sheetrock will be level with the surface of the surrounding plaster for direct decoration.

When the wooden framework is correctly positioned, fix the uprights to the side walls with screws and wall plugs, then toe-nail the head and sill members to the uprights. Fix the sheetrock in place with galvanized screws or nails, fixing the board with the grey side facing outwards for plastering or the cream side outwards for direct decoration.

With a keyhole or saber saw, cut a 9 × 3in section out of the board and glue a plastic or metal ventilator plate over this hole.

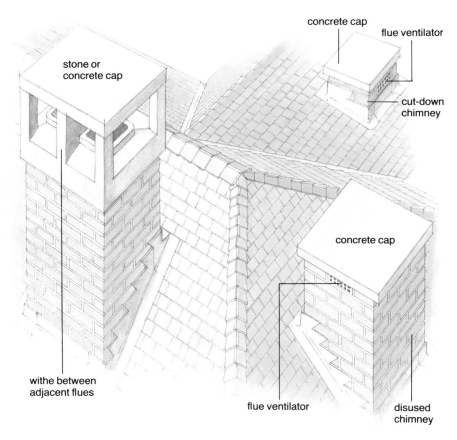

stone or concrete cap

withe between adjacent flues

flue ventilator

concrete cap

flue ventilator

cut-down chimney

concrete cap

disused chimney

RESTORING AN OLD CHIMNEY

Before you attempt to repair or renew a chimney, you must understand how it works. Basically, it is a vertical tube running between the fireplace and the chimney stack. As wind blows over the stack, it should create a suction which draws the harmful combustion gases from the heating appliance up the flue and out of the chimney.

Building codes specify how high above the roof the chimney should terminate and the dimensions of the flue. Many old flues are too wide for modern heating appliances and such flues can be made narrower by using a chimney liner, which will also help to protect the brickwork in the chimney from damage.

Most chimneys are built with a bend in them to prevent rain from falling straight down the flue and on to the fire.

Capping a chimney
The simplest way to cap a chimney is to fit a capping cowl into the flue cap. This will seal the flue from rain penetration while at the same time allowing a gentle airflow to keep the flue dry. Alternatively you can remove the caps and mortar and bed a concrete flue cap in cement mortar over the flues.

Another method is to replace a couple of bricks at the top of the chimney stack with vent blocks (to give an airflow) and then bed a paving slab in mortar at the top of the stack. Remem-

ber to allow for an air vent at the base of the flue as well if the fireplace is also being sealed.

Lining a chimney
A flue lining serves several useful functions. It cures any problems of a faulty flue, protects the brickwork against tar deposits and keeps the chimney warmer, thus improving the draw of combustion gases.

There are several ways to line a flue and the type to use will depend on the fuel to be burned. Some you can install yourself if you want to save money. Others will involve employing a chimney specialist.

An example of a professional installation is the pumped type of lining, which is suitable for solid fuel, wood, gas and oil-fired heating appliances. Here an inflatable 'sausage' is inserted in the chimney and a free-flowing lightweight insulating aggregate concrete is pumped into the damaged flue around it.

The concrete flows into any cracks and holes in the chimney, seals them and at the same time reinforces the chimney. Once the concrete has set, the 'sausage' is deflated and withdrawn to leave an 'inner' flue with a perfectly smooth internal surface.

The easiest liners to install are the flexible, single-skin corrugated stainless steel ones. Most of these are suitable for gas and oil-

■ It is best not to leave the top of a disused flue exposed to the elements. If just one or two flues in a chimney are no longer used, cover them with a chimney hood. If all the flues are disused, remove the top sections of flue liner and the mortar capping and fit a paving slab on the top of the chimney. Before doing so, remove a brick from two opposite faces of the chimney and fit airbricks in their place to provide some ventilation through the flue. If the chimney itself is in poor condition, cut it down to near roof level before capping it.

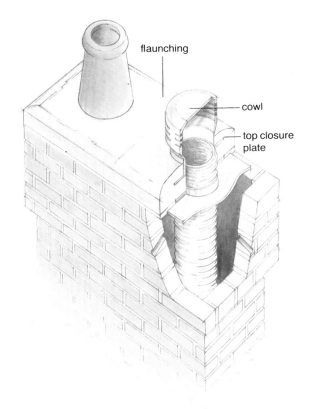

flaunching

cowl

top closure plate

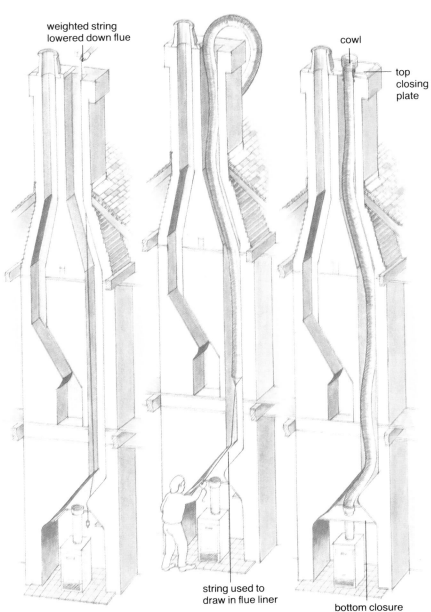

weighted string lowered down flue

cowl

top closing plate

string used to draw in flue liner

bottom closure plate

■ If an old flue is being used in conjunction with a modern boiler, it may be necessary to fit a flue liner. Flexible stainless steel types are lowered down the flue, guided by a weighted string, and are then clamped at top and bottom, ready for a flue cap to be fitted and the final connection of the liner to the boiler to be made.

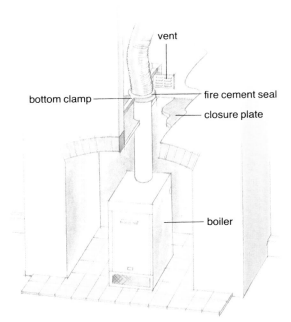

vent

bottom clamp

fire cement seal

closure plate

boiler

burning appliances only, although some are suitable for wood and coal. To install one, you need scaffolding or special staging for safe access to the roof and the chimney stack.

Having swept the flue and removed the flue cap, you feed the liner into the flue from the top. A length of string is attached to the conical end piece, which allows someone inside the house to pull the liner down the flue. When you have fed the liner through, you simply cut it to length and connect it to closure plates at the top and bottom of the flue. You then fit a new flue cap or cowl at the top of the flue.

The third type is the lightweight sectional insulation flue liner, which is suitable for solid fuel and woodburning appliances. The lowest section is installed on a steel plate at the base of the flue and subsequent sections are lowered down the chimney by rope and interlock with each other to form a continuous liner.

Where there are bends, it will be necessary to break into the chimney. While this may not matter in the attic space, it can prove very disruptive elsewhere in the house.

After the liner is fitted, a free-flowing insulating mortar is poured into the chimney to form an airtight seal round the lining.

FITTING A NEW FIREPLACE

Before you fit a new fireplace, make sure you have the flue swept. Then install a new fireback (see above). Now you are ready to fit the new fire surround.

Although there are many styles of surround, there are only three basic types. These are traditional wood, plaster or marble with a cast-iron, marble or composition insert; the raised hearth type; and the brick or stone-built fireplace, which you can make from a kit or to your own design.

For the traditionalist, there are some wonderfully ornate and fashionable Victorian and other period fireplaces available from architectural salvage yards and antique dealers. These can be expensive, so it may be better to opt for a ready-made fireplace. New ones are available from specialist fireplace suppliers in an enormous variety of styles – from reproduction to ultra-modern.

To fit a traditional-style fireplace, first make sure you have a solid constructional hearth at least 6in wider than the fireplace and extending at least 12in into the room. If this has been cut away and the resulting void has been filled with floorboards, you must remove these and the joists supporting them and build up the hearth with concrete so it is level and flush with the surrounding floor.

The first stage is to fit the decorative hearth on a thin bed of weak mortar, comprizing one part cement to seven parts sand. Tap down the hearth pieces so they are completely level. If necessary, make the back hearth level with the top of the decorative hearth by building up its level with fire cement.

Then fit the insert to the face of the opening. It will probably have protruding fixing lugs to enable you to screw it in place to the wall. Fire-resistant rope is used to form a seal between the front edge of the fireback and the

■ The commonest types of replacement fireplace surrounds are formed with machined wooden moldings (below left), often with a decorative tile insert, or are built up in brick or stonework (below right).

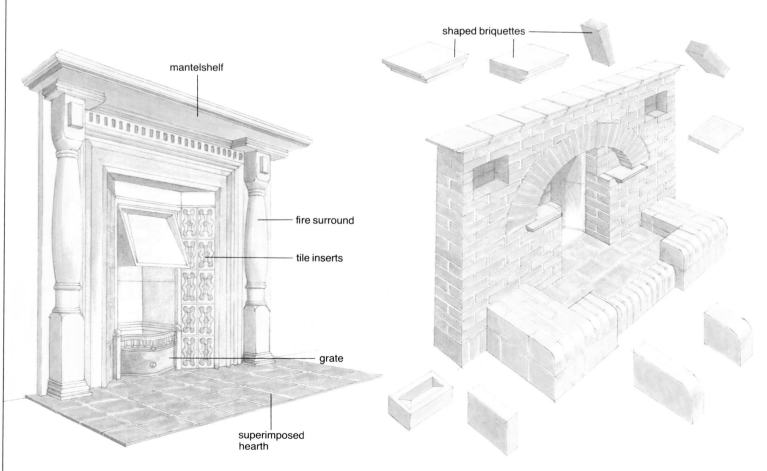

mantelshelf

fire surround

tile inserts

grate

superimposed hearth

shaped briquettes

rear of the decorative insert.

The fire surround stands in front of the insert and is fixed to the wall either by screwing through protruding lugs at the sides of the surround or by screwing through its sides into battens, which you will have to fix to the wall securely with screws and wall plugs. To complete the job, make good any damaged plaster around the edges of the surround.

With a raised hearth fire, you will probably have to brick up the bottom of the fireplace opening about three courses high and cast a reinforced concrete hearth in place at this level. If you are installing a prefabricated type, you will have to fix a pre-cast hearth at this level. In this case, follow the manufacturer's installation instructions to the letter to ensure that the new hearth is fitted correctly.

To cast a raised hearth, first fill in with crushed brick at the base of the bricked-up opening. Next make up a smooth tray for molding the hearth using plastic-faced board. Build up a reinforcing mesh by wiring together 3/8in steel rods, which should be inserted into holes bored into the brickwork at the back and sides of the opening. Pour the concrete into the mold, press it down and smooth it off. When it has set, remove the mold. You can then tile the surface of the hearth.

With brick or block-built fire surrounds, you must lay the decorative hearth first and then construct the fireplace as if building a wall against the chimney breast. Screw brick ties into the wall at regular intervals to ensure the fire surround is properly secured to the chimney breast as it is built up.

Take care not to get mortar on the face of the bricks or blocks and make sure there is either a stone or metal lintel above the fire opening to support the surround at this point.

If you want to install a wooden mantelshelf, bed this in mortar on the surround and hold it against the wall using mirror plates screwed to the back of the mantelshelf and buried in the wall plaster when the wall is made good.

INSTALLING A NEW CHIMNEY

A balanced flue heating appliance, whether gas or oil-fired, can be fitted on any outside wall. But if you want to install an open fire or a woodburning stove, you must build a chimney. This is not, however, as difficult as it sounds, since chimneys are available in kit form and can be installed internally or externally. You will need to obtain local building code approval if you propose to install one.

First you must lay a concrete constructional

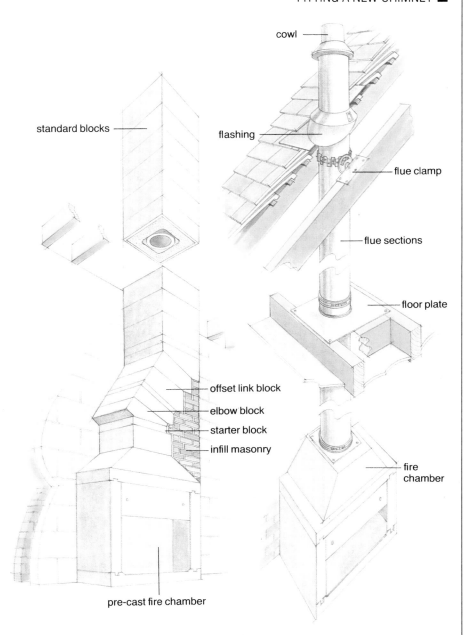

standard blocks

cowl

flashing

flue clamp

flue sections

floor plate

offset link block

elbow block

starter block

infill masonry

fire chamber

pre-cast fire chamber

hearth where you want the fireplace. The next stage is to install a fire chamber, which is available pre-cast from lightweight concrete sections in a range of sizes.

Then you need to build up prefabricated flue sections from the top of the fire chamber. Use 9in sections for an open fire and 6in sections for a room heater. The 9in flue is suitable for either type of fire and allows you to keep your options open should you want to change to another heating appliance at a later date.

The flue sections can be taken up through the house to the roof or fed outside and then up. If kept inside, the flue can be boxed in with wood and sheetrock to form a chimney breast. If taken outside, it can be left in its natural state or clad with bricks or stone to blend in with the walls of the house.

■ Several types of prefabricated chimney are available for domestic installation, and are far quicker to construct than a conventional chimney. The new flue can be taken up within the house or built against an outside wall.

Organizing the Kitchen

The size and shape of an existing kitchen will depend on the age and style of the property. In an older house, designers were usually more generous about space and the kitchen was normally a reasonably large, workable area which could accommodate a table and chairs for eating, as well as the regular facilities.

In more modern homes there has often been a desire to economize on space and therefore kitchens have tended to become more compact space-saving areas. In some cases the kitchen and dining room are combined. This arrange-

ment, of course, requires considerably more thought in terms of planning and layout to make it as practical and functional as possible.

Before planning your kitchen, you must decide what level of expenditure you are prepared to allocate to it, since there is a wide range of options available.

If you are prepared to spend a reasonable amount of money on the kitchen, there are plenty of specialist designers who will be only too pleased to give a bid for redesigning the whole kitchen lock, stock and barrel. They will take on the job of installing the entire room, right down to the last cabinet, fixture, electrical appliance and light switch.

If your budget is more limited, most of the large home builders' supply stores offer a kitchen design service of variable quality. Normally this is a free service and is well worth investigating. If you do not like the plan – or the price – at least you have the benefit of some basic ideas to use in your own design.

Whichever route you decide to take, you must ensure that the new design incorporates

■ Kitchen design is very much a matter of personal taste. The choice between modern and traditional styles is less important than practical things like having an efficient layout and providing adequate services and storage facilities.

■ The key to an efficient kitchen lies in keeping the 'work triangle' as small as possible. This represents the route taken between the food preparation area, the stove and the sink; in a badly-designed kitchen the cook can spend unnecessary time and effort walking constantly from one end of the room to the other. The layouts shown here give an idea of efficient kitchen layouts for four different floor plans.

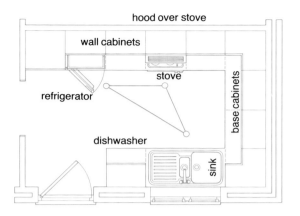

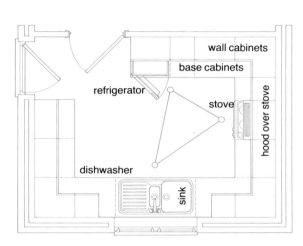

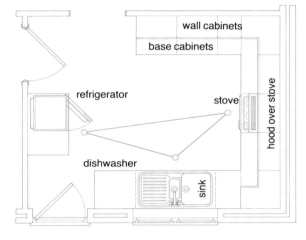

all the basic requirements of this room. These obviously include a sink, dishwasher, cooking facilities, refrigerator, freezer, food and utensil storage space, a waste compactor and disposal system and adequate working surfaces. To this one might add a washing machine and drier.

LAYING OUT THE KITCHEN

The first determining factor for any layout is normally the location of the sink waste line. While it is fairly straightforward to run water pipes and electrical lines behind kitchen cabinets, the run of the waste pipe to the drain should be kept as short as possible with the minimum number of bends.

One important aspect to remember is that there must also be a continuous slight drop in the pipe from the sink to the existing drain. If you need a run of more than about 5ft, you should use a larger size of pipe.

Before you establish the position of the sink, bear in mind that about 75 per cent of the working time in the kitchen is spent here. So the surroundings should be as pleasant as possible. This normally means placing the sink by a window.

With the location of the sink decided, the

next item to consider is the dishwasher. One of the most common problems encountered with a dishwasher is where to put it, since there is often not enough space in the kitchen for all the appliances you want. There is no doubt, however, that a dishwasher is a great timesaver and also cleans more efficiently than a manual operation since it uses stronger detergents and much hotter water. This gives it priority as far as finding space is concerned.

A washing machine may be situated in the kitchen, mainly because of easy access to hot and cold water and waste facilities. But there is no reason why it has to be there. While not every house has a utility room, there may well be a space elsewhere near the soil stack where a washing machine could be installed.

A further point to remember is that the cold water supply to washing machines and dishwashers must be fitted with a double check valve to prevent the possibility of back siphonage of contaminated water into the mains supply should its pressure drop.

The next items to be located are the cooking facilities. These should be near the sink but not so close that an electrical switch or component can be touched while your other hand is in the sink. This also applies to outlets.

The refrigerator should also be situated in the vicinity of the sink to minimize the amount of walking while preparing food. With regard to working surfaces and storage space, these are normally determined by the position and number of the wall and floor cabinets.

Although it is obviously impossible to have all your requirements located within the same area, you should try to plan or rearrange your kitchen so that it 'works' in the most convenient way, but safely.

CHOOSING SINKS

There are many types of sink available nowadays in a range of styles and materials – and, of course, price. So your choice will not only be determined by what you like the look of but also what you can afford.

Sinks made of stainless steel, which contains chromium and nickel, are impervious to all household chemicals and heat. They cannot be cracked or broken, but can and will get scratched. The finishes available range from polished high gloss to satin matt.

A sink made from polycarbonate, a very tough plastic which is colored right through, is also resistant to household chemicals and heat. Scratches can be polished out, although tex-

tured finishes are available that do not even show such marks.

There is also a new material made up from natural minerals polymerized with resin. It is heat-resistant up to 350°F and resists all normal household chemicals. It is very hard and will not crack or chip under normal usage. It can be cleaned using standard household detergents. Other similar versions of this type of material are available.

The latest flexible enamelled sinks are very much better than the old enamelled ones. They do not chip or crack and can be easily cleaned.

With the exception of stainless steel, all these types of sink come in a variety of colors to blend in with the color scheme you have chosen for your kitchen.

With regard to shape, there are countless combinations. The traditional style of one rectangular bowl with either a single or double draining board is still available. One of the more recent trends is for multiple bowl sinks, where the bowls may be of standard size or what are known as half bowls, which are much smaller. These are, among other things, very useful for vegetable preparation and soaking. Circular and other unusual shapes are also available to suit all tastes. Most sinks are inset, fitting into a specially shaped hole cut into the countertop.

■ Double and triple-bowl sinks (left and right) are the most popular style in modern kitchens, allowing different tasks to be carried out at the sink simultaneously. The smaller bowl is often fitted with a waste disposal unit, while the larger bowl can have removable baskets and drainers. A swivel mixer serves whichever bowl needs filling, and can be pushed out of the way if necessary.

There are also special purpose shapes, including one that fits round a corner. This can be particularly useful in a kitchen where space is limited. The other practical aspect of this shape is that it utilizes a space that is otherwise awkward for things like cabinet storage, so releasing the more useful straight runs of work surface for other purposes.

CHOOSING FAUCETS AND FITTINGS

Once you have selected the type of sink you want, give some thought to your choice of faucet. You can still have the traditional separate hot and cold faucets, especially if you have chosen a single-bowl sink, but you must make sure that the sink has mounting holes provided for them.

Mixers are far more popular nowadays and are a must with two-bowl sinks, so that the swivelling outlet can fill both bowls and can also be pushed out of the way when necessary. You can choose between the standard deck-pattern mixer, which needs two holes in the sink surround or countertop, or the monobloc mixer which has a smaller, neater body containing two narrow pipe tails designed to pass through a single hole in the sink or countertop. Some mixers also incorporate a retractable brush head and spray unit linked to the hot water supply which is useful for rinsing dishes.

Many of the latest models now incorporate ceramic discs instead of the traditional rubber washer, and their handles turn through just 90° from off to full on.

On some sinks a pop-up waste system is either fitted or available as an extra. This solves the problem of where to put the plug and avoids the unsightly and unhygienic chain.

Most of the multiple bowl sinks come complete with their own waste and overflow fittings, but normally you will have to supply the trap for the waste outlet.

ORGANIZING WASTE DISPOSAL

Most of the waste in the kitchen is generated at the sink. It makes sense, therefore, to arrange for its safe disposal here. One of the most common methods was in a bin on the inside of the door of the cabinet under the sink. Most manufacturers of cabinets can supply a bin of this type to suit their units. Although it is a very convenient system, its one limitation is normally the small size of the bin itself.

However, in most modern homes a kitchen sink waste disposer is the answer. This is an electrically operated grinder which is fitted to

the sink waste outlet.

There is a removable perforated disc fitted into the drain hole during normal sink use to prevent cutlery and other smaller items slipping down into the waste disposer. When you want to dispose of waste, you remove the disc, turn on the cold faucet and switch on the disposer. As you drop the waste down the hole into the disposer, it is ground up and runs away with the water. However, waste disposers are less suitable for houses with cesspools or septic tanks instead of mains drainage.

These disposers can be used for all vegetable waste, apart from very fibrous matter. They can also demolish bones, fruit pits, fat, grease and coffee grounds. With every disposer comes a full set of operating instructions and the necessary wrench to release any blockages that may occur.

ARRANGING COOKING FACILITIES

There is a very extensive range of stoves available, which is constantly being added to. Most models nowadays use either gas or electricity although you may prefer the traditional range-style stove that can be run off oil or solid fuel and combines covered hotplates on top and two ovens below.

The choice between gas and electricity is one that usually comes down to personal preference. It is normally claimed that electricity is cleaner, while gas is more easily and instantly controllable. Both of these arguments are hotly contested by the respective utilities authorities.

Gas stoves are available for use with natural gas or, for areas that do not have piped

■ A waste disposal unit beneath the sink can dramatically reduce the volume of waste food and preparation leftovers that would otherwise end up in the dustbin.

■ The stove is the heart of the kitchen, and should be sited so that other kitchen facilities can be placed conveniently round it. Gas and electricity are the most popular fuels, but solid fuel range-style stoves still have some devotees.

supplies, bottled gas is available at a slightly higher price. The stove will require some modification to use this fuel.

The traditional all-in-one stove is still widely used and available with an eye-level or lower level grill. It is supplied as a drop-in unit that fits tightly between two cabinets with the cooktop at the same height as the counter.

The stove can, however, be made up of as many as two separate components. The cooktop itself fits into a pre-cut hole in the counter; the oven can be fitted into a special unit at a number of different heights. Generally speaking, it is more expensive to install separate units. But it does allow for more versatility to suit individual requirements and tastes.

Ovens come in both standard and fan-assisted versions. All gas appliances supplied nowadays have electronic ignition, which needs an electricity supply, and all ovens have a flame failure device which turns the gas off if the flame is somehow extinguished. Some of the more modern cooktops are also offering this safety feature now.

Many gas appliances are now available with automatic controls which enable you to present the time you want to turn your stove on – or off, for that matter – if you are out of the house.

All gas appliances must be installed by a registered plumber. Another point to bear in mind is that cooktops with combined gas and

electric burners are generally more difficult to install and service than one-fuel types.

Electric stoves are available in the same basic configurations as gas ones. They need a 210–220 volt supply and have to be connected to a dedicated power circuit.

Various types of cooktops are available, including those with a single flat surface which is very easy to clean. One point to bear in mind, however, is that some electric cooking elements remain very hot long after they are switched off. This could be a danger to inquisitive young children or elderly people.

Electric ovens come in a variety of forms. One of the most popular is that which gives three different cooking methods. These include the traditional method with the heat from the bottom of the oven, convection types with a uniform oven temperature coming from a fan at the rear of the oven, and variable grilling using a large grille in the top of the oven, which can be thermostatically controlled.

Microwave ovens have proved very popular in recent years and modern developments mean you can do as much with them now as with the standard oven. They are of course ideal for quick food preparation, and many are fitted with browning elements to improve the look of certain dishes. Many of the latest models also boast a variety of other useful features such as lots of power levels, one-touch power programs

that let you set the oven more quickly, automatic cooking programs that cook, reheat or defrost particular dishes at the touch of a button, multiple-sequence settings so you can pre-set several different cooking stages, and an autostart control which sets the oven off while you are out.

Although you can buy built-in models, it is probably true to say that most microwave ovens are still free-standing and can therefore be situated anywhere in the kitchen.

CHOOSING STOVE HOODS

You can fit a hood over the stove or cooktop to help reduce the problem of fumes and steam. Most models also have a light fitted to illuminate the cooking area. Stove hoods are available in two basic types.

The simplest one to install is fixed to the wall at the recommended height above the cooktop and is connected to a 15-amp socket outlet. This type has a built-in fan with two or three speeds. The fumes are drawn up into the hood, where they pass through a mesh filter. The cleaned air is then passed back into the kitchen above the hood. The filters are very effective, but will need changing from time to time to maintain their efficiency.

The second type is fitted in a similar manner but the fan has a duct connected to it that allows it to blow the fumes outside the house.

■ A stove hood is essential for getting rid of steam and cooking smells. The concept of a lower-than-usual cooktop makes it easier for the cook to keep an eye on things.

■ Appliances such as refrigerators and upright freezers can be concealed within built-in cabinets to give the kitchen a streamlined look.

Although harder to install, it is more effective.

Stove hoods are ideal where you do a lot of cooking and want to keep the air in the kitchen as clean and fresh as possible without having to rush to open the windows all the time. And it is really essential if you are using a skillet.

CHOOSING REFRIGERATORS AND FREEZERS

The refrigerator is available in many shapes and sizes to suit any kitchen requirement. If you get one that fits below the working surface, it allows more space for other functions such as preparing food.

Wherever you site it, you must leave plenty of room around it to allow free circulation of the air needed to cool the heat exchanger at the back. Failure to do this will result in much higher power consumption, poor temperature control and a short life for the unit.

Some manufacturers make special versions of their standard cabinet units that contain a refrigerator. This means it can blend in unobtrusively with the rest of your kitchen units.

Combination refrigerator/freezers are a useful compromise for a couple or a single person but cannot really do the job of the individual freezer in coping with the demands of a family. So do not be tempted to put more unfrozen food in than the freezer can handle.

Freezers come in two basic types – upright and side-by-side. The upright version is easier to keep tidy and easier for you to keep a check on what you have inside. But the commercial-style chest freezer holds more frozen food per cubic foot. One other snag with the upright freezer is that when the door is opened more of the cold air is lost. Manufacturers have gone to

great lengths to prevent this, but some loss is inevitable as the freezer is used.

The same precautions should be taken with the siting of freezers as with refrigerators to make sure that enough air can circulate around the heat exchanger. Another point worth remembering is that nothing else should be plugged into the same outlet. This should ensure that the freezer is not turned off by mistake, with the possible loss of its contents.

CHOOSING LAUNDRY APPLIANCES

The majority of washing machines sold today are top-loading automatics, which are all around 2ft in width. They obviously have to be sited close to both a water supply and the kitchen waste line, with easy access for loading and removing clothes.

Rotary clothes driers take up a lot of valuable space and need special arrangements for discharging the damp air. This can be through a permanently installed wall vent or a large tube hung out of a convenient window while the clothes drier is in use.

Dishwashers normally take up similar space to washing machines and have the same plumbing and electrical requirements. As the doors open downwards, they must be positioned in a suitable area that allows for this.

FITTING LAUNDRY APPLIANCES

The main problem with siting laundry appliances is that they normally need both hot and cold water, an electrical supply and a suitable drainage system. They are generally sited in the basement, but can go elsewhere in the house if necessary.

While the first three requirements should not pose any major difficulty, drainage can be a different matter altogether. Another possible site, therefore, is in or near the bathroom. A conveniently situated garage may be suitable, but you must make sure it is completely weather- and frost-proof.

Plumbing in a washing machine is quite a simple operation. The water supply for the machine is taken from the nearest hot and cold water supply pipes.

The easiest way to break into an existing pipe is to use a tee fitting connected to a short length of matching pipe and a small in-line shut-off valve, followed by a further length of pipe terminating in a threaded connector to which the machine hoses are linked. This enables you to isolate the machine easily in case you need to get it repaired. You then run your pipework

∎ Where space is at a premium, washing machines and clothes driers can sometimes be stacked one above the other. Dishwashers can be fitted neatly underneath sink drainers or countertops.

from these valves to a convenient position at the rear of the washing machine.

When installing the cold water supply from the main supply line, you must fit a double-check valve before the shut-off valve to prevent back-siphonage unless the machine itself incorporates one. You then screw the hoses from the washing machine tightly by hand on to the threaded ends of the valves.

The drain hose from the machine can be

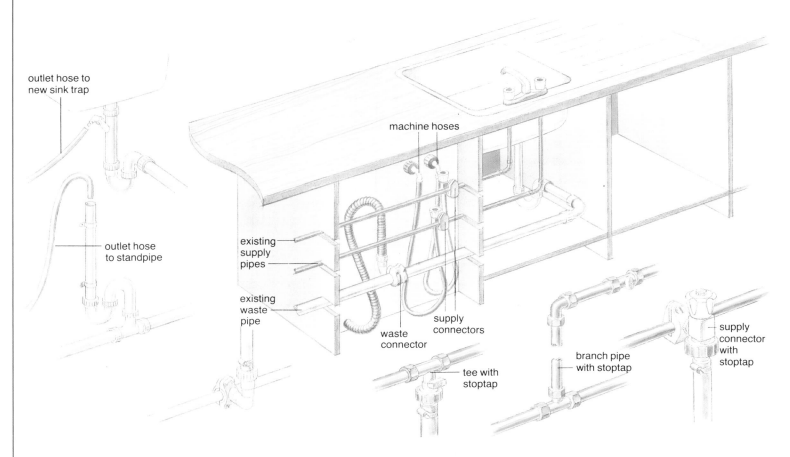

outlet hose to
new sink trap

machine hoses

outlet hose
to standpipe

existing
supply
pipes

existing
waste
pipe

waste
connector

supply
connectors

supply
connector
with
stoptap

tee with
stoptap

branch pipe
with stoptap

hooked into a vertical piece of drainpipe with a trap fitted at the bottom. This pipe should be a minimum of about 2ft in length. Finally connect an outlet pipe from the trap directly into the drainage stack.

It is important to leave an air gap around the top of the vertical pipe and the hose from the machine. If there is no gap, the water could be siphoned out of the machine.

You can also connect washing machine and dishwasher hoses direct to special traps fitted beneath the kitchen sink waste outlet.

CHOOSING COUNTERTOPS

Apart from the very expensive versions, countertops come in three basic forms, in a range of widths and thicknesses. They are all made from laminate-faced particleboard. The widths are to suit standard cabinet sizes. The front edge can be square, postformed (rounded) or with a molded beading fixed in position. Thicknesses are usually around 1½in.

Countertops can be cut to length and shape, but care should be taken since laminate will chip very easily. It is best to score the surface with a sharp knife along the line of the cut first. It is not possible to cut a postformed profile around a corner and any mitred ends should normally be covered with a strip of laminate, which is usually supplied with the countertop. Holes for a sink, cooktop unit and similar fittings are best cut with a jigsaw or saber saw.

Countertops are normally screwed on the underside to light brackets fixed to the wall and then up through the tops of the cabinets. It is this fixing that usually gives such kitchen furniture its rigidity. For special applications you can get custom-made countertops. However, these can be very expensive.

CHOOSING STORAGE UNITS

There are many suppliers of kitchen units who offer a vast choice of styles, colors and individual shapes. Care is needed if you decide to mix units from different suppliers, since they are not all interchangeable.

The commonest material used for these units is particleboard, with special fixings supplied. The quality of the board varies, with the higher priced units generally being made with better grades or with solid wood.

Most of the drawers operate on steel runners, which are finished in a variety of ways to achieve smooth, silent operation. Doors are

■ A washing machine needs a water supply – sometimes cold only, or more commonly both hot and cold – and also some means of discharging its contents into the waste water system. It is best to site the machine close to existing water and waste pipes in order to make the connections easier. Water supplies to the machine can then be connected up via a conventional tee and branch pipe with a stop tap on it, or by means of special connectors. The machine's outlet hose can be taken to an open-ended standpipe, or can be connected directly either to a special sink trap or to the sink waste pipe using a special connector.

normally hung with special hinges that can be adjusted in three directions to ensure the doors align accurately and shut neatly. These hinges also incorporate a spring return to hold the doors shut, thus eliminating the need for catches that used to be a constant source of trouble.

The way in which the doors are finished is one of the main features affecting the choice of unit or system. The cheaper models normally have plastic laminate-faced particleboard doors. As the price increases, the finish improves. Top of the range are solid wooden doors. These incorporate attractive molded contours, which can take different forms – from basic panelling to more complex styles.

How the cabinets are supplied again depends on the price you pay. The less expensive ones normally come as factory-assembled carcases to which you have to fit doors, drawers and other internal fittings. Although the quality of these instructions has improved considerably over the years, there are still some manufacturers who leave much to be desired in this respect. As the price increases, the cabinets are normally delivered pre-assembled and very carefully packed.

The height of the base cabinets that fit beneath countertops varies between manufacturers – from 34 to 35in. Most units are designed with a depth to suit 24in wide countertops, although some are available for the smaller size of 20in.

Cabinets can be bought in standard lengths from all suppliers, although not all lengths are

■ Kitchen base and wall cabinets meet every possible storage need, and many have special internal fittings for particular storage requirements (below). Installation is quite straightforward and adjustments are easily made to line up cabinet and drawer fronts (above).

available in all styles. The normal dimensions include 12, 16, 20, 24, 32 and 36in.

To take up the odd spare space, manufacturers produce a range of ingenious devices such as towel rails and ironing boards that slide away underneath the countertop when not in use.

You can also choose from a range of taller cabinets to house ovens, refrigerators or for food storage. These are normally 2ft wide. The side panels can normally be obtained in white or colored laminate to suit your decor.

To provide added storage, wall cabinets are available in matching styles and colors. These are normally about 2ft 4in high and 11in deep and come in a similar range of lengths to the base cabinets, with various shelf and door configurations.

You can also get bridging units, which are about 11in high and come in a limited range of lengths. They are intended to be fitted high on the wall between two deep cabinets, thus allowing you to work comfortably and safely on the surface beneath them.

INSTALLING THE CABINETS

Once you have finalized plans for your kitchen, selected and obtained all the cabinets you need, it is now time to fix them in place. But first you must empty the kitchen as far as possible and clean off the walls. If the floor is uneven, this must be levelled to ensure the base cabinets sit squarely.

You must also make sure all the necessary utilities are in place, particularly those running along the kitchen walls. Incidentally, cabinets

are designed with a space at the back to allow for pipe and electrical lines. You will obviously not be able to finalize, for example, the plumbing for the sink until the cabinets are in place. But you can fit the main pipe lines to their approximate final positions.

You should also install any electrical outlets or stove connections. In some cases you may have to cut a hole in the back of a unit to accommodate an outlet where the two coincide. Ideally, however, you will have planned beforehand the position of these to avoid such a problem. For example, outlets should preferably be sited above the countertop and below the wall cabinets.

With regard to any gas supply, you will not be able to install this yourself. So you should leave sufficient access to the nearest gas line for a later connection.

The first cabinets to be installed should be those in corners. Normally this will involve screwing to the floor and wall as appropriate using special brackets. Make sure the top of the cabinet is absolutely level. You can then fix the adjoining units, using the screw holes drilled for that purpose to lock each one together.

You are almost certain to find that the wall is not square or straight – particularly at the corners. The important thing to remember is that the front of the cabinets need to be joined accurately together for a straight, flush finish. This is the part that is visible. But you do not have to worry if there is the occasional gap at the back, since the countertop will cover this. Continue fitting the cabinets until you have completed the planned run round the kitchen.

The next stage is to fit the countertops. These can be bought in standard lengths and joined where necessary end to end using the special joining strips available. If you have to make a right-angled join using preformed countertops, you can buy special jointing strips that enable you to make a neat and hygienic joint.

You will have to cut the required holes to accommodate a sink or cooktop in the countertop. Normally manufacturers supply a template for this purpose or the exact dimensions for the hole. Mark this out accurately on to masking tape stuck on to the countertop. This will ensure you do not accidentally erase the mark before you have finished cutting.

Drill a ¼in diameter hole in the waste material near to the edge and insert the blade of a jig saw/saber saw through it. Make sure you fit the small plastic anti-chip guard to the saw and carefully cut out the required shape. It is best to take care to cut out the exact shape with your saw, since it is a very slow process to

■ Storage cabinets are now available to fit every usable space in the kitchen, from awkward corners (above) to the wall above the sink (left). Tall storage units (above right) take care of food storage, while slim shelves beneath wall cabinets (right) keep smaller ingredients conveniently to hand.

clean up the edges afterwards.

Before installing the sink, apply a strip of bath caulk to the underside edge before screwing up the special clamps that locate it. This helps to ensure a watertight seal. You can now complete the plumbing for the sink.

To fix the faucets, you may find it easier to use connector pipes, since these overcome the problem of bending pipes accurately. Then connect up the waste. All sinks normally take 1½in connections and the waste needs to be connected to a suitable trap. The pipe must then fall at a slight gradient – roughly 1·5° from the trap.

You are almost certain to find that the back edges of the countertop do not fit snugly to the wall. It is more than likely you will want to fit tiles above, so a gap of about ¼in is acceptable without posing any problems. If the gap is larger than this, you will have to scribe the rear edge of the countertop to shape to fit the contours of the wall behind.

To achieve a really neat, watertight finish between the countertop and the wall or tiles, you can use one of the many sealing strips available. These are very easy to fit and separate corner and joining pieces are available to cope with these awkward areas.

FINISHING TOUCHES

With all the wall and floor cabinets and their countertops installed, you can turn your attention to adding the finishing touches to your new kitchen. What to put on the walls will be your first concern, and it is worth thinking twice before settling on the obvious choice: ceramic tiles. They certainly look good and present a durable and easy-to-clean surface, but they are expensive to buy, time-consuming to fit, prone to causing condensation if they are on cold external walls, and very difficult to remove if you want a change of color scheme in the future. It is well worth considering using a tile-effect wallcovering if you want the look of tiles, or an easy-clean vinyl wallcovering otherwise. And if you want plain color, stick to paint – easy to apply round all sorts of obstacles, easy to keep clean and easy and inexpensive to redecorate. It is ideal for ceilings too.

As for the floor, you need a surface that is hard-wearing, easy to keep clean and also comfortable underfoot – you stand up more in the kitchen than in any other room in the house. Without doubt the best combination of all these features is provided by either resilient sheet flooring or by special low-pile synthetic fiber kitchen carpets.

Bathrooms and Showers

The bathroom is often called the 'smallest room' and unfortunately in many modern homes this is all too often true. Glossy magazines frequently carry pictures of luxurious bathrooms occupying a space two or three times the size of the average. For many, the reality is very different.

Whatever the size of your bathroom, there are general problems that arise in any event and these must be tackled to ensure the efficiency of this vital area and your enjoyment of it.

One point you should bear in mind is that as far as this room is concerned, small definitely can be beautiful and with careful planning there is much you can do even in the most confined spaces, thanks to the wonders of modern bathroom fixtures.

SOLVING PROBLEMS IN THE BATHROOM

It is often said that there are no permanent solutions to bathroom problems. Fortunately nowadays many products are available that at least keep problems at bay for longer periods. The range is extensive and forever changing, so you should keep a check on what is available. Some work well, others offer reasonable benefits and inevitably there will be the occasional gimmick. So beware before you buy.

Dripping or leaking faucets are a common problem, easily dealt with (see opposite). Another problem sometimes inherited when moving into a house is staining below the faucets where they have been allowed to drip continuously.

In the case of a cast-iron or steel bathtub, the stain may respond to one of the more aggressive bath cleaners. Another way of dealing with such stains is with descaling liquids. If properly applied, this can be quite effective, but you must follow the manufacturers' instructions carefully to avoid damaging the bath surface.

Another problem is a blocked bathtub trap, where the usual culprit is hair. To gain access to the trap normally means removing the panel at the side of the bathtub. Where this is of wood or Masonite, it is usually held in place by screws, sometimes mirror screws with chrome-plated dome-shaped heads that unscrew out of the

■ Rewashering a dripping faucet (right) is one of the commonest plumbing maintenance jobs. It involves removing the handle by releasing its retaining screw, unscrewing the spindle mechanism and then fitting a new washer to the piston which closes down onto the seat inside the faucet to shut off the water flow.

■ Bathroom design revolves around fitting three or four basic ingredients – a shower, a lavatory, a toilet and often a bathtub or bidet too – into what is often not an over-generous floor space.

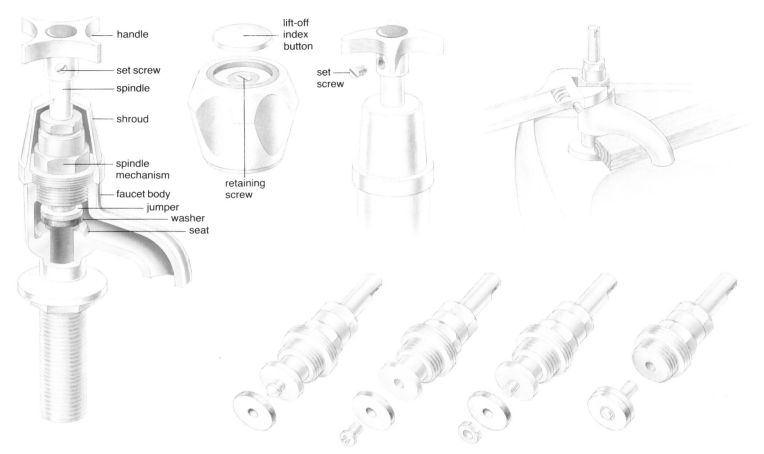

- handle
- set screw
- spindle
- shroud
- spindle mechanism
- faucet body
- jumper
- washer
- seat

lift-off index button

retaining screw

set screw

main screw. Plastic panels tend to be clipped in place below the rim of the bathtub.

Of the other common problems in the working of the bathroom fixtures, the main ones affect the toilet – either water running in continuously or the flush not operating correctly. With the former, the trouble lies in the tank valve and should be dealt with as soon as possible, since this can be very wasteful.

Repairing the tank valve

First take off the top of the tank and look at the valve. It will be either a piston-operated type or a diaphragm type. In either case, the first thing to do is turn off the water supply. This may mean turning off the main stopvalve, although you might find a stopvalve below the toilet tank or on the supply pipe feeding it.

One frequent piece of advice is to bend down the rod or arm connected to the float. While this may provide a temporary cure, it does not remedy the basic trouble in the valve, which will eventually have to be sorted out.

To repair a piston valve, first remove the split pin holding the arm in place using a pair of pliers. Take off the arm and shake the float. If it sounds as though there is water inside, replace the float with a new plastic one.

Unscrew the knurled cap at the innermost end of the valve with a pair of pliers and take out the valve itself, using a screwdriver in the slot where the arm is fitted. Look inside the body at the valve seat, which should be a continuous ring with no scratches or grooves in it. If it is damaged, the whole valve must be replaced – ideally with the more modern diaphragm type.

Now look at the end of the piston that fits against the valve seat. In this there is a small rubber disc (or washer), which presses against the seat, and this is where the problem is most likely to be. If the disc is damaged, replace it. The end of the piston screws off the body, but the joint is often impossible to see. The easiest way to unscrew it is to hold the end with a self-grip wrench and insert a stout screwdriver in the slot to turn the piston body.

Once you have taken the end off, remove the old rubber disc, clean out the piston and insert a new disc. Do not be tempted just to turn it over and use the other side, since this will soon wear down and the problem will recur. Smear some petroleum jelly on the thread and replace the end of the piston. Clean up the outside of the piston, removing any wrench marks with fine wet and dry abrasive paper.

Refit the arm and float using the old split pin –

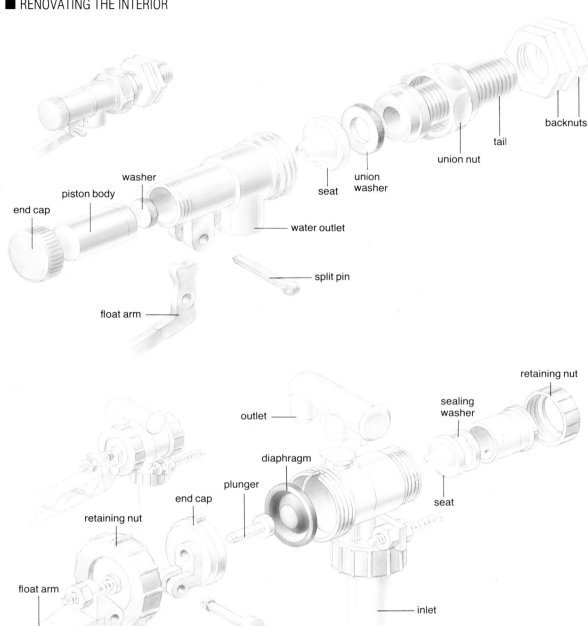

end cap

piston body

washer

seat

union
washer

water outlet

split pin

float arm

union nut

tail

backnuts

■ Old brass ballvalves have a piston which is operated by the float arm. As the water level in the cistern falls, the float drops and the lever moves the piston and its washer away from the seat, allowing water to flow through the valve. Debris within the valve can prevent the washer from closing on the seat, allowing the valve to drip; so can a worn washer. In both cases, turn off the water supply to the valve and dismantle it so it can be cleaned out and a new washer can be fitted.

outlet

diaphragm

plunger

end cap

retaining nut

float arm

sealing
washer

retaining nut

seat

inlet

or replace it with a new brass one. Refit the cap to the end and turn on the water. The valve should cut off the water at the correct level, which is marked on the inside of the tank. This should be at least 1in below the warning pipe. If the level is not correct, carefully bend the arm up to raise it or down to lower it. Support the arm when you are bending it so there is no strain on the valve.

Some of these valves have a silencer tube which runs down into the water. These are not recommended by most plumbers, since back siphonage of water can take place. You should remove this tube if one is fitted.

The more modern diaphragm valve is fitted either through the side of the tank or, with more modern versions, at the top of the plastic tower that rises from the bottom of the tank. The water is discharged from above the valve to prevent any possibility of back siphonage. Although there are some slight variations of this valve now on the market, the same basic instructions apply as far as maintenance is concerned for all models.

To gain access to the valve, you must undo the large serrated plastic nut nearest the float. This nut unfortunately sometimes locks on to the body. If so, pour boiling water over it to try

■ The commonest problem with toilet tanks (right) is a failure of the siphon mechanism, usually due to a worn or split diaphragm. With a close-coupled tank, disconnect the supply pipe, undo the fixings to the pan and lift the tank away so you can undo the siphon backnut. With a separate tank, disconnect the flush pipe and take this opportunity to check that this pipe is clear by pulling some rag through it with a weighted string.

Next, uncouple the lever mechanism, lift out the siphon unit, pull out the lift rod, remove the washers and slide off the old diaphragm. Fit a replacement and reverse the dismantling sequence to reassemble the mechanism.

and release it. If this does not work, you may have to use a self-grip wrench on the nut and another wrench on the body. Turn it anticlockwise, looking from the float end.

You can now remove the diaphragm to inspect it and, if punctured or damaged in any way, replace it. Check the plastic seat it presses against, which should be smooth, clean and without any scratches or grooves. If the seat is faulty, you can remove it by unscrewing

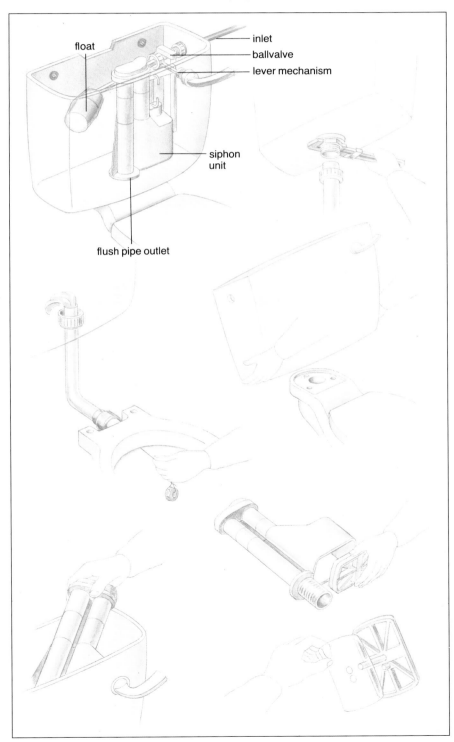

float
inlet
ballvalve
lever mechanism
siphon unit
flush pipe outlet

the other large nut on the body. Make sure the new seat you fit has a hole the same size. Before reassembling the valve, lubricate the threads with petroleum jelly. Use only hand pressure (no wrenches) when replacing the nuts to avoid stripping the threads.

To adjust the water level, never try to bend the float arm. If you have a tower valve, first check that the support screw at the opposite side to the float arm is resting lightly but firmly against the side of the tank. This is to stop the tower bending with the pressure from the float. If it is not touching the side, loosen the locknut and turn the screw by hand until it is in firm contact with the side of the tank. Then tighten up the locknut.

You will see that the float arm is fixed to a pivot bracket with a locknut on either side. To alter the level, slacken one locknut and tighten the other, thus moving the float arm through the bracket. To lower the level move the arm towards the valve body; move it in the opposite direction to raise it.

Replacing a diaphragm

This is necessary when the flush handle does not work properly and you have to pump it to get the toilet to flush.

There are two basic tank arrangements – wall-mounted with a short flush pipe connecting to the bowl, or close-coupled, where the tank sits on an extension of the top of the toilet. With the wall-mounted type, it is not necessary to remove the tank. For the close-coupled type, however, it has to be removed. The following instructions apply to a close-coupled tank. Once the tank is removed, the method is the same for both types.

First check that the water level is correct. If not, adjust it as already described and try again. If it still does not work properly, turn off the water supply and flush the tank fully. Then empty out all the remaining water with a jug, mopping up any left in the bottom with an old towel or cloth.

You must now disconnect the water supply pipe and then undo and remove the wing nuts below the tank. Check whether the tank is screwed on to the wall, then lift it off. Do not lose the rubber gasket.

Disconnect the operating linkage from the handle and undo and remove the large backnut beneath the tank that holds the siphon assembly in place. Lift out the siphon and you will see the old diaphragm on the plunger in the siphon tube. This will either be split or torn, so remove it.

Fit the new diaphragm, carefully trimming it to size as necessary with a sharp pair of scissors. It should fit well to the sides of the tube without dragging. Use the plunger as a guide. Then refit the plunger to the siphon, clean out any debris and use a non-setting caulk to assemble the siphon to the tank. Screw the backnut up tight.

When reassembling the tank to the toilet, do not forget the rubber gasket. Reconnect the water supply pipe and the flush linkage and finally turn the water supply back on. Make sure that none of the joints leak. The tank should now flush correctly.

Low-flow toilets

In many areas of the country, water conservation has become a critical issue. The vast amount of water that has traditionally been used to flush toilets in particular can no longer be afforded. Many state building codes have been amended recently to require the installation of toilets that require less water for flushing, and low-flow toilets using about 1½ gallons of water per flush (as opposed to the traditional 3½-gallon flush) are now available from all the major manufacturers. Public education programs have encouraged this switch to a more efficient use of water, and homeowners should be aware of the new codes when installing new toilets.

Coping with condensation

Condensation occurs whenever warm, moist air meets a cold surface, which obviously happens frequently in a bathroom. It can play havoc with paintwork, leading to rot in wooden fixtures such as window frames and, in severe cases, it can cause problems with the carpet or flooring

■ Whether a bathroom is small and simple (above) or large and well furnished (below), it needs to be warm and also well-ventilated. Radiators and towel rails provide the heat, while an extractor fan quickly gets rid of steam.

when it runs down the bathroom walls.

It is also responsible for the black mold that forms on ceilings and at the top of walls. If left, this can be very difficult to remove. Aggressive cleaners can sometimes solve the problem. There is also a fungicide you can paint on the walls and ceilings which will prevent the growth of this mold. It is transparent and effective for quite long periods.

The ideal solution is to overcome or reduce condensation in the bathroom and one way of doing this is to cut down the amount of cold surfaces. These include ceramic tiles – a particular favorite in this type of environment – and you would be well advised to avoid the temptation of using these on all your walls. Obviously the area around the bathtub, lavatory and shower is best tiled this way. But warmer surfaces like cork tiles or tongued and grooved panelling, which are sealed with polyurethane varnish, or vinyl wallpaper can happily be used on other wall surfaces and all help reduce the level of condensation.

An unheated bathroom merely aggravates the problem, since any tiled surfaces will naturally be that much colder. Various forms of heating can be installed, the most economical and practical being a heated towel rail. You can buy an electric version, which must be permanently wired in, or install one that runs off the central heating system.

Other heaters commonly used in the bathroom include an infra-red radiant heater. Since this type is only switched on when the bath-

■ Bathtubs and lavatories can be boxed in neatly to give the room a streamlined look and also to provide much-needed storage space for toiletries, cleaning materials and so on.

mended that the calculations allow for three complete changes of air per hour in a bathroom. When the room is not in use, ventilation naturally diminishes. So it is quite in order to exceed this figure when taking a bath or shower. When you buy an extractor fan, the manufacturer always quotes the amount of air that it will extract in cubic feet per minute. A simple calculation will enable you to select a fan with sufficient capacity for your bathroom.

You should bear in mind, however, that any air removed has to be replaced from somewhere. If you shut the bathroom door and keep the window closed, the fan will not be able to 'extract' any air. You can, of course, gain 'new' air by leaving the window open. While this may be acceptable in the summer, it will not help your condensation problem on a cold, damp, winter morning. The best arrangement is to allow air to enter the bathroom from inside the house. You can do this by deliberately leaving a small gap underneath or at the top of the door. About ¼in should be sufficient.

Another advantage from fitting an extractor fan is that it will help to get rid of the inevitable smells from the toilet quickly.

Giving tiles a facelift

After a number of years the grouting between ceramic tiles will become discolored and spoil the overall effect of what was once a clean, shining surface. By freshening up the tile joints, you can give these areas a real facelift so they look like new again.

If the grouting is in poor condition, rake it out with a suitably thin sharp tool, such as an old hacksaw blade. This can be a tedious operation. Then replace it with new waterproof grouting. Mix this according to the manufacturers' instructions, which may include a recommended standing period before use.

Apply the new grouting with a rubber spreader, making sure you work it thoroughly into all the gaps. Allow it to dry and then wipe off the surplus with a damp cloth. If you find that you have left too much in some gaps, wait until it is dry and then scrape it off with a piece of slim wooden dowel.

If the grouting is in good condition but stained, you can paint it with a special preparation available in a range of colors to match or blend in with your tiles.

The gap around the bath and the lavatory should be properly sealed to prevent water getting in behind the fittings. Existing seals will age and break up or become discolored. The best solution is to remove them and use one of the special silicone rubber caulks now available

room is occupied, however, it has a somewhat limited effect on condensation.

Never be tempted to use a standard electric heater in the bathroom, since this is a potential killer. Electricity and water form a lethal combination. All outlets installed in bathrooms must be gfi (ground fault interruptor) units to comply with local wiring codes.

The other method of reducing condensation is to reduce the amount of moist air. This can be done by fitting an extractor fan, but its position is important. The window is a popular place to fit one, mainly because it is easy and cheap. But this is often not the best location. You should position the fan where it is likely to remove the air that is most moist. Over a bath or shower is the ideal position and you should do this by fitting the fan so that it can exhaust through an exterior wall. There are a number of models available that come complete with the necessary fittings for this type of installation.

When installing an extractor fan, it is recom-

in a variety of colors to suit your bathroom suite. They are applied with a caulking gun and full instructions are given as to their application. However, the compound is very sticky and difficult to remove once it has cured. So you must remove any excess immediately.

Because these caulks remain flexible, they are able to accommodate any movement in the fittings without cracking. The problem is that after a time black mold tends to form on them. The easiest way to deal with this is to cut out the old caulk with a sharp utility knife and reseal the offending section.

Retiling a bathroom

If you decide you want a change of color scheme in a tiled bathroom, you have two choices: to remove the old tiles and start again, or to tile over the existing tiles. The second option is infinitely preferable to the first. For a start, trying to hack tiles off a wall clad in sheetrock (drywall) is likely to result in considerable damage to the wall surface, and the job is extremely tedious and time-consuming to carry out. In contrast, tiling over tiles is no more difficult than tiling on a bare wall; modern tile adhesives are strong enough to bond to existing tiles so long as they are clean and free of grease or other surface contamination.

The only problems you will have to contend with when tiling over tiles are what to do where

the tiling meets door and window casings and baseboards, and where the tiling stops part-way up the wall. In the first case, nail on thicker timber if necessary to form an edge for the tiles to butt against, and in the second, nail up some decorative wood molding to disguise the double thickness of tiles and give the area a neat finished edge. You could even fix up a shallow shelf level with the top edge of the tiled area and use it to display toiletries.

Keeping showers working

One of the most common problems with showers is when the head becomes blocked due to excess scale, particularly in hard water areas. Since this is a gradual process, it is not always noticed until the shower becomes really weak. Regular treatment here will eliminate any serious effects.

Take the head off the shower and, if possible, dismantle it. There are a number of descaling solutions available which take varying amounts of time to work and are applied in different ways. Among these are some 'environmentally friendly' products that are less aggressive, but equally effective – and safer to use.

While tackling this problem, you may be able to descale some of the working parts of the shower itself. But be careful if you have to put any parts of a thermostatically controlled shower into boiling water. Check first with the

■ Bathrooms benefit from good natural light; hang translucent blinds or curtains to provide the necessary privacy when the room is in use.

manufacturers' instructions.

One other problem frequently encountered with ordinary showers is when someone turns on another tap in the house and the shower temperature changes dramatically. This can generally be overcome by fitting a thermostatically controlled mixer valve.

Low-flow shower heads

If you plan to fit a new shower head in your bathroom and you want to make your own contribution to the cause of saving water, it is worth considering the use of one of the new low-flow heads now available. These can save an enormous amount of hot water. For example, at normal household pressure the conventional shower output of 12 gallons per minute can be reduced to less than a quarter – around 2½ gallons per minute. Assuming that one five-minute shower will be taken each day, more than 17,000 gallons of hot water can be saved each year, representing a huge saving in water-heating costs.

MAKING BATHROOM ALTERATIONS

If you are considering any alterations at all in your bathroom, it is worth thinking about the whole room and not just individual parts. There is little point in replacing a single fixture now if in the future you are likely to change the whole lot. Equally any amendments to the plumbing should be done altogether, rather than having

further inconvenience and upheaval at some later date, when you finally decide to put in that shower you have been promising yourself.

Whereas there is usually a lot more scope in the traditionally larger bathrooms in older properties, the average small modern bathroom may not appear to offer much opportunity for changes. With a little careful thought, however, it is often possible to use the space available much more effectively.

If, for example, you install a shower, you will find you no longer need a large lavatory as its use diminishes. Alternatively, buy a small corner bathtub, which takes up less space than a normal bathtub yet still allows you to use that facility, perhaps with the addition of a shower fitted over it.

By replacing the toilet with a more compact version and the lavatory with a smaller model, you have already created considerably more space. This can be left to give your bathroom a more spacious feel or it may be big enough to allow you to fit the larger bathtub or shower cubicle you have always wanted.

Draw up a scale plan of your bathroom and put in the fixtures you would like to the same scale. This way you can estimate accurately how your ideal bathroom might work. There is a minimum recommended area of free space around bathroom fixtures that allows easy access and safe and comfortable use. These spaces can overlap, however, since you can only use one fixture at a time.

■ Bathrooms are much easier to plan than kitchens because they contain fewer essential ingredients – usually just a shower, lavatory and toilet, although larger rooms may have space for a bidet or a bathtub too. Each piece of equipment needs enough 'activity space' around it to allow it to be used safely and comfortably; the arrangements shown here suggest some workable possibilities.

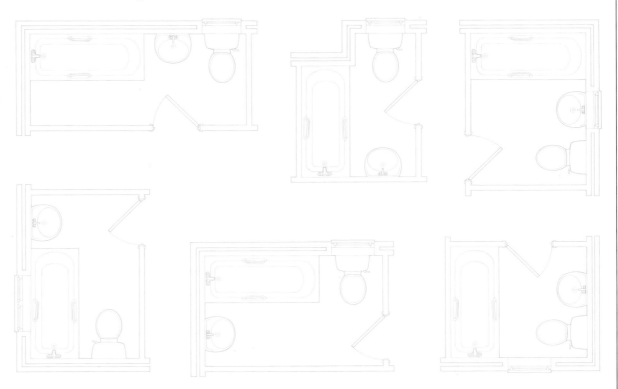

When planning, it is best to leave the toilet in the same position, since moving the large diameter waste pipe can be difficult. Most of the other fixtures, however, can be accommodated in different positions. It may be necessary to raise the bathtub, however, if you propose moving it to the other side of the room. This is to give sufficient fall in the waste line over its new, longer run to the soil stack.

REMOVING AN OLD BATHTUB

■ Corner bathtubs take up less floor space than is at first apparent, and can make better use of bathroom space than a conventional rectangular tub does.

One of the first problems you are likely to come across when refitting your bathroom is that of removing the old bathtub. Quite possibly it is a cast-iron one and therefore very heavy and awkward. The easiest way is to break it up first, which can be done in two ways, both of which are noisy and messy.

First turn off the water and disconnect and remove the old faucets and waste connections. You will probably need a wrench to remove the faucets. You can then break the tub with a sledgehammer, but make sure you have protected your eyes and your ears. Start in the middle of the sides, which is the weakest point. One snag is that there is not always enough room to get a good swing on the hammer.

The other method involves first drilling a line of ¼in diameter holes across the tub about 1in apart. Then drive in a tapered punch to split the tub in two. You should be able to remove these pieces – or repeat the operation, cutting it into four roughly equal quarters.

REMOVING OTHER FIXTURES

Removing an old lavatory is a much simpler job. Start by disconnecting the waste line from the trap, and undo the pipe connections to the faucets. With a free-standing lavatory, unscrew the fixing brackets supporting the bowl and lift it off the pedestal. Then remove the wall brackets, unscrew the pedestal and lift this away too, ready for the replacement lavatory to be installed.

Removing a toilet can be more difficult, especially if it discharges into an old cast iron soil pipe. Start by disconnecting the water supply to the tank, and flush it to remove the bulk of the water. Scoop and mop out the rest. With a separate tank, disconnect the flush pipe next and unscrew the fixings holding the tank to the wall so you can remove it. With a close-coupled tank, undo the screws securing it to the lavatory bowl and to the wall, and lift it off the bowl. Next, undo the screws holding the pan to the floor or wall and lift it away from the soil pipe connector; with plastic pipework the pipe will simply pull out, but with cast iron you may have to break out old, hard caulking first. Take great care as you do this not to crack the cast iron spigot on the soil pipe; it is preferable to break the outlet from the toilet with a cold chisel and hammer, and then to remove the remaining pieces from the pipe afterwards.

CONNECTING THE NEW FIXTURES

If you are positioning new fixtures in their original position, you should find you can connect the new faucets using the existing pipework. For any slight variations, you will probably find it easiest to use flexible pipe connectors. If the waste pipes are of metal, it is a good idea to replace the system with plastic pipe and fittings.

■ Showers can be taken in the bathtub, with a shower curtain to keep splashes under control, or in a separate shower cubicle.

■ **Above** Careful planning can squeeze the essential bathroom components into even the most unpromising room shapes.

FITTING A SHOWER

A shower is a very useful addition to any bathroom and will bring considerable savings in water and heating costs, not to mention the easing effect on the morning 'rush hour'. Of course, a shower can also be fitted quite easily elsewhere in the house – for example in a downstairs cloakroom. There are four basic types from which you can choose the most suitable or convenient. Only the first two types are commonly installed.

Mixing valve shower
Installing this type involves replacing the bath faucets with a mixing valve with a shower connection. One thing you must check is that the existing hot and cold supply lines can be easily reconnected to the threaded tails on the new mixing valve; they may need extending.

With the mixing valve in place, you will have to fit the shower head to the wall and also put up a suitable shower enclosure. This can be a simple screen fixed to the wall and pivoted into place, a curtain running along the bath or an enclosed curtained space.

Thermostatic shower
This type also uses the domestic hot water supply and is subject to the same restrictions as faucets with regard to the feed of water. It does have the advantage that it can be positioned anywhere in the bathroom – or elsewhere – and

■ Shower cubicles can be bought as kits and fitted into a convenient corner (left), or can be built from scratch as part of a full-scale bathroom remodelling project (right).

■ Matching vanity units, mirrors and wall cupboards (below) help to give the bathroom a carefully co-ordinated look.

gives a better flow rate and better control of water temperature.

If you live in a hard water area, make sure the shower you buy is suitable for hard water and will not be affected by scale, particularly in the mixing valve.

Pumped shower

Pumped showers are sometimes used in situations where the local water supply is drawn at low pressure. They provide an invigorating shower and the rose is usually adjustable to give variations in the pattern or volume of water spray that is provided by the shower head.

These showers, which often take their supply from a cold water storage tank, comprise four main components – the shower head with its fixings; the mixer valve; the pump with filters and flow control valve; and a transformer. The shower head and mixer valve can either be fixed on to a wall or sunk into it with the connecting pipes concealed under tiling.

The pump motor usually works at low voltage for safety and is switched on and off by a flow valve, which detects the sudden flow of water when the shower is turned on. The pump can be positioned in any convenient location near the shower and is connected by feed pipes to the mixer valve and the water supply.

The transformer converts full mains voltage to the special low voltage required and again can be positioned in a suitable dry location reasonably near the pump.

Electric shower

This type of shower, which can be fitted over the bath or in a separate enclosure, is occasionally recommended for use in remote locations where full-scale plumbing arrangements do not exist. The water is heated electrically as it passes through the shower. Because it takes a high current, it is best to leave the installation to an electrician.

If you are considering buying one, remember that the hotter the shower the less water flows. The higher wattage versions give better flow than the low wattage ones, which in some cases do not really provide a sufficient water flow to keep you warm in a cold bathroom. Make sure you take professional advice if you live in a hard water area since some models are affected by a build-up of scale.

INSTALLING A BIDET

A bidet can be a useful addition to a bathroom if space permits. It is, however, subject to quite stringent water supply controls to prevent any possibility of contaminating mains water by back siphonage. If you wish to install a bidet, you must inform your local plumbing inspector.

Bidets come in two types, the most common being the over-the-rim type which can be likened to a low-level lavatory. The other, more expensive type has an ascending spray to provide the necessary rinsing facility. With either type, the waste must discharge through a

■ The advantage of free-standing lavatories (top) is that they take up very little floor area – a boon in small bathrooms. Mirrors help to make the room seem both lighter and larger.

Built-in lavatories (above) provide extra storage space and help give the bathroom a streamlined appearance. A rooflight provides natural light in a windowless room.

separate waste pipe into the soil stack and on to your drainage system.

The water supply to the over-the-rim bidet can be taken from the domestic supply in the same way as a lavatory if either separate faucets or a mixing valve with two separate channels are fitted. If a single outlet mixer faucet is fitted, then check valves must be fitted to the hot and cold water supply lines to prevent any risk of water being siphoned back into the mains should the supply pressure drop.

In the case of the ascending spray bidet, quite different rules apply and you should check with your local plumbing inspector before you commit yourself to fitting one.

Creating more space

As the family grows, a once spacious house can begin to burst at the seams, making life very crowded and increasingly difficult. Perhaps an elderly relative has come to live and will need his or her own room. Or possibly having a spare bedroom will make all the difference when planned or unexpected guests arrive.

In some cases the existing space can be adapted so that, for example, a large living room becomes a living and dining room, leaving the original dining room free for conversion, maybe, to a first-floor bedroom-sitting room. In other cases, walls might be rearranged to change the layout of the house. Here you should first seek expert advice to ensure you are not going to affect the basic structure. Or you might decide to partition a large room to create two smaller ones.

These are just a few of the possible options available and you should consider all the various opportunities carefully before looking at other possibilities, such as building an addition. That, of course, may be your choice, but it will involve more work and greater cost.

So the basic choices available are either to convert existing accommodation, including an attic or basement if you have one, or to build on. The first option depends on whether the space is suitable for conversion and the second on whether you have the land available.

If you have complete freedom of choice then cost, convenience and looks will be the major considerations. Should you have a neighbor with a similar property that has been altered in any way, then it is a good idea to see what that conversion or addition is like inside. The new room may be the wrong shape or size or perhaps has involved altering the interior layout in some way that might not appeal. But at least it will give you some food for thought.

On the outside of the house, have a good look at the way an addition or attic conversion has affected the appearance of the property. Sometimes it can do so adversely.

CONVERTING AN ATTIC

It is impossible to say whether an attic conversion will be cheaper than an addition. So much depends on the type of house and therefore the amount of work involved. A local engineer or architect should be able to give you a reasonable idea, before you go to the expense of having plans drawn up which a builder can use as a basis for producing bids.

The advantage of an attic conversion is that you do not use up any valuable yard space. The extra room will already have a roof (the existing one) and there is no need for excavating foundations or getting involved in the messy building work associated inevitably with making additions to the building.

First you have to decide what is the end use you intend for your attic space. For example, you may just want an occasional play area for the children – somewhere for them to lay out a toy village or train set, for example. Or you may want a crafts room for dressmaking or photography. This kind of occasional use will involve little in the way of large-scale structural work and any conversion should be relatively quick and inexpensive to carry out.

■ An attic conversion below a steeply pitched roof can have a spaciousness other rooms can ever aspire to. A window in the gable end wall allows an outside view, while rooflights admit plenty of natural light.

If you decide you want proper habitable rooms – an extra bedroom or maybe a bathroom, for example, with all the amenities of plumbing, heating and electricity – then it will be a different matter altogether. Most alterations must comply with local building codes as far as the strength of floors, sound and heat insulation, ventilation and means of escape in the event of fire are concerned. This will obviously involve much more work and expense (see Fire safety in attic conversions).

Making sure your conversion complies with building codes is essential. So it is best to get professional advice on layout and design and to consult with your local building inspector at an early stage in the project. Not only will such consultation avoid problems during construction, but it will also help you to get the most practical design for your conversion and to make the best use of the space.

Checking the roof

First, though, you need to make sure your roof is suitable for conversion. Not all of them are.

In general, house roofs are constructed on site by fixing individual wooden frame members together. The basic shape involves a braced triangle. The sides (rafters) support the roof and the base (joists) stop the bottom of the rafters from moving outwards. They also provide support for the ceiling below. The strengthening members linking the triangles (purlins) run along the roof space and hangers and struts provide extra support.

Designs vary, but all such roofs can be converted by taking out individual sections and putting additional supports in the correct place to take the various roof loads. Looking at it from the inside, such a roof structure may seem an awkward place in which to fit a new room. But it can generally be easily adapted.

In more modern houses, the roof has probably been constructed using the trussed rafter system. Here, prefabricated triangular wooden frames span the main house walls.

If you have a roof like this, a full-scale conversion is not possible, because you cannot remove or reposition any of the trusses without seriously weakening the roof structure. However, you can improve access and lighting and use the space for storage.

Planning the work

Once the plans for the proposed conversion have been finalized and a permit has been issued, you have several options as far as getting the job done is concerned.

You can do everything yourself, which is the

Fire safety in attic conversions

If you are planning to add an attic conversion to an existing two-storey house, you must satisfy your local building codes. The following points on providing safe means of egress and fire-resistant construction may have to be complied with, but you should always contact your local building inspector for advice first.

● The existing stairway to the second floor to be enclosed in a fire-resistant partition and to lead to a final exit from the building.

● Every existing door to a habitable room (including a kitchen but not a bathroom) opening onto the stairway to be fitted with a door closer. Any new doors fitted as part of the attic conversion may have to be fire doors.

● Any glazing in the walls of the enclosure or in doors opening onto it to be fire-resistant.

● The new stairway leading to the conversion may be a continuation of the existing stairway enclosure or may have to be in a separate enclosure that connects with the existing stairway at second floor level.

● The new storey to be separated from the others by fire-resistant contruction.

● Each room in the attic conversion to have an openable window or rooflight which can serve as a means of escape or a rescue point.

least expensive method. But converting an attic from scratch is not really a do-it-yourself job. Although there are many ways in which you can save money, two important aspects – strengthening the attic floor and installing a staircase – will normally require professional help. And in some older houses, for example, there may be no building paper under the roof, which might mean having to provide a waterproof roof lining.

One way in which you can save money is to use a builder to carry out the major alterations and then do the finish work or arrange for individual sub-contractors to do it for you at a separately negotiated price.

Jobs you may be able to do yourself include installing windows, laying floor coverings, building partition walls and ceilings, extending the electrical, plumbing and heating lines into the attic and tackling the final decoration, making good and putting in fixtures and fittings. So there is still plenty you can do yourself.

If you do decide to undertake some of the major work, then be prepared for a long job. Alternatively, of course, you can hand the entire job over to someone else – ideally a conversion specialist or a reputable building contractor. This is expensive, but it will be the quickest and easiest method.

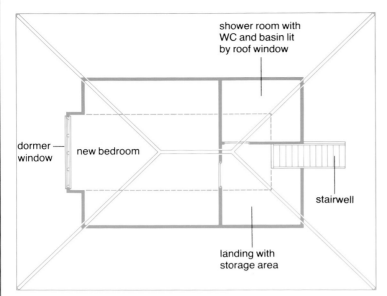

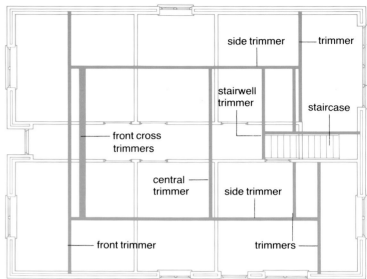

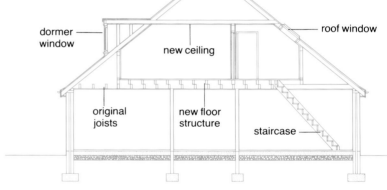

■ These outline plans for a typical attic conversion (above) show the extent of the new work, the positions of extra joists needed to support the additional loading and a cross-section through the building. Detailed plans must always be submitted for official approval before conversion work starts (below right).

Laying an attic floor

Although you may decide to leave the job of putting down the attic floor to a contractor, it is worth knowing what is involved. The main problem here is that existing roof joists stop the sides of the roof and walls moving outwards, but they are usually not strong enough to carry a floor with people walking on it.

There are three methods of strengthening the joists. The first is to bolt new joists of the same size to the existing ones to spread the load (known as sistering). Secondly you can install new, larger joists between the existing ones. Finally you can position a beam below the existing ceilings at right angles to the joists so as to reduce their span.

The simplest type of floor to lay on the joists is flooring-grade particle board, screwed to the joists. You can, however, lay floorboards if you prefer. Do not, however, lay any flooring until other jobs, particularly any extensions to wiring and plumbing, are completed. But putting down at least some of the flooring temporarily will provide a solid platform on which to work. When putting in the flooring, it is well worth

■ Dormer windows projecting from the roof slope were the traditional way of lighting attic rooms.

■ Rooflights, installed in the plane of the roof slope, are less obtrusive than dormers while admitting more light to attic rooms. They can also act as fire escapes in an emergency.

■ A typical use of an attic conversion is to provide an extra suite of rooms, perhaps to house an elderly relative.

taking it right through to the roof edges and creating access doors in the walls of the attic so that the eaves space behind the walls can be used for additional storage.

Once the floor is laid, put in the windows so you can work by natural light. Then install the plumbing, electricity and heating you require. This may involve reorganising the route of existing utilities and this is most easily done before you start building partition walls on the new floor structure.

Choosing attic windows

There are two types of window – the dormer, which is built out from the roof rafters, and the skylight, which fits into the slope of the roof itself. The latter is made by specialist manufacturers and comes with a range of accessories, such as blinds and awnings.

Skylights can have pivoting sashes so that they can be rotated right round for cleaning purposes and can be fitted working entirely from inside the roof, which makes installation less hazardous. They may also provide an escape route in the event of a fire. Frames are in softwood with metal cladding, and the windows are supplied complete with flashings.

Putting in utilities

Running electricity into the attic is a straightforward operation. You can extend the upstairs lighting circuit, which will already be there in

■ Since rooflights are designed to fit between the roof rafters, there is no reason why several should not be installed to increase the amount of light reaching the room.

the floor area of the attic. As far as the power circuit is concerned, it is a relatively simple job to run lines from the upstairs circuit for any outlets you require in the attic room.

Providing water supplies is also a simple plumbing job. If the main house runs are inaccessible then an alternative is to provide hot water by either gas or electric instantaneous water heaters. Gas has to be installed by a competent plumber. You must not do it yourself. Electric heaters are different. You can install these yourself, provided you understand the job completely. If in any doubt about your abilities, employ an electrician.

If you have space for only a small bathroom, you can put in a shower cubicle instead of a bathtub. Installing waste lines should not prove too difficult, especially if the shower is positioned directly above an existing bathroom.

Putting in walls
The walls in the attic will be a wooden-frame partition construction covered with sheetrock (drywall). These can have insulation added within the timber framing and insulating sheetrock can be used for greater effect.

Once the wall framing is in position, you can complete running in pipework and wiring. Then cover the walls, remembering to build in access doors to any storage areas and pipework concealed in voids in the eaves. Remember, too, to insulate any plumbing or heating lines.

You will need a vapor barrier of heavy gauge polythene fitted on the warmer side of the insulation – that is, under the cladding – to prevent moisture from inside the room causing condensation within the partition frame. If you are using insulating sheetrock, choose a type with a built-in vapor barrier.

The ceiling is created in a similar way. Unless you are following the angle of the sloping roof, you will need to put in new horizontal joists. These must be nailed on to the existing rafters and will form the surface on which to nail the sheetrock. Insulation can be installed on top of this as you would when insulating a standard attic space.

Providing access
You can either install a permanent staircase or fit a retractable attic ladder. Check with your local authority to see which is acceptable. An attic ladder is not usually allowed as access into a fully habitable room, although it can be perfectly acceptable for a storage area that is used only occasionally.

The problem with a staircase is the amount of space it takes up in the landing or room below, as well as the amount of headroom it needs. You may have to install a dormer window at the top. If there is not room for a normal staircase, there are two other possible choices.

A spacesaver staircase has a steeper pitch than normal stairs and the individual treads are specially shaped to take either the left or right foot. So you have to make sure you walk up them in the right way. Most attic conversion firms offer spacesaver stairs as an option. The other option is a spiral staircase.

BUILDING AN ADDITION

If you decide to put an addition on the property, its location will be critical. You must make sure you still have access to the back of the house or garden. Existing drains will need protecting and inspection chambers within the addition must be fitted with double-sealed covers.

If you are thinking of building on to any part of the house wall that incorporates a window, you may have to make special provisions for extra light and ventilation for the rooms affected.

Wood-frame addition
Building a wood-frame addition is the quickest way of getting extra living space, so long as the land is available. Once the foundations are in place it is relatively straightforward to erect the wall framing, add the roof and make the

■ The most important part of designing a home addition is ensuring that when it is completed it looks as much a part of the original house as possible. This involves careful matching of things like external wall surfaces, door and window styles and the pitch of roof slopes.

structure weatherproof before attending to the internal fittings. Building a single-storey addition is well within the capabilities of the experienced do-it-yourself builder, but it is advisable to leave two-storey work to a builder.

Brick-built addition

At its simplest, your addition may just be for a first-floor utility room. More complicated ones could involve adding on two storeys to accommodate extra bedrooms or a bathroom, with possibly a new or extended kitchen or an extra living room underneath.

A brick-built addition is an ambitious project. You have to prepare proper foundations and have skill in laying bricks, plastering, roofing and so on. If you are building a kitchen or bathroom, extensive plumbing and electrical work may also be involved. You might, therefore, be happier to do the planning and the finishing off and leave someone else to handle the main construction work.

Purpose-built addition

If all you want from your addition is a comfortable room for use in the warmer weather, then a sunroom would suit your needs. And double glazing will help make it habitable in colder weather. Unless you can afford a custom-made model, you will have to choose from the range

■ Careful attention to proportions and detail can result in an addition that blends in perfectly with the original building and its surroundings.

of prefabricated options available.

The choice is between the modern and the traditional. The less expensive types have slim aluminum glazing bars, curved eaves and sliding screen doors to guarantee maximum sunlight. More expensive versions offer delightful replicas of period styles with delicate framing in timber or cast aluminum, often with traditional French doors and decorative finials.

Depending on the model, some companies give you the choice of either building the sunroom yourself (with the aid of comprehensive instructions) or of opting to have it built by the supplier or a franchised builder.

You can do some of the work yourself – for example, preparing the foundation and doing the final decorating – or you may choose to complete the entire installation job yourself. Pricing is flexible according to individual needs.

In order to gain the full benefit of the sun, it is advisable to build a sunroom on a south-facing wall. However, if there are other buildings or trees in the way, you may have to choose another, less sunny site.

Of course, you do not have to build a sunroom on the ground. You can construct it at second-floor level on to a suitable existing flat roof. This is a good way of creating extra space in smaller properties without the benefit of a garden. However, you must discuss your plans with your local zoning or building inspector first.

CONVERTING A BASEMENT

It is relatively easy and obvious to assess what you might be able to use a basement for, if your house has one. Since it will either be completely below ground or semi-sunk, the most important consideration will be dampness.

Most often, the problem will be one of damp areas on floors, walls and ceilings. These can be treated with a brush application of a suitable waterproofing solution. If water is definitely seeping in through cracks or holes, then more comprehensive waterproofing will be needed. Condensation is sometimes the main problem, simply because the basement is so cold. The addition of some heating will solve this problem.

The next important aspect is ventilation. Clearly this will not be a major problem if the basement is to be used as a workshop or storage area. But if you hope to create a living area, then you must conform to local building codes concerning window size and opening.

Without getting involved in very costly excavation work, a completely underground basement cannot be given windows. However, a semi-basement will probably already have a

small window and it may be possible to enlarge this to comply with the building codes.

Extending plumbing and electrical requirements to the basement should not cause any problems since these services should be readily available from the floor above. And there is certain to be an existing staircase. This might be suitable or you may have to adapt or, at worst, replace it with a new one.

Depending on its overall condition, you will probably find you have to reline the walls and lay a new solid floor – or at least lay a smooth covering over the existing one.

■ Sunrooms are a popular way of gaining extra living space without the complications of building a conventional addition.

■ Basement conversions face two major hurdles: keeping dampness out, and letting light in. The former can be more difficult to achieve than the latter.

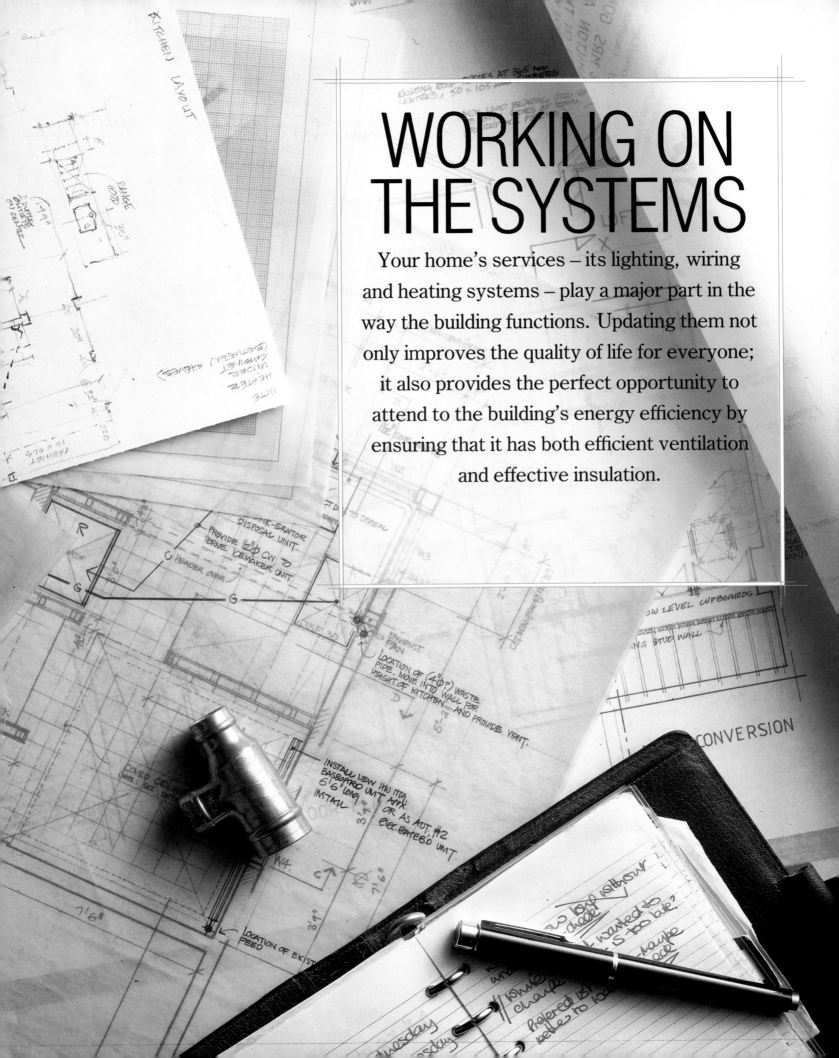

WORKING ON THE SYSTEMS

Your home's services – its lighting, wiring and heating systems – play a major part in the way the building functions. Updating them not only improves the quality of life for everyone; it also provides the perfect opportunity to attend to the building's energy efficiency by ensuring that it has both efficient ventilation and effective insulation.

Lighting

Lighting is a vital function in every home, yet all too often it is the most neglected aspect of interior design and planning. It is as important as the paint colors, wallcoverings and furnishings, which are generally chosen with such care and deliberation.

Too often just a standard ceiling light, possibly backed up by a table lamp, is used to light a room. This might provide adequate illumination, but that is all: there is no atmosphere, no excitement, no subtle shadows, no contrast and no sparkle to fascinate the eye and help you enjoy your surroundings.

Just like the decorations and furnishings, lighting needs to be planned from the start. It is not something to be added on as an afterthought once the decorating has been finished.

When you have analyzed your needs room by room, you will probably find you want to put in more than one lighting circuit in some rooms. For wall, cornice and recessed lights, any new cable will need to be concealed. Adding extra ceiling lights will involve gaining access from the floor above. And additional table or floor-standing lamps may require more outlets to eliminate potentially dangerous extension cords. With any of this work, you will not want to upset decorations you have just spent much time and money putting up.

Any lighting system in the house must do two things – give you light where you want it and enhance the overall look of the room or area it affects. Choosing the right type of fixture and positioning it correctly is the key to creating a balance between light and shadow.

Uniformly bright lighting offers no contrast and the result is harsh and cheerless. Conversely, deep shadows are depressing. An acceptable level of lighting is needed throughout the room to avoid harsh shadows. In addition, you will want local pools of light for tasks such as reading and sewing and for highlighting features such as alcoves or ornaments.

One basic rule is to ensure that naked lamps (bulbs) are never visible, whether you are standing, sitting or lying down. Avoid this by careful choice of fixtures and shades and also by positioning fixtures carefully.

■ Many homeowners pay scant attention to the lighting options available nowadays, yet a well-designed lighting scheme can be a highly attractive feature of the house . . . whether viewed from indoors or outside.

■ **Right** The entrance hall is the first room your visitors will see, so make an effort to show off its features in a welcoming light. Here an array of individual track-mounted fittings turns a hallway into a miniature picture gallery.

Electrical safety

Before planning any extensions or alterations to your home's electrical wiring system, it is essential to make sure that the circuits and any protective devices fitted to the system are in good condition and capable of supplying the demand.

Start by inspecting the system controls – usually sited next to the main service switch. In a modern home you will find a multi-way switchboard, fitted with an array of miniature circuit breakers which provide overload protection to individual lighting and power circuits in the home. In addition, there may be another protective device fitted called a ground fault interruptor which guards against users receiving electric shocks or current leakage through poor insulation causing an electrical fire. Older homes will have rewirable fuses rather than circuit breakers, and these may be in separate switch-fuse units – a sure sign of an out-of-date system.

Next, check the condition of the circuit cables running away from the switchboard. Unless they have grey or white PVC sheathing, they should almost certainly be replaced – a job you may prefer to leave to a qualified electrician.

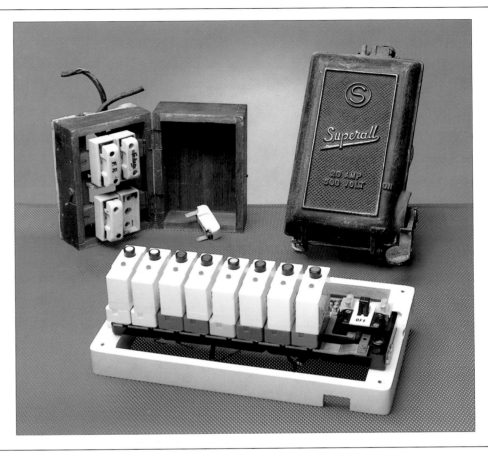

LIGHTING ACCESS AREAS

Apart from any aesthetic considerations, access and traffic areas such as entrances, halls and stairways are potentially high risk ones as far as accidents are concerned. So safety is of paramount importance when planning lighting here.

With entrances, you may want to make a specific feature of the front door by aiming a spotlight at it, illuminate a stained glass panel from inside or highlight an interesting group of plants. Consider outside lighting at low level as well, so that the path or any steps are clearly visible. Make sure, of course, that all exterior lights are fully waterproof.

Halls, corridors and stairways must be adequately lit and operated by switches at either end. Make sure each landing and flight of stairs has its own light, preferably at the top and bottom if flights are long. Individual stair treads must be clearly visible and not concealed in deep shadows.

A linear fluorescent light is particularly suitable for narrow areas, as are wall-washers directed up or down, especially if you also want to illuminate hanging pictures or objects. For good general lighting, use a row of canlights (potlights) or track-mounted spotlights.

■ Lighting in access areas performs two purposes. It should make the hall and staircase appear welcoming, and it must also illuminate the stairs themselves for safety reasons.

LIGHTING LIVING ROOMS

Living rooms have to cater for a range of family activities, so the lighting must be versatile. An ornate ceiling fixture will provide an attractive feature and general lighting when lit. Back this up with wall lights in alcoves, perimeter lighting behind curtain valances to direct light upwards or downwards, and wall-washers to grace a long wall with diffused light.

One striking effect is to spotlight individual features of the room. To achieve this, install track lighting in different positions and add small striplights above favourite pictures. Wall-washers or spotlights should be individually switched or dimmer-controlled, so you can vary the light level at will.

Activities such as reading, sewing and home-work need good localized lighting. And since the site for these activities may move around the room, plug-in lights are often the most flexible. Adjustable lights on desks can be moved to shine on the surface for writing or using a word processor keyboard, for example, again without glare being a problem. To prevent excessive glare from the television screen, provide sub-dued lighting behind it.

■ In living rooms, lighting has to provide background illumination, task lighting for reading and similar hobbies, and highlighting of individual features such as pictures and ornaments.

■ In kitchens, top priority must be given to providing good task lighting for countertops, and also for specific areas such as stoves and sinks. In addition the room needs adequate general background lighting. Tungsten lamps offer a warmer, more flattering light than fluorescent tubes, and make food look more appetising too.

LIGHTING DINING ROOMS

A rise-and-fall hanging light over the dining table will illuminate both the table and guests. You will also need some background lighting such as wall-washers, valance lights or accent lights on pictures or ornaments to illuminate other areas of interest in the room. Dimmers can be used for both types of lighting, to cater either for family meals or more intimate occasions. Background lighting will also be needed to pick out the all-important serving areas.

LIGHTING KITCHENS

Arguably this is the most critical room in the house as far as planning lighting arrangements is concerned. It is a real workroom, which can also be used for eating, and it is occupied at different times of the day, both summer and winter. So the lighting has to be flexible to cope with the various ever-changing demands likely to be made on the room.

Overall lighting from a ceiling fixture or fluorescent tubes should be sufficiently strong to wash the whole room with light. If you have

two fluorescent tubes and control them with individual switches, you can vary the lighting as required. A fixture controlled from a dimmer will provide similar options. An alternative is to install canlights (potlights), again with optional switching or dimmer controls.

With work surfaces, the sink and the stove, you have to be sure the lighting is strategically placed so that it illuminates the intended area and not someone's back, as can often be the case with ceiling fixtures.

Wall-mounted spotlights or recessed canlights can be adjusted to beam directly on to the work surface. Striplights below wall cabinets are also practical and effective in this respect.

Should you have a dining area or breakfast bar, then a rise-and-fall fixture that can be lowered sufficiently not to glare into people's eyes while they eat is an ideal solution. A strategically placed ceiling-mounted spotlight can make a viable alternative.

A stove hood incorporating a light is important to illuminate a cooktop, and an oven with a built-in light source is also essential. If you have a walk-in pantry or storage cabinet, then this would benefit from some lighting – possibly a

type that is activated by a trip switch when you open the door.

Finally, do not forget that kitchens are meant to be aesthetically pleasing as well as functional, so the odd spotlight highlighting an appealing house plant or dinner service on a shelf is certainly worth incorporating into your overall lighting scheme.

LIGHTING BATHROOMS

Bathrooms should not be purely cold, clinical, functional rooms but places of relaxation, so that washing and bathing become really pleasurable activities.

If your overhead bathroom light provides a stark look, with the light glaring on all those shiny surfaces, fit a lower wattage lamp and then augment it with wall lights or washers for a softer look, maybe even with colored lamps.

Emphasize the mirror instead – with striplights or small, low-wattage lamps. You can also get striplights with shaver sockets incorporated, specially for use in bathrooms.

All fixtures must be safe to use in damp conditions. Lights should only be operated with dry hands for safety's sake. Outlets in the room must be specially earthed with ground fault interruptor units.

If you enjoy reading in the bathtub, try a canlight positioned directly above it. But make sure that lights close to extra wet areas are properly enclosed in waterproof casings.

■ In the kitchen, it is vital to have good illumination for all work areas – the stove, the sink and the countertops. Lighting beneath wall cabinets is one excellent way of providing this. In addition you need overall background lighting, perhaps from directional ceiling-mounted fittings, and lighting above the table if you have room for one in the room.

In the bathroom, you need restful general lighting, plus good task lighting at the lavatory for shaving and applying cosmetics. Make sure all fixtures used in bathrooms are enclosed for safety reasons, and always use UL-approved types over bathtubs and in enclosed shower cubicles.

■ In bedrooms, having some restful background lighting is a must; dimmer control is particularly effective here. You also need localized lighting for reading in bed or making up at a dressing table, and here wall and table lights can be the perfect solution. Above all, provide two-way switching so you can turn lights on and off without having to get out of bed to do so.

LIGHTING BEDROOMS

In any bedroom where you have a central hanging light, this should be under dimmer control to create a restful atmosphere. And two-way switching of all lights is important so you do not have to get out of bed to switch them off at night or on in the morning.

For reading in bed, remember to include adequate illumination. But make sure fixtures are flexible so that light can be directed away from a sleeping partner. An additional task light may be required over the dressing table and closets will benefit from a fluorescent tube inside to illuminate the contents.

The lighting in children's bedrooms must be flexible to cope with various activities that go on there and be adaptable as the child grows. For the youngest, good background illumination is the most important. A dimmer allows the main light to be left on very low, while youngsters go to sleep. Equally an ornamental child's night-light provides security.

A ceiling track system will cope with changing requirements and provide background or indirect lighting, as well as highlighting posters, a desk or play and storage areas. A Luxo or similar style lamp could provide additional light for studying and clip-on or portable spots are ideal for reading. Make sure to provide one each for the upper and lower levels in bunk beds and position them well out of the way of the bedding for safety's sake.

LIGHTING CONSERVATORIES

Conservatories and sunrooms are unusual because they are largely composed of glass which means that, in darkness, unwanted reflections and shadows are inevitable.

It is largely a question of experimenting with an assortment of spotlights, low-voltage lamps and even candlelight. A single light source is unlikely to be sufficient. Make sure all lamps are well shielded to cut down reflections from the glass as much as possible.

CHOOSING LAMPS AND TUBES

There are four main considerations that determine whether a filament lamp (bulb) is suitable for a particular application – wattage, life rating, finish and cap fitting. You need to specify all four carefully when you are buying new lamps.

The amount of energy a lamp uses is measured in watts. The light given off is roughly in proportion to the wattage. So, for example, a 150 watt lamp will produce roughly twice as much light as a 75 watt one of the same type. The amount of electricity used is directly proportionate to the lamp wattage; that means a 150 watt lamp will use twice as much electricity as the 75 watt one.

Lamps (bulbs) can be clear or frosted. Clear lamps transmit the most light, giving brilliant illumination. But they do create harsh shadows and so are most often used where a sparkling effect is desired, such as in a chandelier or inside enclosed fittings with opaque diffusers.

Frosted lamps have internal finish that gives a more even light with more diffuse shadows and are therefore the most popular for general lighting use.

A lamp should have a life of around 1,000 hours, subject to normal usage. Double-life lamps are intended to last for 2,000 hours, though there are fewer ratings to choose from – usually 40, 60, 100 and 150 watt.

Filament lamps have an Edison screw fitting, with large and small sizes available. The most common lamp is the familiar pear-shaped type, which comes in 15, 25, 40, 60, 75, 100 and 150 watt sizes and in both clear and frosted finishes.

Colored lamps (bulbs)

Lamps are available in a range of different shades including pink, red, amber, yellow, blue and green. And they are usually rated at 15, 25, 40 and 60 watt. They have a poor light output for their wattage, with the darkest colors being the weakest.

Globe (spherical) lamps have a frosted finish to enable them to be used without a shade. They come in several different sizes. The choice of rating is not so wide – 25, 40 and 60 watt in the smaller sizes, together with 100 and 150 watt in the larger ones.

Candle lamps are available in plain and twisted versions. They are mainly used in candelabras and in some decorative wall fittings. Both shapes are generally obtainable in both clear and frosted finishes.

Night lights are rated from 8 to 12 watts and provide continuous light at low cost for children's rooms and access areas where required.

Reflector spots, which are used with spotlights, come in two types – ISL and PAR. The former gives a soft-edged beam and is often used for spotlights, canlights (potlights) and uplighters. The ratings available are from 40 to 150 watt. PAR reflectors, which are more expensive, have a beam of exact width for highlighting specific objects. These come in 100 and 150 watt ratings.

Tungsten tubes are used for lighting display cabinets, mirrors and other fittings and are available with single cap (3½in long and 25 or 40 watt) or double cap (9 and 11in and 30 or 60 watt) in either a clear or frosted finish.

Lamp life

Vibration will shorten the life of any lamp, so avoid siting light fixtures near to doors and ensure they are securely fixed. You do not need to be reminded of their fragile nature.

Fluorescent tubes use less energy to produce the same light output as bulbs. The equivalent of a 100 watt bulb would be an 18 to 36 watt tube, depending on the type. However, unlike bulbs, their light output falls off considerably over a period of time – up to 25 per cent – and they may need replacing some time before they actually fail.

According to the type you buy, the efficiency of tubes does vary. For normal use, the options include high efficiency and poor color or good color and poor efficiency. The more expensive models do, however, offer good color and efficiency. They come in 2, 4, 6 and 8ft lengths and in 1 or 1½in diameters.

In each category there is usually the choice of a warm or cold effect. Colored tubes are also

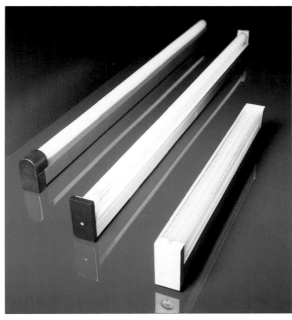

■ **Above** Track lighting offers tremendous scope and flexibility in lighting design, since different types of fitting can be mixed to create a range of lighting effects.

■ **Left** Lamps (bulbs) come in a wide range of types, shapes and colors. When choosing which to use where, remember to specify whether the fitting accepts bayonet cap or screw bulbs, and take care not to exceed the recommended maximum wattage for the fixture or lampshade.

■ **Right** Fluorescent lights are more efficient than tungsten lamps in terms of the amount of light they produce, but can make rooms look cold unless a 'warm' tube is chosen.

■ **Left** Enclosed fittings range from the simple wire-reinforced bulkhead light to globes and fittings with ornamental cut-glass shades. Recessed or semi-recessed canlights (potlights) are ideal for casting pools of light without causing undue glare.

Fluorescent lights may seem costly to buy, but in the long-term they do pay for themselves with their long life and low running costs. It has been estimated that a fluorescent light can be up to five times more efficient than a tungsten filament lamp.

Choosing spotlights

Spotlights offer a high degree of flexibility since they can be mounted in a variety of different places, can be adjusted individually and can be controlled separately using normal lightswitches or dimmers.

Wall-mounted spots can provide task lighting for reading or sewing, for example, or can be used to cast highlights on pictures or ornaments or throw a wash of light on to a wall or ceiling. Single spots are mounted on their own baseplate. Cluster spots, where two or more lights are mounted on the same base, are also available. Ceiling-mounted spots can also be fixed on a base, while track-mounting allows the position of the lights to be altered to suit your lighting requirements precisely.

Choosing a lamp for a spotlight is almost as important as choosing the fixture itself. Different width beams are available to suit different lighting effects. For illuminating an area, a precise narrow pencil beam is best. Where a less concentrated illlumination is wanted, a wider beamed lamp should be used. Framing spots, which produce a precise straight-edged beam, can be particularly effective for lighting individual ornaments.

Choosing canlights

Canlights or potlights are permanently fixed ceiling-mounted fixtures that, as their name implies, have recessed tubes that direct light downwards. They can provide general illumination, task lighting or creative lighting effects.

Eyeball canlights are similar to adjustable spotlights mounted in the ceiling itself. Lamps with different beam widths give some flexibility in their range of uses and the beam direction is fully adjustable.

Flush-mounted canlights are fixed in the ceiling so that the face of the lamp is level with the surface. They are available with either fixed beams or adjustable ones that can be narrowed or broadened slightly.

With recessed canlights, the lamp is set back a few inches behind the plane of the ceiling in a brass or silver-finished metallic tube. These may require a deep ceiling void to accommodate the tube and in some cases can only be fitted into suspended ceilings. In either case, care must be taken to prevent overheating.

available for use with illuminated ceiling panells and in other decorative situations.

Low-energy compact fluorescent lamps provide an alternative to the tungsten lamp for general use. It is claimed they last up to five times as long and use only a fifth of the energy. As they are cool-operating, they can also be used with ultra-slim fixtures and types of shade that cannot take tungsten filament lamps.

Low-energy lamps are available in 16 and 28 watt ratings. The light output of the former falls between that of a 60 and 100 watt lamp, while the latter is equivalent to a 150 watt lamp. One point to bear in mind with these bulbs is that they may require a special ceiling fixture or a plug-in adaptor.

Heating and Ventilating

Central heating provides the ideal overall system for keeping your home warm and comfortable to live in. Whereas modern homes are normally built with some kind of all-round heating, older properties may only have partial heating, low-level background heating or in some cases none at all. If so, better heating should be a major consideration in any improvement plans you draw up for the house.

With partial central heating, only a section of the house will be covered by the system. The other parts are either unheated or rely on isolated space heaters.

A background system enables the house to be fully heated to a temperature of about 58–62°F. Where additional heat is required to boost this level – for example, in a living room –

another source of heat such as a wood or solid fuel stove is used.

With a full central heating system, all the rooms in the house are heated to the desired temperature from a series of heat sources – normally baseboard convectors or radiators.

Of course, heating is also needed to provide domestic hot water for the kitchen, bathroom and possibly a lavette, a bedroom vanity unit or shower cubicle. This is normally supplied by a separate water heating system.

There are various ways of distributing heat around the home. These include baseboard convectors and fan-coil units. Forced hot air heating systems are normally only used when they can be incorporated into the house as it is being built.

■ Every room in the house needs controllable heating and adequate ventilation. In most homes this means having a convector or radiator and an openable window, but increasing use is being made of more advanced technology to remove stale air and recycle it after filtering it and heating or cooling it.

■ Modern wood-burning grates offer the comforting looks of a real fire with the bonus of greatly increased thermal efficiency.

SELECTING FUELS

The range of domestic fuels available offers a wide choice, depending on the system, the individual units and, of course, availability and supply. It includes solid fuels such as wood and coal, as well as natural gas, electricity and oil – and even solar power.

Solid fuel heaters have advanced considerably from the old days of open fires. Solid fuel can usually be delivered by truck and, provided you have sufficient storage space to cope with bulk deliveries, you can take considerable advantage from off-peak summer prices.

Gas is the most popular form of fuel in many regions. It is clean, instantly controlled, reasonably stable in price and generally available in most areas. In more remote spots where there is no mains supply, liquid propane gas can be used instead. This comes in replaceable cylinders or, for larger houses, is piped from the delivery truck into permanently installed pressurized storage tanks.

Oil provides a similarly clean and versatile domestic fuel, but it is subject to fluctuations in price. And you will need space for a fairly large storage tank, which must be accessible from the road to take the necessary deliveries.

Electricity is also a viable option for home heating. Very few homes are without a mains supply, whereas gas is still not available in some outlying areas.

Still troubled by hesitant technology and high front-end costs, solar heating is another alternative worth considering. Its efficiency depends on the region of the country and the extent of its installation.

SAVING HEAT

All the heat produced by any home heating system is, of course, eventually lost to the atmosphere. To delay this, insulation is required. The better the insulation, the longer the heat will remain in the home and consequently the lower your heating bills will be.

Attic insulation
The attic floor should be covered by at least 6in of insulation material. The cost of the insulation can be recovered in three to four years.

Wall insulation
The external walls of your house should be filled with suitable insulation material, professionally installed. The cost of this operation can normally be recovered in about five to seven years.

Double glazing
If properly installed, double glazing reduces the heat lost through windows and eliminates the 'false draft' effect caused by the cold surface of a single glazed window. New low-emission glass cuts the heat loss still further. It is difficult

to calculate the cost recovery period for this, since there are many different forms and it can be expensive to install.

Draftproofing
It has been estimated that the air gaps present in the average house are the equivalent of having a 10 sq ft hole in an outside wall. Insulation to prevent drafts is cheap to buy and easy to install, which means it is very cost-effective. Do not, however, seal rooms completely when fitting draftproofing.

Hot water storage tank
This must be covered with an insulation jacket, which should be 4in thick. The cost of the jacket can be recovered in a matter of weeks. Most modern tanks have the insulation already fitted in the form of an integral outer covering.

HOT WATER HEATING SYSTEMS

Many older homes have a hot water system, with water heated in the boiler being pumped round the system to individual baseboard convectors or fan-coil units. Some installations use the one-pipe loop system, with a single flow and return pipe supplying the convectors via venturi tees that ensure each one receives an adequate water supply. On two-pipe systems there are separate flow and return pipes, with the flow through each convector being controlled by its shut-off valve. A small expansion tank is fitted close to the boiler to cope with the increase in volume of the water in the system as it heats up.

If a heating system of this type is in good working order, regular servicing of the boiler and occasional maintenance of the other system components may well be all that is needed to keep it going for years. The boiler can be replaced by a more fuel-efficient modern type if desired, and it is also possible to fit replacement convectors to the existing pipework if the existing ones look old-fashioned or are in poor condition. So long as the boiler has sufficient spare heating capacity, it may even be possible to add extra convectors to the system to provide better heating in existing rooms or to supply extra heating to any future additions or conversions you may want to make to the house. Get a professional to advise you on the circuit layout and pipework sizing if you propose to add more than, say, one new convector to the existing system.

Apart from problems with the boiler, the only other maintenance the system may need is the curing of minor leaks from joints on the pipework and from the connections to the

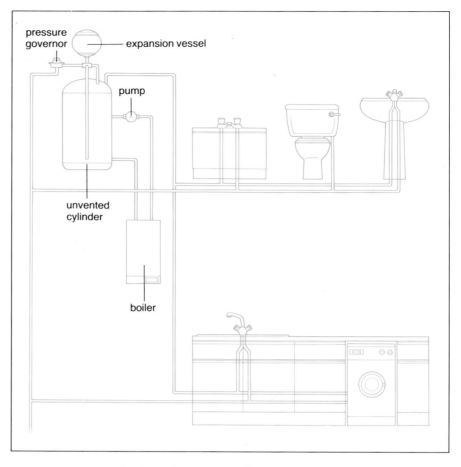

convectors as and when they occur. You may be able to make the repair yourself – by tightening up any screwed connections, for example – but leave other repairs to a plumber.

ELECTRIC SPACE HEATING

Your house may have electric space heating – usually in the form of electric baseboard heaters, but possibly ceiling-mounted radiant heating panels, wall-mounted fan-assisted heaters or hydronic baseboard units. Individual heaters can be replaced with new ones if desired, so long as the electrical system is in good condition – have it checked by an electrician if you have any doubts – and it is a relatively straightforward job to add extra individual heaters supplied by new circuits run from the house's main service panel – again a job for your electrician.

WOODSTOVES FOR SPACE HEATING

In areas where wood supplies are plentiful, woodstoves are another popular form of space heating. These stoves must be installed to comply with both the manufacturer's instructions and the requirements of your local building codes – in particular to avoid fitting them too

■ Pressurized hot water systems take cold water direct from the mains supply. They must be installed by professionals to ensure that they operate completely safely.

close to combustible building materials. For example, the stove must stand on a non-combustible hearth which extends to at least 18in in front of the stove door, and should be 36in away from any stud wall surface unless a non-combustible heat shield is fitted to the wall. Where an uninsulated stove flue passes through the house wall, it should be kept at least 18in below combustible ceiling surfaces, and if the flue passes through the ceiling and roof structure adequate clearances must be provided to keep the flue away from any combustible framing. Finally, the flue pipe or any chimney into which the stove discharges must rise at least 2ft above any structure within 10ft of it.

WARM AIR HEATING

More modern homes in cooler zones will generally have a warm air heating system, with a boiler running on gas, oil or electricity providing a supply of warm air which is blown through a main supply duct and smaller take-off ducts to registers or diffusers around the house. With a system of this type, there is nothing to go wrong except the boiler, which may need replacing with a modern, more fuel-efficient model if it is showing its age.

It is generally possibly to extend a warm-air system by adding new supply ducts and registers, but the most difficult part is routing the new ducts within the existing house structure. When such a system is newly installed, 6in diameter round sheet metal ducts are usually used, and it may be possible to build an enclosure for the new duct in the corner of a room to supply the second floor. However, for conversion and extension work on an existing system it is better to use a 3 × 12in rectangular duct which can be fitted between floor joists and within the stud space of exterior walls. When planning the route of a new supply duct, try to keep bends to a minimum since each twist and turn in the duct creates extra resistance to the air flow.

Making a connection into the main supply duct is relatively straightforward, involving cutting a hole in it with metal shears or a metal saw blade and fitting a take-off collar. The collar is secured to the duct with self-tapping screws after the joint has been caulked. Then sections of new duct are added one by one, with all joints wrapped in duct tape to minimize air losses, and the run terminates at the new register. In addition, any ducting that passes through unheated areas such as a crawl space or attic must be insulated to avoid major heat losses.

Warm air systems can also provide cooling if an outdoor compressor and condensing unit is added to the system. This unit circulates cold refrigerant to evaporator coils sited within the main air supply ducts, enabling the main fan to blow cold air round the system in warm weather when the boiler is switched off.

TYPES OF BOILER

There have, over the years, been significant advances in the design and efficiency of home heating boilers. The commonest domestic units run on oil or gas – either piped in or stored in cylinders or storage tanks.

Oil-fired boilers
Oil is certainly, with gas, the most common fuel used for home heating. You need a large storage tank installed, which must conform to regulations concerning its siting. You may even need building code permission for this. Access from the road for the fuel delivery tanker should be made as easy as possible.

With an oil-fired boiler, a pump forces the finely atomised oil into the combustion chamber where it is fired in a pressure jet burner with the help of air. Because of the various working

■ Hot air systems deliver warmed air to individual rooms via a network of ducts and diffusers, and can sometimes supply domestic hot water too. However, installing them in an existing house can cause major internal disruption.

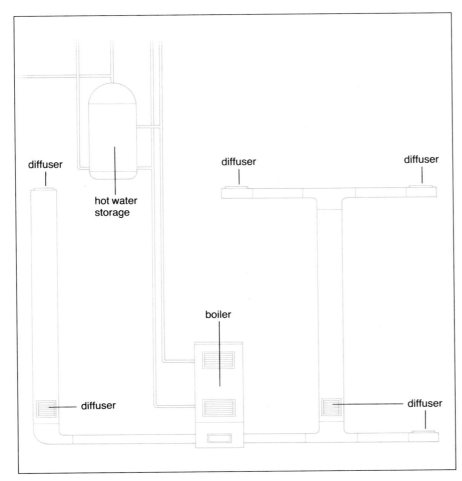

diffuser

hot water storage

diffuser

diffuser

boiler

diffuser

diffuser

most common type fitted. They are small and can be sited in any room, as convenience dictates. Most have a balanced flue, which means they are fitted on or close to an exterior wall, with the flue passing through to the outside. The air for combustion is drawn in through one part of the flue and the products of that combustion are exhausted back into the atmosphere via the other.

Liquid petroleum gas is available as a fuel for central heating systems, where piped gas is not connected. It is worth checking first with your local gas company whether there are plans to install gas mains in your area in the future. The price of the initial installation is considerable and the running costs are higher.

The normal gas supplied is propane, which is available either in cylinders you can exchange yourself (if you are willing to handle these heavy objects) or delivered by tanker to your own permanently installed storage cylinder. The positioning of cylinders is subject to stringent safety regulations and you must check with your local supplier about a suitable location.

Most natural gas boilers can be easily adapted for propane by a change of jets and pressure regulators.

CONTROLLING THE HEATING SYSTEM

With a hot water heating system, the simpler the control device, the easier it is to run. But the degree of precise control over individual

---

parts and the high powered flame, such boilers are noisy and odor-producing. For this reason, you will want to site yours away from the normal living areas of the home – normally in a basement. In all cases an external flue to roof level or internally lined chimney is needed. The burner must be serviced regularly by a qualified technician, and the oil filter on the supply pipe from the tank should be cleaned from time to time to ensure an efficient oil flow.

The oil supply companies run very good technical advisory services, if you are thinking of having one of these boilers installed.

Gas-fired boilers
Gas is the other common fuel for central heating. Its use is strictly covered by safety regulations and it is illegal to connect any appliance to the gas supply yourself. This has to be done by a licensed plumber.

For installation purposes, the flue must be sound and will probably have to be lined. An approved flue cap must also be fitted. The air for combustion is taken from the room or via a ventilation duct unless it is a balanced-flue type, so you must ensure that arrangements are made for adequate permanent ventilation.

The traditional free-standing boiler was normally fitted in the basement. The modern free-standing boiler is normally much slimmer – and quieter in operation – and can therefore fit into a more convenient space. Some of these boilers are fitted with a separate flue up to roof level, although most are now installed with a balanced flue – see below.

Wall-mounted boilers are now probably the

■ Central heating boilers can be floor-standing (**above**) or wall-mounted (**below**), and can have either a conventional flue that discharges into a chimney or a balanced flue that passes through the wall behind the appliance.

■ Individual thermostatic radiator valves (**far right**) provide better temperature control in individual rooms than a system with just a room thermostat, since each room can be heated to different temperatures if required. Some have the thermostat mounted on the valve body; others have remote sensors which eliminate the effect of the hot radiator on the valve's operation. The valve replaces the radiator's normal on/off valve.

room temperatures is limited. Boilers are supplied with their own control system as protection and any further controls that you may wish to fit must be compatible with this.

In any system, there are basically two aspects of control to be considered:

● The times at which the system operates.

● The basic temperature of the water.

Timing is usually controlled by an electrically operated programmer. This normally gives a selection of periods throughout any 24 hours when the boiler is switched on. Temperature is controlled by the boiler thermostat. This switches the boiler off when the correct level has been reached and back on again when the temperature drops.

The system can supply heat to individual zones of the house if motorized valves are installed on the circuit pipework. The controller is programmed to operate the valves at pre-set times and so to divert hot water to individual zones of the house.

Room temperature control

Not all rooms need to be heated to the same temperature. The following is a rough guide to optimum levels of heat:

● Lounge/dining room – 70°F

● Kitchen/bathroom/bedrooms – 65°F

● Hall/landing – 60°F

These temperatures are used in the initial calculations that determine the number and size of convectors fitted when your system is being designed. It will, however, be necessary to have some other form of control.

The most popular method is to install a room thermostat. This is fitted to the wall in an area where you want to keep an optimum average temperature and where there are likely to be major fluctuations in temperatures. You should bear the following points in mind when deciding on its position:

● The room in which it is sited must be heated solely by the central heating system, otherwise another source of heat could effectively switch off the heating in that zone.

● It should be positioned about 5ft up from the floor and away from convectors, wall lights and other forms of heat – or cold, for that matter, such as draft sources.

Most thermostats have a calibrated dial with maximum and minimum settings. But other, more sophisticated models are available. One incorporates a clock and reduced temperature settings. This enables the thermostat to control the boiler to give a variety of temperatures at different times during the day. The device is useful if you are out at work, when a low level of heat is maintained, with the temperature increased when you return home in the evening.

Another type of thermosat is useful since it

■ As far as heating controls are concerned, the bare minimum any system needs includes a room thermostat (**right**) and a system programmer (**far right**). The former turns the heating system on and off to maintain a pre-set room temperature, while the latter switches the boiler and pump on and off at pre-set times.

can automatically switch the heating on if the temperature drops to near freezing level or below, thus preventing possible frost damage. This is particularly sensible if you are spending some days away from the house in winter.

One further point to bear in mind when incorporating controls is to be aware of the possibility of one control over-riding another so you can avoid a potential loss of heating at a crucial time. For example, if the boiler is programmed to come on at about four in the afternoon but the room thermostat is set very low, the system may well not switch on.

AIR CONDITIONERS

Air conditioning equipment is a must in many homes, especially those in warmer zones. Without it, summer temperatures simply become unbearable. When choosing it, there are several important factors to take into account.

The principle of air conditioning is exactly the same as the mechanism that makes a refrigerator work. The refrigerant liquid is pumped round a continuous closed-circuit loop through two sets of coils. First of all it enters the evaporator coil, where the liquid absorbs heat from the surrounding air and becomes a gas. It then passes through a compressor which turns the gas back into a liquid, and on to the condenser coil where it gives up its heat to the air again. For household air conditioning, the evaporator coil is situated indoors, where the cooling effect is required, and the condenser coil outdoors.

There are two main types of domestic air conditioning equipment. The first is the individual room unit; this has the evaporator and condenser coils fitted into a single casing, and is installed within a window opening or a hole cut in an exterior wall. The second has the coils housed in two separate enclosures, so that the noisy compressor/condenser section can be placed out of doors. Small split units of this type still cool just one room; larger versions can cool the whole house.

Some air conditioners can also be run in reverse to extract heat from the outside air and use it to heat the interior. They are known as reverse-cycle air conditioners or 'heat pumps'.

How big a unit?

The first step you have to take is to work out how much cooling capacity is needed. It's best to call in a professional to do this for you, but the calculation below will give you a rough guide. Measure the room, work out the floor area and then multiply the figure in sq ft by 24 to

get the number of BTUs needed to cool it. As an example, you will need about 12,000 BTUs (equivalent to 1 ton of cooling capacity) for a room with a floor area of 500 sq ft.

Other factors that must be taken into account include how well the house is insulated, how many windows and outside walls each room has, and where in the country you live.

Systems and components

As mentioned earlier, air conditioning can be provided by individual room air conditioners or by means of a whole-house system. This may be a combined unit like a large room unit, or else a split system. The latter has the evaporator coil unit positioned within the house – often in the roof space – and this distributes cooled air to every room in the house by means of ducting; the compressor/condenser coil is sited out of doors, and the two units are linked together by relatively unobtrusive pipework carrying the refrigerant. The combined 'single-package' unit is cheaper than the split system, but is of course much noisier.

With either system, the ducting is run either above the ceiling or below the floor to serve outlets in each room. The return flow of warm air to the evaporator coil unit is usually via a single inlet on the unit; small gaps beneath room doors throughout the house are usually adequate to ensure a free flow of air back to the unit, to balance the amount of cooled air being delivered. Some systems have parallel return

■ **Above and right** The compressor unit driving a split air conditioning system is situated outside the house. This not only reduces the noise levels when the system is in operation; it also facilitates regular servicing of the equipment and any maintenance work that has to be carried out.

exterior wall. There are several features to look out for when choosing one, perhaps the most important being whether the unit is fixed in place or can be slid out for servicing. A thermostat to prevent wide temperature fluctuations should be fitted, and the unit should have at least two fan speeds. Filters remove airborne dust from the air, and should be easy to remove for cleaning. Air direction control allows the air flow to be directed upwards, downwards, to the left or the right; some models are fitted with automatically-oscillating louvers to do this.

FITTING A ROOM AIR CONDITIONER

The installation of a room air conditioner is well within the capabilities of the average handyman. Only everyday tools are needed, and no special skills will be required beyond the ability to mark out and saw accurately.

The most common method of installation is known as 'through-the-wall', and involves creating an opening in an exterior wall big enough to receive the unit. It is therefore important to check the thickness of your exterior walls before choosing a unit, so you can be sure that the body is long enough to avoid obstruction of the grilles when it has been installed.

One you have chosen the unit, your next task is to find the optimum position for the unit. Ideally, it should go on a wall that does not receive any direct sunlight, and should be positioned at least 2ft above the floor. If it's near an existing electrical outlet, so much the better. Then check what sort of wall construction you have – probably timber studs with exterior siding, possibly an outer veneer of masonry – so you can make sure you have the tools needed to cut through it.

Forming the opening
Although you can in theory locate your room air conditioner anywhere on the wall surface, it makes sense to keep the amount of carpentry needed to a minimum by making an existing timber stud form one side of the new opening. You must therefore locate the stud positions in the area where you plan to install the unit, first of all by tapping (a dull sound indicates the presence of a stud) and then with test drillings. Mark a vertical line on the surface of the wall to indicate the edge of the chosen stud.

Now check with the installation instructions to find out how big the actual opening needs to be to allow for the necessary lining (see below). Mark a line across the wall, level with the bottom of the opening, and extend it until it

ducting running from each room to take warm air back to the coil unit.

This type of air conditioning can treat individual zones of the house at different times – living areas by day and bedrooms by night, for example. Electrically-operated dampers linked to a timer control switch the airflow between zones as required. The big advantage of this sort of installation is that the equipment can be smaller and cheaper than that needed for continuous whole-house treatment.

Somewhere between whole-house systems and individual room air conditioners come what are called multi-split systems. Here a number of fan coil (evaporator) units are linked to a single large condenser unit outside the house. Individual controls on each fan coil unit mean that the desired temperature in each room can be set to ensure optimum comfort coupled with economical use of electricity.

Linked systems of whatever type can provide all-year heating and cooling or just air conditioning, but it can be difficult (and expensive) to have ducted systems installed in an existing house, and the equipment must be professionally installed. However, individual room units can be easily fitted by any competent handyman.

ROOM AIR CONDITIONERS

Room air conditioners are designed to be installed either within a window opening or, more commonly, set in an opening cut in an meets the next stud. Then complete drawing up the rectangle on the wall. Use a keyhole saw or a power saber saw to cut round the rectangle; stop the cut when it meets an intermediate stud and cut carefully through the sheetrock (drywall) at this point. Prise away the cutout.

As you make the saw cuts, look out for any pipe lines or electrical wiring concealed within the wall; it may be necessary to reposition the cutout slightly to avoid them. Don't make the cutout immediately above the position of a wall outlet, in case the cable runs down to it.

If the cavity between the studs contains insulation, cut this away carefully to expose the inner surface of the outer wall sheathing. Check with the fitting instructions to see how big the cutout in the exterior wall has got to be, and mark this on its inner surface (remember that one vertical edge of this cutout will be against the edge of one exposed stud; its bottom edge will be 2in above the bottom of the inner cutout to allow for the thickness of the lining – see below). Now use a drill to make a hole through the outer wall surface in each corner of the marked rectangle. Join up the four holes on the outside to give the dimensions for the cutout.

Use a saw of the appropriate type to cut through the exterior wall sheathing, after removing siding or shingles as necessary. Then saw right through the exposed studs, level with the top and bottom edges of the interior opening, and lift out the unwanted sections.

Lining the opening

Cutting away one or more studs will weaken the structure of the wall, so the next stage is to strengthen it by adding framing members round the edges of the opening. This extra reinforcement is also necessary to carry the not inconsiderable weight of the air conditioner itself. Follow the fitting instructions carefully if these detail a special technique for lining the opening; use the technique below otherwise.

Start by cutting a length of wood of the same cross-section as the existing studs and long enough to reach between the two studs flanking the opening; this will form the new 'sill'. Rest it on top of the cut-away stud, nail down through it and check that it is precisely level; then toe-nail through each end into the studs.

Repeat this process to fit a similar header over the top of the opening, again toe-nailing the ends to the studs and nailing up through it into the cutaway end of the intermediate studs. Check that the gap between header and sill is wide enough to admit the cabinet.

Now cut two short vertical studs to fit between the header and sill, and toe-nail these

in place to the side studs to complete the lining. Again, check the spacing to make sure the cabinet will fit. If your earlier marking-out of the exterior cutout was accurate, it should match up precisely with the lining. If there are any small inaccuracies, trim them off now. You can if you prefer leave marking and cutting the opening in the exterior wall surface until you have completed the lining framework.

Fitting the unit

Once the lining has been completed and you are certain that everything will fit, you can begin to install the air conditioner itself. Again, be sure that you follow the manufacturer's instructions to the letter; here, briefly, is what is involved.

The first step is usually to fix the exterior support brackets that help carry the weight of the protruding external section of the unit. Fix these by screwing through the exterior cladding into the timber framing of the wall itself. Then you can slide the empty cabinet into place in the opening, pushing it through until it rests on the brackets and protrudes from the wall on the outside by the required distance.

Next, mark and drill holes in the cabinet so you can screw it to the lining. Generally you should provide two fixings at the top and four at each side. Note that screws are not driven down through the base of the cabinet into the sill. Use screws 1in long to secure the cabinet in place within the lining.

With the cabinet in place, you can neaten the interior edges of the opening by pinning mitered lengths of decorative molding round them, fitting them flush against the edges of the cabinet. Caulk all round the edge of the exterior opening to ensure that moisture cannot penetrate, and add moldings here too if you wish, to match the casings round doors and windows.

All that remains is to slide the air conditioner chassis into place in the cabinet. The units are surprisingly heavy, so don't try to do the job on your own; get someone to help you. Lift it at a slight angle until you can support its lower rear edge on the front edge of the cabinet. Then raise the unit to the horizontal and slide it backwards into the cabinet as far as it will go. The fascia should finish up neatly flush with the edge of the cabinet itself. Finally, fit the front grille to complete the installation.

Most room air conditioners are rated at about the 10,000 BTU mark, and can take their power from an ordinary wall outlet. Make sure that the grounding connection is correctly made within the plug; then simply plug in and switch on. Test all the operations of the unit fully to make sure that everything is working properly.

Improving air quality

Good ventilation is essential for the health of both the home and its occupants. Without a steady supply of fresh air, the interior of today's well-insulated homes would soon become stuffy and moisture-laden, concentrating unwanted smells and causing condensation to form. In addition, fuel-burning appliances such as boilers and cookers can burn improperly if starved of oxygen, causing the build-up of fumes.

The best way of providing controlled ventilation within the house is to fit extractor fans in rooms that are major sources of moisture and unwanted smells – in the kitchen, in the bathroom and in any separate toilets. These should be powerful enough to extract 2 cu ft of air per second in a kitchen, ½ cu ft per second in a bathroom, and the volume of the room within 20 minutes in separate toilet compartments. In addition, all rooms in the house should have some means of background ventilation to the outside air, to allow fresh air from outside the house to be drawn in to replace that extracted mechanically. In modern homes this ventilation is usually provided by so-called trickle ventilators let into the tops of window frames; air bricks in external walls do the same job in older homes. Each habitable room should have ventilators or airbricks with a total open ventilation area of about 6 sq in.

Extractor fans (above right) come in a variety of shapes and sizes, and can be installed in windows, walls or ceilings. Ducting can be used to take the extracted air to the outside where necessary.

Portable air conditioners (above) are the instant solution to the problem of over-heating in hot weather. The air in the room is drawn in over a refrigeration coil within the unit, and is then blown back into the room. At the same time as cooling the air, the unit removes moisture from it, so helping to reduce humidity levels and improving comfort. Small units of this sort simply plug into an ordinary outlet; more sophisticated units which can also act as heat pumps in cold weather are built in and separately wired up.

A humidifier (left) does just what its name implies, releasing controlled amounts of water vapor into the room where it is sited to counteract the dry-air effect created by many heating systems, which can affect people with chronic chest problems such as asthma.

Insulating the Home

When you insulate your home you are effectively slowing down the rate at which heat escapes through different areas – the roof, walls, windows and floors. The longer you can keep any heat inside, the less fuel you will need to use up to keep all the rooms within the house at a comfortable temperature.

This in turn will mean lower energy bills and the money you save will soon cover the cost of the insulation materials used. When this has been recovered, which could be in less than three years in some cases, you can start counting the savings.

In a typical two-storey house, roughly a third of the total heat lost goes through the walls, a quarter through the roof, a quarter through windows and a sixth through the floor. These ratios will vary with the house design, of course, with single-storey homes losing proportionately more heat through the roof than through the walls, and buildings with large areas of glazing losing more heat there than a home with fewer, smaller windows.

The location of the house and its architecture, for example, can alter the heat loss figures – and therefore your insulation priorities. Anyone living in a terraced house with just a few small windows would see double glazing as being of less importance than the owner of a modern single-family house with large picture windows. While the single-family house will lose more than a duplex through its external walls, with a ranch house the major area for concern will be the roof.

There are various ways in which the different parts of any house can be insulated. But in all cases, most of the jobs involved can be handled successfully by the competent homeowner.

THE ATTIC

There are two main ways to insulate the attic. You can use rolls (of mineral wool or fiberglass) or loosefill material (vermiculite, a lightweight expanded mineral, or polystyrene granules) sold in bags. Though the two methods are comparable in terms of cost and efficiency, fiberglass blanket is the more popular.

You can also have loosefill insulation, usually mineral wool or fireproofed cellulose fibres, blown into the attic by specialist companies.

Blanket materials are generally easier to handle than loosefill types, unless your attic

■ **Above** Insulation materials for walls include foam or glass fiber which is blown into cavity walls – a job solely for professional installers. Alternatively the inner face of cold exterior walls can be lined with insulating sheetrock (drywall), or with ordinary sheetrock over a layer of insulation batts or rigid polystyrene.

■ **Left** For insulating attics, blanket-type fiberglass or mineral-wool blankets are the most widely-used materials, but loose-fill materials such as expanded vermiculite are useful in attics full of obstructions.

■ **Opposite** Pipe tape or slip-on sleeving is ideal for insulating pipework (top), while proprietary jackets are available for hot and cold tanks (right).

contains a lot of obstructions or has irregular joist spacings. The rolls are normally 16in wide to match the standard joist spacing and common thicknesses are 4in and 6in. Choose the former if there is already some insulation and simply lay it on top of the existing material. If there is none at all, then you should use the thicker blanket.

It is worth checking the thickness of any existing insulation if you move to another house. An older house could well have an inadequate layer, which may need topping up with a new layer. It is also worth remembering that over a period of years blanket insulation can naturally compress and shrink in thickness.

Apart from being awkward to handle, loosefill materials have another drawback. To be as effective as the blanket type, they need to be laid to a greater depth – at least an extra 1in. There are not, however, many ceiling joists deeper than about 6in, so there is nothing to contain the top of the insulation unless you are prepared to fix extra wood along the top of each joist. So before you commit yourself to using this type, it is advisable to check the size of joists in your attic.

Many people find that insulation materials irritate their skin, while loose fibers and the ever-present dust in the attic can also be a problem. So it is advisable to wear gloves and a face mask when laying any insulation there.

Ventilation is essential in any attic to prevent condensation forming in the winter months and causing rot in the roof structure, as well as dampening the insulation and thus making it ineffective. This means providing extra ventilation openings at the eaves by fitting grilles in the soffit boards or by installing additional vents in gable walls. Never pack the eaves with insulation, since this will tend to cut off the airflow. Special eaves vents are available which fit between the joists and prevent the insulation material from restricting the flow of air. Remember to insulate the top of the trap door leading into the attic.

Thorough insulation makes it even more vital to insulate any pipes within the attic, since it is going to be even colder in winter. The pipes can be wrapped in fiberglass or molded foam tubes. Molded foam tubes have a slit along one side, which enables you to push them over the pipes. You then tape them to keep the insulation securely in place. Pay special attention to bends, making sure you do not leave any of the pipe surface exposed.

Do not forget to insulate the hot water storage tank if you have one. A purpose-made insulating jacket is by far the best to use and you will recover its cost in a couple of months.

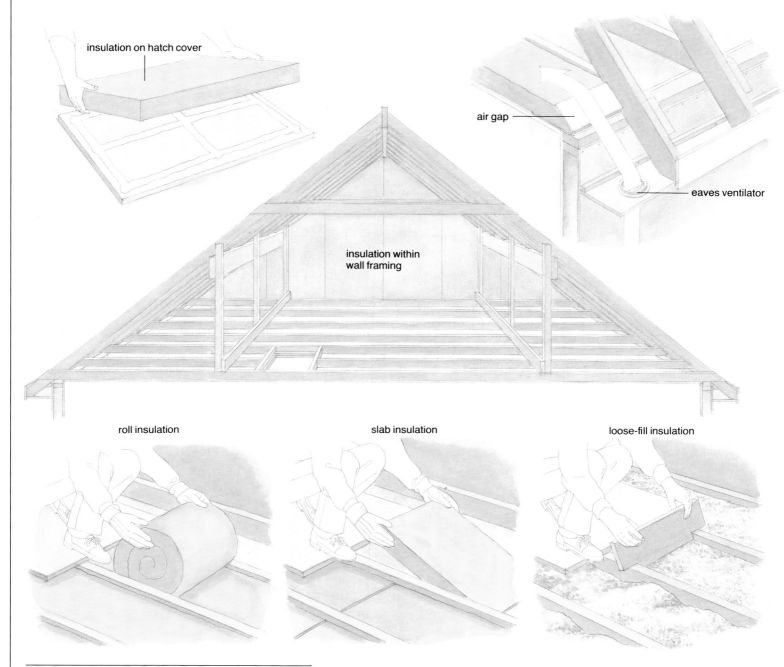

insulation on hatch cover

air gap

eaves ventilator

insulation within wall framing

roll insulation

slab insulation

loose-fill insulation

THE RAFTERS

If you use the attic as an organized storage area, possibly as a workshop or play area, then you must insulate between the rafters to keep the area reasonably warm in winter. There are two basic ways in which this can be done.

The simplest method is to use a waterproof or foil-backed building paper. This will check any drafts and rain from being blown in through the gaps between the shingles. The foil-backed type reflects heat and provides a far better standard of insulation than waterproof paper.

The paper is stapled to the rafters in horizontal strips. Always work down from the top of the eaves, overlapping each layer by a couple of inches. Remember that the foil must always face inwards to reflect heat.

Before you fix the last strip above the eaves, tuck a layer of building paper into the eaves between each pair of joists. This will ensure that any rainwater running down the paper will drain away into the eaves. Make sure you do not block this area completely and cut off the ventilation. Staples can tear the paper and any wind blowing through the roof may extend the damage over a period of time. Therefore it is a good idea to reinforce the fixing points by firing the staple through a square of card at each individual fixing point.

■ Attic floors can be insulated by laying fiberglass blankets or semi-rigid insulation batts between the ceiling joists, or by spreading a loose-fill insulating material such as vermiculite to a uniform depth. Remember to insulate above the hatch, and to leave clearance above the insulation at the eaves for ventilation via vents in the soffits.

An alternative method is to fix a proper 'ceiling' direct to the rafters using sheetrock or drywall, although this will, of course, be more expensive. First fix strips of waterproof paper, foil-backed paper or roofing felt between the rafters, followed by insulation blanket. To secure the edge of the paper or felt, use thin battens and pin through the material into the sides of the rafters. Leave an air gap of about 2in up to the sheathing. Finally attach the panels of sheetrock or fibre insulating board to the rafters with nails to complete the job.

FLAT ROOFS

If you are having a flat-roofed addition built, then insulating the roof is easily done at the building stage. Existing flat roofs pose more of a problem since it is not easy to get at the voids above the ceiling.

It is possible to add secondary roofing above the existing one and sandwich insulation between the two. But this is a very expensive solution and not likely to be cost-effective for many years – if ever. Should the existing roof be in need of replacement, however, then this method might be a possibility.

Other methods should be tackled from inside the house. Taking down an existing ceiling is a fairly clean exercise if it is a modern sheetrock (drywall) type, but quite a dirty job if you have to knock down a lath and plaster construction.

Polystyrene slabs or insulation blanket are fitted between the roof joists and a layer of polythene stapled to the joists. The polythene prevents condensation forming in the roof void and damaging the insulation. It also serves as a vapor barrier to moisture created in the room below which, in the case of a kitchen or bathroom, could be considerable. You can then fix a new sheetrock ceiling to the joists.

You must ensure that the roof space remains well ventilated, otherwise the roof structure could become moist and start to rot. Allow for a 2in wide gap between the top of the insulation and the underside of the roof and drill ventilation holes in the soffits on both sides of the roof so that there is a continuous cross-flow of air.

An alternative method involves adding a sheetrock ceiling to the interior surface, while sandwiching insulation material in between the old and new ceilings.

First you need to nail a framework of spacers about 4in below the existing ceiling. Then add insulation blanket or polystyrene slabs between the two surfaces, followed by a polythene vapor

■ If the attic space is being used to create a habitable room, install insulation behind the walls and above the ceiling forming the new room. Insulate the floor of boxed-off eaves areas as before, but remove any insulation under the floor of the room itself.

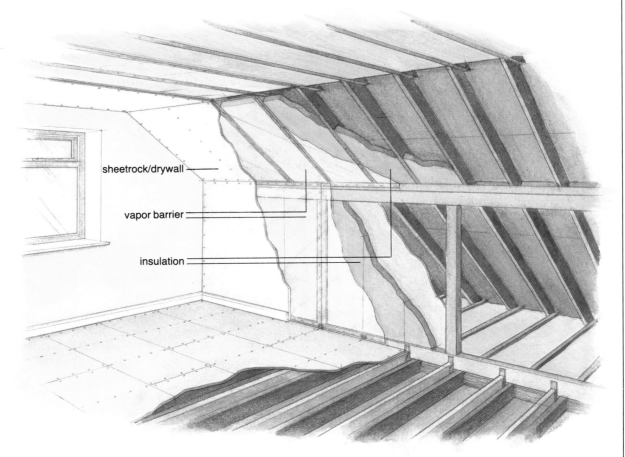

sheetrock/drywall

vapor barrier

insulation

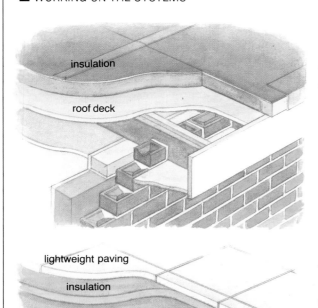

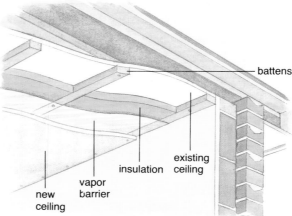

■ **Far left** If a flat roof surface is in poor condition, add insulation above the roof decking by using insulation boards, finished with an additional layer of built-up roofing.

■ **Left** If the fascia boards can be removed, slide pre-cut rigid polystyrene insulation boards into the voids between the joists.

■ **Far left** If the roof decking is in good condition, simply lay insulation slabs over it, topped with lightweight paving slabs.

■ **Left** Alternatively, add insulation below the existing ceiling and cover it with a vapor barrier and a new sheetrock ceiling.

barrier and a layer of sheetrock. Alternatively, you can nail sheets of insulating board directly to the ceiling. This board incorporates a vapor barrier and a layer of rigid foam insulation.

Another option is to fix a new tongued and grooved board ceiling and fill the cavity above with polystyrene slabs or insulation blanket. Since wood itself has excellent insulation properties, this is a particularly effective method.

Finally, you can use a proprietary suspended ceiling comprising a framework of metal channels supporting insulating tile panels.

THE WALLS

In older wood-framed houses where insulation is virtually non-existent and the dismantling of the wall to install conventional fiberglass batting would be prohibitively disruptive and expensive, the use of blown insulation can be very effective. This can be carried out only by experienced professional operators with the appropriate equipment.

On a clapboard house, a row of clapboards is carefully removed at the level of the sill and top plates and a 1in diameter hole is drilled through the sheathing between each stud. The insulation – either cellulose or fiberglass – is then blown into the voids between the studs, where it settles into a solid layer and dramatically reduces heat losses through the house walls. Once installation is complete the clapboards are replaced, leaving virtually no evidence of any disturbance. This method can also be used to fill between the joists in the attic.

If your house has masonry cavity walls, then the simplest method of insulation is again to have the cavity filled. The process, which is covered in the section on external walls, is not a do-it-yourself job and the installation should be tackled by a specialist company.

Houses with solid walls can be insulated externally (see page 76), but more often the job is done working on the inside of the house. There are various methods and the one to choose depends on whether you want to retain the impression of a solid wall or prefer a decorative finish of cladding or panelling.

If the wall to be insulated has no switches, doors or windows, then the job is very straightforward. However, where these obstacles exist, then the work is much more tricky. Switches and outlets will have to be repositioned on the new wall surface and baseboards removed and refixed. You will also have to cut round window and door frames.

There are several types of sheetrock (drywall) you can use, but two in particular are relevant here. The one you choose will probably be determined by the surface condition of the wall being insulated.

If the wall is flat, you can use vapor-check thermal board and stick it directly to the surface with a special adhesive and secondary nail fixing. Thermal board is standard sheetrock bonded to a backing of expanded polystyrene with a polythene film sandwiched in between.

Where the wall is uneven, you will have to put up a framework of timber to provide a level surface on which you can then fix standard (general-purpose) sheetrock. This has an ivory colored side over which you can paint or paper directly after taping and filling the joints.

All sheetrock is supplied in standard dimensions of 8 × 4ft, although 10ft lengths are available too. Such board is popularly used in 3⁄8in and 1⁄2in thicknesses.

Sheetrock can be cut quite easily using either a fine-tooth saw or a utility knife, which is more convenient and less messy. Holes and other cut-outs, to accept light switches and outlets, for example, can easily be made with a keyhole saw or power saber saw.

When working with sheetrock, bear in mind that it is very cumbersome and awkward to handle and you should have two people to carry it. To position it accurately on the wall against the ceiling you will have to make a lifting device, which you can cut from a block of wood.

Having lined the walls, you then have to replace the baseboards and reposition any outlets and switches. Your new wall is then ready for decorating.

Using panelling

Another method of insulating old masonry walls is to panel them. You can use tongued and grooved boards or large decorative Masonite panels. Either material is quite straightforward to fix and has the dual function of being decorative as well.

Wall boards are available as either V-jointed boards in knotty pine or cedar or as pine shiplap. The boards are fixed to 1½ × 1in sawn softwood support strips, which are fixed at 16–20in centres for 3⁄8in thick boards and 20–24in centres for 1⁄2in thick boards. They can be fixed horizontally or vertically.

You must allow for a slight gap behind the boards to enable air to circulate. This will be achieved automatically where the support strips are fixed vertically. With horizontal fixing, use packing pieces behind the strips. Then add insulation material between the strips.

■ A cheaper alternative to external wall insulation (page 76) is to add insulation on the inside of exterior walls. Either line the walls with battens and add insulation and a vapor barrier before nailing up new sheetrock (drywall), or fix insulating sheetrock direct to the wall surface with adhesive.

The boards can be fixed by nailing through the faces and punching the heads below the surface. Make sure you fill the holes afterwards. An alternative is to use very thin finishing nails through the tongues at an angle so that they are covered by the next board. The other option is to use special metal clips. Tap the boards firmly together as you fix them, using a wooden block between the edge and the hammer head as protection.

To finish off at ceiling level, fix quadrant molding to conceal the sawn board edges, remembering to leave a small air gap. At the bottom, you can either leave a small gap as well or fit a new baseboard.

To fit decorative panels, you need vertical support strips to provide a fixing for each edge, plus horizontal battens at 16in intervals. If the corners are out of true, leave a small gap so that the board is positioned horizontally. You can cover this later with a piece of molding. Again leave a small gap at the bottom for possible expansion and cover this with baseboard.

After fixing insulation between the supports, you can secure the panels either with pins (punched below the surface with holes filled) or with adhesive. Pins are really only suitable for boards with vertical grooves that resemble planking, since they can then be easily concealed within the grooves.

Where you are using wall panel adhesive, apply a generous layer to the supports and press the boards firmly in place. If a wall is perfectly flat, you can fix the panels directly.to the wall surface.

USING CORK TILES

Cork tiles offer a reasonable measure of insulation, but are really intended to reduce condensation on cold walls. The thicker the tile is, the better the insulation provided will be. The surface must be smooth, flat and dry and you should fix the tiles with either a contact adhesive or special cork wall tile adhesive.

INSULATING FLOORS

A solid floor does not normally have to be insulated, since a straightforward floorcovering is sufficient to keep it warm underfoot. A wooden floor, however, is a quite different matter, since it is essential that some air flows constantly beneath it to keep the joists and boards free from damp. Vents in the perimeter wall are there to ensure ventilation from the outside, so never cover these over or you will be inviting trouble from rot in the floor.

Tongued and grooved floorboards are rarely drafty – apart, possibly, from at the edges below the baseboard, where there is often a gap. Unless there has been acute movement caused through shrinkage, the tongues should remain engaged in the grooves to create an effective barrier to drafts.

With square-edged boards, however, there will almost certainly be gaps at some point. If you find only the occasional one, then the simplest solution is just to plug it. This can be done by injecting a bead of flexible caulk along the gap. The caulk never sets and so is able to expand and contract with any slight seasonal movement of the boards. The alternative, with larger gaps, is to fill them with wedge-shaped pieces of wood.

If you discover gaps all over the floor, you can take up the boards and relay them, butting them tightly together again (see Flooring). The problem would, however, have to be extreme to go to this trouble. Most people would settle for the simpler option of covering the complete floor with sheets of Masonite. You will have to do this anyway if you are putting a flexible covering such as vinyl or cork on the floor.

Standard Masonite is ⅛in thick and ideal for living rooms and general areas. In kitchens and bathrooms it is better to use tempered boards to cope with the higher moisture levels.

The boards must be properly conditioned before you lay them so that they do not react adversely to the atmosphere of the room and possibly warp later on. To condition them, moisten the textured side with about 1 pint of water per board. This can be sponged or sprayed on. Then stack the boards on edge for 48 hours. Use small blocks of wood to keep each board separate.

Which way up – either textured or smooth side – you lay the boards will be determined by the floorcovering you are intending to use. With carpets it does not matter. But for cork, vinyl or wood it does and you should first consult the manufacturer's instructions. Generally speaking, if an adhesive is to be used, then the textured side will provide better grip. If self-adhesive tiles are being laid, then the smooth side is better. Where the floorcovering is being laid loose, either way will do.

When laying boards, you should stagger the joints between each, rather like laying a course of bricks. Cut them in half to make 4ft squares and start laying them against the longest wall in the room, cutting smaller pieces as necessary to complete each row. Start the next row with the offcut from the previous one to keep the joints between adjacent rows staggered.

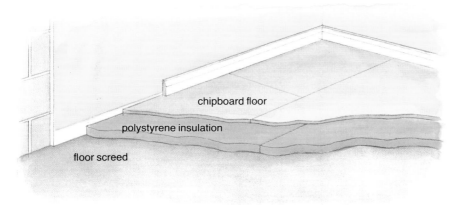

chipboard floor

polystyrene insulation

floor screed

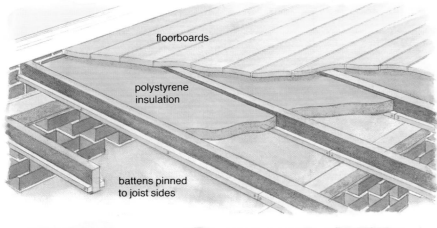

floorboards

polystyrene insulation

battens pinned to joist sides

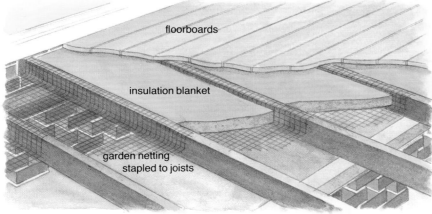

floorboards

insulation blanket

garden netting stapled to joists

■ **Top** Insulate solid concrete floors by laying expanded polystyrene over them, followed by a new floor surface.

■ **Center and bottom** Insulate beneath suspended wood floors either by supporting expanded polystyrene on battens pinned to the joist sides, or by stapling fiberglass mesh to the joists to support blanket insulation between them.

Sealing the baseboard

Although any gaps below the baseboards can also be sealed with a flexible caulk, it is usually better to use a wood molding. This should be pinned to the baseboard, not the floor, so that the boards can still move naturally.

Insulating under floors

In extreme cases such as in a very severe climate or where the room is over a garage and therefore particularly cold, you may have to take more severe measures.

If there is enough space under a suspended wooden floor to crawl into, it is quite easy to fix

insulation between the joists under the floor-boards. You can use rigid polystyrene, cutting it into strips and resting it on nails driven into the sides of the joists. Alternatively, you can suspend lengths of insulation blanket between the joists using garden netting stapled to the joists as support. If there is only a narrow space under the floor, you will have to lift all the floorboards first. This will inevitably cause a lot more disruption within the room concerned.

This method is the best way of insulating rooms above cold, ground-floor areas such as integral garages.

Insulating concrete floors

With concrete floors, to add insulation you will have to raise the existing floor level significantly. The work involves laying 2in thick rigid polystyrene boards over the concrete and then putting down sheets of flooring grade particle board or a fine concrete screed on top. The effect will be to raise the floor level in the room by about 2¾in.

Obviously here you will have to strip the room completely, repositioning baseboards (which will anchor the new floor surface in place), trimming the bottom of the doors and adding a sloping filler strip – unless, of course, you are also treating the floors in adjacent rooms in a similar way.

Reducing drafts

A house that has not been draftproofed can never be kept really warm and comfortable. And there is nothing more unpleasant than icy cold drafts whistling around you on a cold winter's night.

Although draftproofing can be time-consuming, it is not expensive. In fact, under normal circumstances you can look forward to recovering the cost of adding full draftproofing to a house within three years.

Plan any work sensibly, since there are circumstances in which it is not advisable to eliminate all drafts completely. In kitchens and bathrooms, for example, you will want to seal off major drafts, but minor ones help ventilate the area and combat condensation.

Fuel-burning appliances need ventilation, so you should consult your fuel company for advice before applying any draftproofing in areas where these are sited.

In rooms that are heated by electricity or central heating radiators, it is still advisable to leave the odd window untreated, since the normally small amount of draft from this will ensure that the room does not become stuffy.

When you are working out what draftproofing

materials you need, doors and windows should be top of the list. But do not forget other areas such as mailslots, keyholes and, of course, those major culprits like floors and any disused chimney flues.

For window and door frames, you will find there is a variety of different materials to choose from, the simplest and cheapest being self-adhesive foam and brush strips. Supplied in rolls, they are simply stuck to the appropriate place on the frame so that the door or window closes against them.

Other, more expensive devices include V-shaped lengths of plastic, phosphor bronze or aluminum, which are pinned to the frame. The door or window then compresses the V shape when shut, sealing out any drafts.

For the bottom of doors you also have several options. All are simple and quick to fit, although some are more sophisticated and more effective than others.

The basic type is a strip of wood, metal or plastic housing a rubber, brush or plastic insert that grazes along the floorcovering when the door is closed to form a sound seal. You just cut it to length and pin or screw it to the door. If you have the type with pre-drilled screw holes, you should trim where necessary from both ends to ensure the remaining holes are evenly spaced. You can, of course, drill new holes in the strip if you have to.

There is also a rise-and-fall excluder, which will lift above the floorcovering as the door opens and then fall back into place when the door is closed. Another type comes in two parts, one fitting to the bottom of the door and the other to the threshold. The two parts interlock when you close the door.

On the front door, make sure you fit a mailslot flap and keyhole cover. Newspapers left in the slot can let in quite a draft, but you can overcome this problem by fitting a special excluder. This comprises a plastic frame housing brushes, which will mold themselves around any shape pushed through them.

Sealing fireplaces
A disused fireplace can be a source of considerable draft and heat loss from the room. If you want to retain the appearance of an open fireplace, the simplest method is to push some fiberglass blanket up into the throat of the flue, leaving a small air space so that it remains ventilated. Remember, of course, to remove this if you ever decide to use the fire.

A more permanent solution is to seal the chimney stack outside by removing the caps and replacing them with paving slabs. If you do

■ Draftproof sliding sash windows by pinning on proprietary excluders down the edges and across the meeting rail. Check that the window still slides freely.

■ Use self-adhesive foam excluders to draftproof casement windows and doors, sticking the strips into the rebates so they are fully compressed when the window or door is closed.

this, you will have to incorporate a couple of air vents in the top of the stack.

Inside the house, you can of course block off the fireplace opening with plywood, bricks or lightweight blocks. Again, allow for ventilation by incorporating a ventilator; one measuring about 4 × 2in should be sufficient.

Underfloor fresh air vents
The increasing use of solid fuel stoves and draft-controlled fireplaces in older houses can cause draft problems. These units demand a continuous source of air for efficient combustion to occur, and if it is not available they can induce cold drafts through the exterior walls and the floor. They can also seriously deplete the

oxygen content of the air within the house, especially if efforts have been made to prevent the infiltration of fresh air into the house through draftproofing.

One means of solving this problem is to build in a separate underfloor vent pipe, usually 1–2in in diameter, which connects the stove or fireplace directly to the outside air. In this way the large volume of air needed to support combustion can be brought to where it is needed without causing uncomfortable drafts.

FITTING DOUBLE GLAZING

Exactly how much heat double glazing will save is debatable; much depends on the number, orientation and size of the windows. It is generally estimated that about 10–15 per cent of heat goes out through the windows of the average house and that this can be halved with an efficient, well-installed system.

Double glazing is not a short-term investment. Its initial cost will take many years to recover. However, it will make the house much more comfortable by reducing drafts and cold areas around the windows.

Whereas most people install a system to reduce heat loss, in some cases insulation against unwanted outside noise is the main objective. For thermal insulation, an optimum gap of ¾in is needed between the two panes of glass, whereas for good sound insulation the gap should be about 4in.

Buying double glazing
There are two ways to obtain double glazing. The most costly is to get a specialist company to install hermetically sealed units – generally the most efficient. Installation involves taking out the existing window frames and installing new ones. The outside appearance of the property will consequently be altered – slightly or drastically, depending on the type of replacement window frames you choose.

The second, much cheaper method is to fit secondary glazing, which is available as a kit. The advantage here is that the existing windows remain in place so that the outside appearance of the house is unaltered. This type is fixed on the inside, either to the existing window frames or to the surrounding walls of the window reveal.

The simplest and cheapest kit system uses a clear, durable sheet of film, which you can fix in minutes. Cut the film to the overall size of the window, with an allowance of 2in all round. Then fix double-sided adhesive tape or pvc strip around the frame and secure the film to this

around the edges. Finally heat the film with a hair drier to remove all the wrinkles, leaving a perfectly smooth surface. Trim off any excess film with a sharp knife.

A slightly more sophisticated type involves a magnetic system that uses clear rigid plastic instead of glass, but still requires no clips, screws or other similar fixings. You cut the plastic sheet to the size of the window frame and then fix steel strip, which comes in rolls, around the outside of the frame. Apply the matching magnetic strip around the perimeter of the plastic sheet and position this so that the two strips meet. The magnetism will hold the double glazing in place.

Conventional double glazing kits are similar in principle and vary only in detail. A framework of pvc or aluminum accepts the glass and this assembly is then fixed either direct to the existing window frame or to the walls of the windows reveal. The glazing panels can be fixed, hinged or sliding. Hinged or sliding panels will give access to any windows you may want to open, whether casement or top hung.

You will have to buy the glass separately, since this is not supplied with the kit. The correct thickness – either single or double thickness – will be specified by the manufacturer in his literature. Details for measuring the

■ Secondary double glazing consists of panes of glass fixed on the inside of the existing window to create a barrier of still, insulating air between the two panes. The secondary glazing may be fixed, hinged or sliding; avoid fixed panes in rooms where the window may have to be used as an emergency escape route.

overall dimensions of the glass required will also be given and you must follow these instructions very carefully. Measure the windows accurately and then refer to the literature to establish exactly what you need.

Often you will find horizontal channels come in one pack and the vertical ones in another, with all the fittings in a third. It gets more complicated with sliding units, where an additional frame pack is supplied.

In terms of materials, the choice is between pvc and aluminum frames. Since both perform equally well, your decision is likely to be purely an aesthetic one.

Assembling & fitting

There is generally no problem in fixing the double glazing frames to an existing wooden framed window; metal frames, however, are more awkward. If the system you chose is suitable for fixing to metal, then you will need either self-tapping screws or you will have to install a secondary wooden frame around the window on which to mount the system.

It is a relatively straightforward job mounting the double glazing directly on to the window frame. Fixing it into the window reveal, where necessary, can be quite difficult, since rarely

■ Sealed-unit double glazing is factory made to the size required, and consists of two parallel panes of glass sealed together round their edges to trap a layer of inert gas between the panes. The glass can be clear, colored, patterned or given the appearance of leaded lights by placing lead strips on the inner face of one pane.

will a window reveal be exactly square. But it is essential to ensure your secondary frame is perfectly square if the panels are to slide, hinge or close properly.

Check the existing handles and stays. If they project too far, they will prevent you fitting your system to the window frame. If you do not want to fix the glazing to the window reveal, then you will have to change them.

The different systems are all assembled and fitted in a similar way. Bear in mind, however, that if you want a hinged system, you will need to construct a wooden framework on which to mount the secondary glazing and then hang the whole assembly on brackets fixed to the window frame.

Provided both the existing window frame and the double glazing you have put up are both well sealed, the problem of condensation between the two layers of glass can largely be avoided. A point worth noting is that it is advisable to install your system on a day when the air in the room is cold and dry. If damp air is trapped inside the cavity, inter-pane misting will be a constant problem in the future.

Storm windows

The other common form of energy-saving for windows is the aluminum storm window. These are custom-made by specialist companies who work on site and fabricate each window to fit the exact dimensions of the window over which it will be fitted. They are generally made to match the existing window style as closely as possible, and come equipped with an integral insect screen for use in summer when the windows are open. The frames can be painted to blend in with the existing window trim.

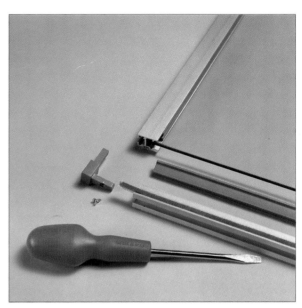

■ **Far left** Start fitting sliding secondary glazing by cutting the side tracks to length. Then screw the side, top and bottom tracks to the frame or reveal (**left** and **below left**). Next, measure and cut to length the channels that frame the glass (**right**), and fit them to the panes (**bottom left**). Finally, lift the panes into the tracks and check that they slide freely from side to side.

WORKING ON THE OUTSIDE

With the building itself renovated and improved to your satisfaction, you can turn your attention to creating or restoring other exterior features of the property, such as driveways, garages, carports, porches and patios. The end product will be a home that has been carefully renovated and thoroughly modernized throughout . . . in other words, your ideal home.

Garages and Carports

It is obviously desirable to get automobiles off the road – and even better if you can have them securely locked away under cover. At the very least, your property should have a parking space or driveway for an automobile, trailer or boat, preferably with a roof over it to create a carport. Ideally, though, you will have a garage where your automobile can be kept protected from the elements and locked up.

If you have a garage, it is worth spending some time checking it for faults – leaking roofs and deteriorating or poorly operating doors are the main problems. With carports, faults are normally few. But you need to keep an eye on the condition of the covering if you are not to loose roofing sheets during fall or winter storms. With an unprotected paved parking space, all that can happen is that the surface may break up.

If you decide to build or extend a garage, remember that this will give you scope for providing additional facilities such as a do-it-yourself workshop or hobby area, or space for storing garden equipment, laundry appliances or a large chest freezer.

■ Since the automobile became an essential rather than a luxury, many homes have been built with the garage as an integral part of the house structure. It may be built out to the front of the house (above and right) or positioned alongside it (left). Such integral garages often have an internal door giving access direct to the house, avoiding a dash to the front door on wet wintry nights. The traditional pair of side-hung timber doors is still found on many older properties (right), but up-and-over doors are now the norm for most homes.

CARRYING OUT ROOF REPAIRS

If you discover a leaking roof, check from the underside to see if you can trace the source of the leak during rain. This can be particularly difficult with a flat roof, especially if the underside is lined, as it should be, with insulating material.

The problem, as has already been discussed in the section on roofs, is that rain can enter at one place and travel a considerable distance along roofing joists before it shows itself as a damp patch on the garage ceiling.

With a leak in a flat roof, scrape away any gravel coating from the affected area. Then paint the roof with flashing primer, which is a bitumen-like product, and allow this to dry. The process takes a few minutes, while the primer changes from brown to black. Then stick a patch of metal-faced, self-adhesive flashing strip over the hole or crack and bed it down well.

The same method of repair can be used for pitched roofed garages, where metal or rigid plastic corrugated roofing sheets have developed holes. However, this is only a temporary measure, since you should eventually change the sheets for new ones.

If the garage is attached, leaks often develop between the roof and where it joins the house

■ **Right** To repair a corrugated garage roof, free the fixings securing the damaged sheet so you can slide it out. Buy a sheet of replacement roofing to match the profile of the existing roof sheeting, and cut it to length using a jig saw and a guide batten. Then slide the new sheet into place, drill holes for the new fixings and secure it to the roof joists. If you suspect that the old sheeting contains asbestos, contact your local authority for guidance on its safe disposal.

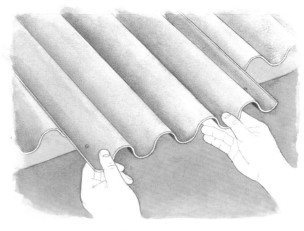

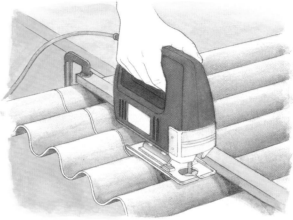

wall. You may also spot the effects of differential movement between the house and the garage where the two buildings meet if the foundations were not built deep enough.

There is little you can do about this. If the building is showing no signs of cracking elsewhere, you might as well leave it. Fill any gaps with non-setting caulk and cover the joint with a self-adhesive flashing strip, which should be able to absorb the movement.

A common roof covering for a carport is clear corrugated plastic sheeting. If this starts to leak, it is often a sign that the plastic has become brittle and is nearing the end of its useful life. So be prepared to strip the roof and fix new sheets.

In the meantime, you can extend the life of the roof by sealing any leaks with self-adhesive waterproof tape, which you just press down over the hole or split. If the damage is extensive, replace individual sheets with new ones with matching corrugations.

CARRYING OUT DOOR REPAIRS

Among the common problems with hinged doors, gaps may appear between the frames and the surrounding wall. You can seal these using non-setting caulk. If the doors are difficult to open and close, oil or grease the hinge.

Look out, too, for rot in the doors or sagging due to loose joints or rot in the door frames, especially round the lower hinge position. You can carry out minor repairs to the doors and frames by cutting out the rot and using a two-part wood filler.

A more satisfactory method of repair would be to insert a new piece of timber or, better still, fit new doors or frames. Repairs are similar to those described for exterior doors.

Up-and-over doors are sometimes made of wood, which is of course prone to rot. Most types, however, are of non-rusting metal. The main problem with either type is usually in the mechanism itself. Moving parts should be oiled from time to time and the channels in which the door gear slides kept well greased. If a door comes off its channel, you may need to adjust the lifting cables. If a door is dented, you may be able to fill the dent; otherwise you may have to replace it with a new one.

EXTENDING A GARAGE

If you have a wooden-framed garage, it is quite feasible to consider extending it to incorporate extra facilities. The work will involve adding to the base and building on the extra section to match the existing structure. Check first with your local authority, however, on the question of whether permission will be needed for the extension work.

If you have a prefabricated garage, it will not be so easy to extend it, unless a similar model is still available from the manufacturer. In that case, all you need do is extend the base and bolt in extra wall and roof sections.

It is more likely, though, that your particular model will be out of production. Here the only choice will be to demolish the existing garage

■ A sweeping driveway not only provides an imposing approach to the house. It also allows ample off-road parking space for visitors, and makes it easy to turn round without the need for reversing out of the driveway onto a busy road.

■ **Above** Cast colored concrete is one of the most attractive and durable driveway surfaces, and can be laid with a smooth or textured surface to any size or shape you may require.

■ **Above right** Paving of various types is one of the most popular surfaces for driveways. For durability, the slabs should be laid in a continuous mortar bed over a concrete base; if they are simply laid over a sand bed the weight of the automobile will shift and crack them.

and erect a new one, built in the traditional manner. This is also a golden opportunity to have both a larger garage and some additional space within it for a workshop or storage room.

PAVING A PARKING SPACE/DRIVEWAY

You might need planning consent for a paved parking space or driveway in the front yard of your house. But you will need permission to create a curb cut on to the highway, if the parking space opens on to a public highway. You will also need permission if you live in a historic district zone.

Make the parking space as large as possible – about twice the automobile's length and double its width. This will give you enough space to open the doors easily and will also allow people to pass comfortably by the automobile when it is parked without scraping the bodywork.

Concrete is practical, but not very attractive. You lay it as for a garage base, as described below. It can be made more attractive with a surface covering of blacktop, as can an existing area of old but sound concrete.

Alternatively, concrete pavers or bricks can be used and here you have the chance to create some interesting patterns. These materials are

available in a range of colors. Laid on a 2in deep bed of sand over compacted gravel, they are ideal for a parking space or driveway.

Paving slabs can be used if well-bedded in mortar over a concrete base. If they are simply loose-laid over a sand bed, they will soon shift and crack under the automobile's weight.

BUILDING A GARAGE

By building your garage, you give yourself the opportunity to create so much more than just somewhere to keep an automobile. It will form an excellent additional storage area for items like bicycles and garden furniture. It can provide a utility area for a washing machine or clothes drier. It will also be somewhere to put a large freezer if this will not fit indoors. Above all, it makes an excellent workshop. And if you build it large and airy enough, it can also make a playroom for the children or a games room for the whole family.

If you want a plain, value-for-money garage with no frills, then a simple wood-framed type is the answer. If you have a masonry-walled house and want the garage to match its appearance, then a purpose-built brick or concrete block garage will be your only option. In the latter case, you can at least be sure of creating a building that will match the style of the house.

You can normally choose from a pitched roof or one that is more or less flat, but in fact slopes to the end or one side. A pitched roof looks more attractive, especially if covered to match the house, and offers useful extra storage space. But it is more expensive.

An extra door for access at the back or side of the garage is often useful and additional windows are important if the garage is to be used as a workshop or utility room. The entrance door will usually be an up-and-over type, either plain or panelled, and made from steel, timber or glass-reinforced plastic. Side-hung doors are an alternative more in keeping with older properties.

With a new garage, you will need to prepare a concrete base. Normally a 4in thick layer of concrete laid over a 4in thick layer of compacted gravel will be sufficient.

You should make the base 6in wider than the garage on all sides and dig out the edges to 8in deep to give an extra thickness of concrete to support the walls. Set out wooden formwork around the slab to support the concrete while it sets and to make it easy to level off the slab.

With a purpose-built garage, you will at least be getting one to suit your requirements exactly. By choosing the materials and style of building carefully, you can effect a perfect match to the house.

If you build the garage against the side of the house, you will get one wall for nothing and save some space. And if you knock a hole for a door in the wall between the house and garage, you will have direct sheltered access.

However, the door must have a one-hour fire rating, be fitted with a metal door closer and there should be a non-combustible step between the house and garage in case of spills of flammable liquids.

If you have the space, it can be a good idea to build a detached garage – and even better if you can build a double one, even if you have only one automobile at present. The extra room will be useful and family needs change remarkably quickly. It may not be many years before you become a two-automobile household.

Obviously, it is preferable to build a double garage side by side. But if you do not have the space for this, you will have to build it lengthways to take two automobiles in tandem.

The minimum internal width of a single garage should be about 10ft – and ideally rather more. The minimum length should be about 20ft and preferably at least 24ft.

CONVERTING A GARAGE

If you decide that you do not want to keep your automobile in your garage, you can generally convert it into extra living space without too much expense. So long as the structure of the building is reasonably sound, all you need to do is to carry out some modifications to incorporate extra windows and close off the existing garage door opening, and to add insulation and

■ Detached garages are common on older properties where space was less at a premium than today. Modern versions can be brick-built, or constructed from a wooden frame with siding or other external wall finish to match that of the house.

■ Carports provide an economical way of creating a shelter for an automobile, recreational vehicle or boat, and can do double duty as a covered play area for children or even somewhere to hang washing to dry in wet weather. Most consist of lightweight roof structures supported on slender poles, and are often built off the house wall.

new surface finishes to the walls, ceiling and floor. If the garage is detached, you will also have to build a linking structure to connect it to the main house.

Before you start work, check your local zoning codes to make sure you are permitted to do away with the garage as a parking space, and also that the conversion satisfies your lot's setback requirements.

If the conversion gets the green light, you can start work. Begin with the floor, which can be covered directly with a new floorcovering if it is smooth, level and dry. However, it is generally better to put down a plywood sub-floor over treated wood sleepers, or to install a new wood joist floor to raise the garage floor level to that of the house. You can then run new plumbing or electrical lines in the floor void.

Next, install any new windows or skylights, remove the garage door and infill the opening with windows, a door or just framing for new siding if you prefer to close it off completely. Line the walls of the garage with sheetrock after placing fiberglass insulation between the wall studs and running in any new electrical or plumbing lines as necessary within the wall structure. Complete the conversion by insulating and lining the garage ceiling.

BUILDING A CARPORT

If you already have a parking space, all you have to do is put a roof over it to create a carport and thus keep the worst of the weather at bay.

Apart from the restrictions mentioned for a parking space, you might need to apply for zoning permission. If you are in doubt, check with your local building inspector or zoning office before starting work.

You can make your own carport by using timber or metal posts to support a light timber framework that will form the roof of the structure. While the posts will support one side of the frame, the other side can be attached to a 2×4in wall plate bolted to the house wall. Set the supporting posts securely in concrete.

To complete the structure, fix lightweight corrugated plastic roofing sheets to the roofing framework. Build the roof with a slight fall away from the house and ensure you allow a minimum headroom under the carport of about 8ft.

If the do-it-yourself approach does not appeal, you can buy carport kits, which are available in aluminum or steel and wood. They contain all the structural components required to erect the building, but you may have to purchase the roofing materials locally.

Porches

A porch is an invaluable addition to a home. It helps stop cold winds blowing into the house every time you open the front door, conserves heat and increases security. It also forms a small addition where you can safely leave a bike, take off and store wet clothes, boots and shoes and stand wet umbrellas.

TYPES OF PORCH

In its simplest form, a porch can just be a canopy over an entrance door. This at least will give some protection to callers to the house and provide a shield for the front door against the worst of the weather.

The roof canopy can be supported by a simple wooden framework fixed to the house wall above the door or by posts at the front outer corners.

One refinement you can make is to fill in between the posts and the wall with trellis panels, on which climbing plants can be grown. This gives some additional protection. You could go even further and enclose the sides with panes of glass and fit a glazed door to the front, thereby creating an enclosed porch.

With some styles of property, the front door

■ **Left** If the house has a recessed porch, it is often possible to fill in the front of the recess to create an enclosed lobby. However, care must be taken to match the architectural style of the house.

■ **Below left** With this type of double porch, infilling can lead to visual disaster and is best avoided.

■ **Below** Building a porch out from the front of the house can create a pleasant additional feature if care is taken over the design and detailing of the addition.

is recessed from the front wall or sited below a lean-to roof. In either case it can be quite easy to create an enclosed porch simply by filling in the recess with glass panels and a door or by building walls beneath the roof.

Where the house has a canopy over the bay windows at the front, you can also quite easily create a porch by adding a curtain wall and door. The result will blend very well with the style of the property. That is very important. As far as possible, any porch you construct should look an integral part of the original house design and should not appear to be an obvious built-on

■ Older properties offer a wide variety of porch designs, from the simple overhanging canopy to more elaborate designs. Often the overhanging roof provided a pleasant place for the occupants to sit out and watch the world go by.

and poorly-designed afterthought.

To allow the maximum amount of light into the hallway, you may want a porch with floor-to-ceiling glass. Alternatively, you may prefer to incorporate low walls up to waist level. Matching the materials you use for these walls to blend with the overall style of the house is an important factor.

With a modern house, or where the property has bay windows with flat roofs, it may be acceptable to have a flat-roofed porch. If your house has a sloping roof, it is better to plan a pitched roof porch, with shingles to match.

The size of the porch may be governed by the recess being filled in. If you are building a porch as an addition to the front of the house, subject to zoning regulations you can make it as wide and deep as you like.

In fact, it may be better to go beyond what could strictly be termed a porch and make it into a lobby hallway, incorporating a downstairs lavette if you wish.

PLANNING A PORCH

Porches are subject to local zoning laws and building codes. These regulations are constantly changing, so you should check your own plans with the local building inspector to make sure your proposed porch meets current requirements.

BUILDING A PORCH

When it comes to building a porch, you have the choice of going for a custom-made design or buying a prefabricated building. You must decide whether you want to carry out the construction yourself or employ a contrator.

If you choose a prefabricated building, most manufacturers offer an erection service. If you employ a contractor, choose a reputable firm,

get written prices from them and check examples of similar jobs done in your area. And always agree the cost, starting and completion dates and payment schedules in writing before any work commences.

Obviously, the choice in prefabricated porches is limited. But if you can find a suitable design in a manufacturer's catalogue, you should get good value for money.

If you decide on a custom-made design, you have complete flexibility as far as styling and materials are concerned. By looking at styles of others in your area, you may be able to design the porch yourself. Otherwise you may need to employ an architect. If you are using a contractor, he may have a design department to take care of this aspect of the job.

INSULATING A PORCH

It is certainly worth insulating a porch. Glass areas including doors should be double-glazed and solid wall areas should have insulation built in within their structure. Timber walls should be similarly insulated, with a polythene vapor barrier between the inner and outer cladding. Alternatively, insulating sheetrock can be used for wall lining. This can be used to line the ceiling as well.

■ The best way of adding a porch to your house is to make the most of existing architectural features, by picking up the line of existing eaves or windows to create a structure that looks part of the original building (**above** and **top left**). If you have the space to build a more substantial porch (**top right**), try to echo the materials and style of the main house in its design.

FINISHING OFF

The porch will need an interior light and ideally an exterior light, too. So put in the necessary wiring for this during construction.

You will also want to incorporate heating in the porch, especially if it contains a half-bathroom. So at the building stage either extend the heating system or incorporate localized unit heaters.

Security is a very important factor, so make sure the porch is fitted with a high security lock. In the case of an open porch, make sure the house door is really secure. The danger here is that a partially enclosed porch may allow an intruder to work on the house's main front door in comparative privacy.

CONVERTING A PORCH

If you have a traditional projecting porch that is seldom used, you can enclose it to expand an existing room or, if it is big enough, to create a new one – a separate study or bedroom, for example. The basic structure is already in place, although because of the porch's exposure to the weather some parts may be in need of some repair or renovation work.

Before you start work, check that the conversion will not block the required daylight and ventilation of adjoining rooms; your local building code office will advise you of the various code requirements.

Begin by removing the existing porch ceiling, its railings and the outer steps, unless these will lead to a new entry door. Then inspect the foundations, the floor, the corner posts and the roof, and repair them as required.

If the porch floor is sound and level, lay a new plywood subfloor directly over it. If it slopes, lay tapered joists across it (if possible, thick enough to bring the porch floor up to the level of the floor in the adjoining room), nailed to new headers at the front and back of the porch, and then lay plywood sheathing over them as before to create a new floor platform.

You can now construct exterior wall frames to fill in between the new floor, the porch roof, the house wall and the front supporting posts. Unless you want to keep the existing wall finish on the back wall of the porch, remove this before fitting the frames and replace it with sheetrock (drywall) or other sheathing later on. With the framing complete, add the new exterior sheathing, fit insulation and nail up sheetrock inside. Insulate the porch roof thoroughly too before putting up the new ceiling. Then finish and decorate the new conversion.

Patios

Whatever size of garden you may have with your house, you should try to make the best possible use of it. One very useful facility is a patio, which not only acts as a link between the house and the garden but also creates another functional area for a whole range of activities.

PLANNING A PATIO

The greatest influence on planning will be the primary use of the patio. For example, will it be used mainly as an outdoor room whenever the weather is fine, with chairs and tables where you can sit and read, eat outdoor meals, sunbathe and entertain friends, or simply as a hard-surfaced play area for the children to use when the grass is wet?

You need to decide whether you want a permanent, built-in table and seating set or whether you want movable furniture. The same decision needs to be made with regard to a barbecue. Do you want a built-in one or will a portable barbecue be suitable? In either case, a built-in table may prove useful, as may some permanent garden seating.

If children are likely to play on the patio when the lawn is wet, a large area of unobstructed paving would be most suitable. You may even need a timber structure like a pergola to support a removable canvas awning, so that the patio can be used even when it is raining.

The size of your patio may well be governed by the area available. With large gardens,

■ Whatever materials you choose to create your patio, aim for an overall effect that blends in naturally with the garden by using curves and broken edges rather than stark squares and rectangles.

where there are no space restrictions, the size could depend on how many people are likely to use the patio at any one time. Bear in mind, for example, peak usage such as summer evening barbecue parties. It is impossible to make a patio too big – unless it dominates the garden. But it could easily be too small. If you are likely to use chaises longues on the patio, the minimum satisfactory size is about 12ft square for two people; double or triple the patio size if you want to seat more people in comfort.

In many cases the aspect of the patio will depend on the outlook at the back of the house. But sometimes it is possible to build the patio out from the back of the house to take advantage of other factors. You may want it south-facing for sunbathing, east-facing to catch the morning sun or west-facing for catching the last of the sun in the evening.

■ If you can incorporate different levels in your garden design, you will create a much more interesting effect. Adding lighting – low-voltage types are the safest – will allow you to enjoy it by night as well as by day.

For such activities as cooking out, it is a good idea if part of the patio is in shade for some of the day. It is usually best to keep it alongside or fairly close to the house, where you can link it with paving so that it is not too far to carry food and other items.

For privacy, you may want to build screen walls, fences, pergolas and awnings into the design. These will have the added advantage of offering a degree of wind protection.

If the ground slopes away from or towards the house, some excavating will be required to create a level area on which to build your patio. Although this will involve making steps and putting up retaining walls, these will enhance the patio's appearance.

It is very important to allow for rainwater to drain away. So build the patio with a slight slope – about ¼in per foot – away from the house. In

Casting ready-mixed concrete

Ready-mixed concrete is one of the most versatile building materials available to the handyman. Not only is it an essential ingredient of many building projects, in the form of strip or raft foundations set in the ground to support walls and other structures. It is also a constructional material in its own right, and can be used to create many outdoor features such as patios, paths and driveways.

The main drawback with concrete is without a doubt its appearance. This obviously does not matter when it is used for something that is largely hidden, such as a foundation slab, but where the material is on show its looks become more important. There are two ways in which the appearance of large expanses of concrete can be significantly improved; color and surface texture.

Color can be affected to a certain extent by careful choice of the sand used as part of the formula, and more drastically by the use of pigments, while the finish given to the slab can add a strong element of visual interest to the project.

In principle, laying concrete in the form of a patio, path or driveway differs little from casting a slab foundation. However, there are several specific points to bear in mind over and above the straightforward casting technique.

Firstly, order all the ready-mixed concrete you need for the job in one delivery. If you use several batches of concrete for a large project, slight differences in shade will be impossible to correct.

You may want to create shapes rather more elaborate than straightforward rectangles and squares. Fortunately, concrete can do this easily so long as you are prepared to spend some time setting out the formwork in the shape you require.

As you plan the layout of your project, watch out for obstacles such as manhole covers and drainage gullies. You will need to plan the levels of your new surfaces carefully unless you are willing to move or reposition the obstacle.

Large areas of concrete cannot be laid as continuous slabs, or they will crack due to expansion and contraction. This means dividing the work up into bays, each separated from its neighbor by an expansion joint of hardboard or bituminous felt if the concrete is laid as a continuous operation. If it is laid in alternate bays, board or felt joints are not needed; a simple butt joint will suffice.

■ When the delivery arrives, try to have it delivered direct to where it is needed via the chute on the delivery lorry.

■ Use barrow to transport loads to areas the chute cannot reach. Protect glazed doors with a sheet of hardboard.

■ Spread the concrete using a garden rake and a shovel. Work it well into the sides and corners of the formwork to avoid hollows.

■ Cast the slab in easily managed bays no more than 10ft long and compact the mix down well with a tamping beam.

■ Lay the next bay in the same way, finishing off with a sawing to-and-fro action of the beam to level the surface of the slab.

■ When you have compacted the slab, apply the finishing texture. For a smooth, polished surface use a steel float.

the case of ground sloping towards the house, you will have to slope the paving away from the house and towards a central swale connected to a large drywell – a pit filled with gravel and stone that can be paved over.

Avoid complicated shapes that involve cutting lots of pavers. For the same reason plan the size of the patio carefully to incorporate standard sizes. When you have got a rough design, mark it out with pegs and string and see if it can be improved. Check that there is enough space for sitting out, see which areas are in shade at those times you are most likely to use the patio and work out where screening will be required.

When you have done all this you can prepare a detailed plan on squared paper with a predetermined scale. This will help you estimate and order exactly the materials you require.

LAYING FOUNDATIONS

When building a patio, you must provide a good base. A layer of crushed stone will give a substantial foundation that acts as a stabilizer between the soil and the paving material.

Remove any top soil to a depth of at least 6in or as deep as required to get the final surface of the patio 6in below the floor level of the house. Lay plastic sheeting over the surface of the excavated base to discourage weed growth.

Firm the soil and spread a covering of crushed stone to a depth of 4in. Then tamp this down and level it, remembering to allow a slight fall from the house. Spread a mixture of sand and gravel over this to provide a smooth, compact surface. This type of base can be used under mortar, sand or concrete – the next layer, depending on what surface material you have decided to put down.

Paving slabs can be laid on an overall bed of mortar. Use a mix of one part cement to five parts sand and, if spreading it, make sure it is 1–2in thick. Use the same mix dry to brush in between the paving. Water it in with a can fitted with a fine spray head.

Sand for block pavers should be laid about 2½in thick. Position the pavers so they are butted tightly together about ½in higher than required. Use a plate vibrator (which can be rented) to work the blocks down to the correct level. Spread fine dry sand over the pavers, then vibrate again to settle the sand into the cracks and lock the blocks in place. Brush away excess sand.

Concrete should be laid 4in thick over the crushed stone base. A mix of one part cement to six parts of combined aggregate will be suitable for a patio area.

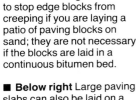

■ **Below** Fit edge restraints to stop edge blocks from creeping if you are laying a patio of paving blocks on sand; they are not necessary if the blocks are laid in a continuous bitumen bed.

■ **Below right** Large paving slabs can also be laid on a sand bed without any edge restraints, but crazy paving must be laid in a continuous mortar bed to stop the paving from subsiding.

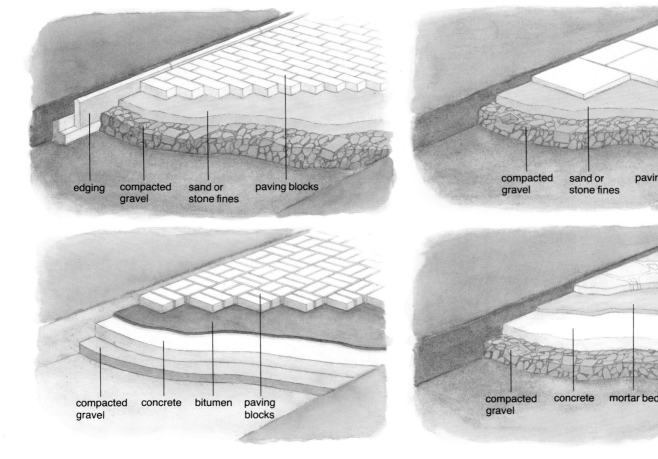

edging   compacted gravel   sand or stone fines   paving blocks

compacted gravel   sand or stone fines   paving slabs

compacted gravel   concrete   bitumen   paving blocks

compacted gravel   concrete   mortar bed   random paving

Conclusion

Having put so much thought, time and effort – not to mention money – into renovating and improving your home, you should certainly be proud of your achievements. But that is not the end of the story. If you do not take measures to look after and protect what you have done, soon you might have to start all over again.

By going through the book, you will have gained a good working knowledge of what is involved in the general maintenance and upkeep of a property. You will also have realized that the time, effort and cost expended in looking after a house is small in comparison to what is involved in putting any faults right.

Take a simple example such as a wooden window frame. Always keep an eye on it and make sure it is well painted. Every few years you should give it an 'overhaul' by sanding, scraping and repainting it. This way, you should have no trouble with it.

Compare the cost of replacement to a small amount of materials and an hour or two of your time, which is all regular checking will involve. If you fail to notice glazing compound or paint cracking, moisture will get in and attack the frame itself. You may be lucky to get away with minor repairs. Alternatively you might have to replace the whole window.

The simple fact of the matter is that to inspect a house that is in good condition takes very little time or effort. With binoculars you can view the roof and chimney stack in close-up. Walls you can check from ground level. Gutters, downspouts and drains you should inspect on a rainy day to see if there are any leaks or overflows. And check closely any wood or metalwork for early signs of rot or rust.

COPING WITH EMERGENCIES

Of course, even the most diligent householder can be caught out. But with constant inspection you should be able to avoid major problems and expense. A damp patch appearing on a wall should signal a quick search for the source of the trouble outside. Prompt action will eliminate the defect before it does any real damage.

To this end it is well worth while keeping a 'first-aid' box of repair materials alongside your tool kit. There is a vast array of tapes, caulks and other waterproofing materials available, many of which can also be used in wet conditions to make immediate repairs.

MAINTENANCE CHECKLIST

FAULT	CAUSE
Chimneys and flashings	
1 Cracked or damaged flue lining.	Old age, failed mortar cap.
2 Cracked or missing mortar cap.	Damp penetration, frost damage.
3 Faulty pointing on stack.	Damp penetration, frost damage.
4 Damaged brickwork on stack.	Damp penetration, frost damage.
5 Damaged flashings round stack.	Old age, wind damage.
6 Dampness penetrating stack.	Porous masonry, failed flashings.
Pitched roofs	
7 Loose or missing ridge shingles.	Failed fixings, wind damage.
8 Out-of-position shingles or shakes.	Failed fixings, wind damage.
9 Missing shingles or shakes.	Failed fixings, wind damage.
10 Damaged sheathing or underlayment.	Missing shingles, rot, wind damage.
Built-up roofs	
11 Torn or cracked roof covering.	Wind damage, temperature extremes.
12 Blistered roof covering.	Protective chippings missing.
13 Torn or damaged flashings.	Old age, wind damage.
14 Puddles standing on roof.	Rot causing decking to sag.
Gutters and eaves woodwork	
15 Overflows from guttering.	Blockages, gutters sagging.
16 Leaks from joints in gutters.	Failed brackets or joint seals.
17 Rot in eaves woodwork.	Failed protective coating.
External walls	
18 Large cracks or bulges in wall.	Subsidence, overloading.
19 Damaged brickwork and pointing.	Old age, frost damage.
20 Cracked or hollow stucco.	Moisture penetration, frost damage.
21 Damaged shingles or siding.	Rot, physical or wind damage.
Doors and windows	
22 Rot in door and window frames.	Failed paint or glazing compound.
23 Doors binding in frames.	Damp penetration, paint build-up.
24 Casements binding in frame.	Paint build-up, failed joints.
25 Sashes binding in frame.	Paint build-up, broken sash cord.
26 Cracked or broken glass.	Accident, slamming, failed joints.
Dampness, rot and termite attack	
27 Internal dampness at ground level.	Failed or bridged flashings.
28 Internal dampness elsewhere.	Penetrating damp, plumbing leaks.
29 Rot in structural timbers.	Penetrating damp, poor ventilation.
30 Termite damage.	Lack of preservative treatment.
31 Condensation.	Poor insulation, poor ventilation.
Wall, floors and staircases	
32 Cracks in wall/ceiling surfaces.	Old age, subsidence, damage.
33 Holes in wall/ceiling surfaces.	Physical damage.
34 Loose or damaged floorboards.	Failed fixings, overloading.
35 Creaks in floorboards or stairs.	Loose boards or treads, overheating.
36 Loose staircase handrail.	Old age, physical damage.

ACTION	MATERIALS

Chimneys and flashings
1 Hack off old mortar cap, reset or replace old liner and renew cap. — New flue liner, bricklaying mortar.
2 Hack off and replace old mortar cap; coat with waterproofing sealant. — Bricklaying mortar, waterproofing sealant.
3 Chisel out areas of failed pointing and replace with new mortar. — Bricklaying mortar.
4 Cut out damaged brickwork and replace with new bricks and pointing. — Replacement bricks, bricklaying mortar.
5 Refix loose flashings, patch holes and repair tears with flashing tape. — Mortar, caulk, flashing repair tape.
6 Repair flashings as necessary, then apply waterproofing sealant to brickwork. — As 5, plus silicone waterproofing sealant.

Pitched roofs
7 Prise off old shingles, then secure new shingles in place with new fixings. — Replacement shingles, fixing nails.
8 Push shakes or shingles back into place, securing with extra fixing nails. — Fixing nails, roofing caulk.
9 Fit replacement shakes or shingles, securing with extra fixing nails. — Replacement shingles/shakes, fixing nails.
10 Cut sheathing back to joists and replace; patch in new underlayment. — New sheathing, underlayment, nails.

Built-up roofs
11 Stick or nail down damaged covering and cover with patch of new material. — Roofing caulk, felt, fixing nails.
12 Make cross-cut into blister, stick down resulting tongues and cover with patch. — Roofing caulk, felt, fixing nails.
13 Refix loose flashings, patch holes and repair tears with flashing tape. — Mortar, caulk, flashing repair tape.
14 Strip old roof covering and decking, renew decking and re-cover roof surface. — New decking, roofing felt and fixings.

Gutters and eaves woodwork
15 Clear blockages; fit new gutter brackets to realign gutter to correct fall. — Replacement gutter brackets, fixings.
16 Undo joints if possible and repair/replace seals; otherwise seal with caulk. — Gutter caulk or new joint seals.
17 Fill or cut out and patch rotten area, using new preservative-treated timber. — Filler, new wood, fixings, preservative.

External walls
18 Professional help essential to discover structural cause and advise on action. — Rebuilding, replacement wall ties.
19 Cut out damaged brickwork and replace with new bricks and pointing. — Replacement bricks, bricklaying mortar.
20 Hack off damaged stucco to sound edge, then re-stucco with new mortar mix. — Stucco mortar, bonding agent.
21 Strip affected area as necessary, then replace damaged shingles or siding. — Matching siding/shingles, fixings, paint.

Doors and windows
22 Cut out rotten wood, replace with filler or new wood; replace glazing compound. — Filler, new wood, glazing compound.
23 Strip paint and plane down door edges to improve clearance, then repaint. — New paint system.
24 Strip paint and plane as 23, remake weak or sagging casement joints, repaint. — New paint system, joint reinforcement.
25 Remove sashes, strip and plane as 23; fit replacement sash cord at both sides. — New paint system, replacement sash cord.
26 Hack out old glazing compound, remove and replace damaged pane. — New glass, glazing points and compound.

Dampness, rot and termite attack
27 Remove damp bridges from outside walls; install new flashings/damp course. — Flashings, damp course fluid, mortar.
28 Locate and rectify source of moisture penetration; repair plumbing leak. — Fillers, sealers, caulk, pipe repair kit.
29 Cut out and replace affected timber; get expert advice for treating dry rot. — New preservative-treated wood, fixings.
30 Professional treatment essential to eradicate outbreak and replace affected timber. — Professional application only.
31 Improve level of heating, insulation and ventilation in affected areas. — Insulation materials, extractor fan.

Walls, floors and staircases
32 Hack out loose material and fill cracks with plaster or interior filler. — Plaster or filler, joint tape.
33 Cut back to studs/joists and patch hole with sheetrock offcut and plaster. — Sheetrock (drywall), plaster, joint tape.
34 Refix loose boards; lift and replace split or otherwise damaged boards. — New fixings, replacement boards.
35 Add extra fixings to secure floorboards to joists and treads to risers. — New fixings.
36 Replace loose fixings or fit new components in place of damaged parts. — New fixings, replacement components.

The same applies to domestic plumbing. Although draining a leaking pipe will stop the immediate problem, if you have pipe repair materials to hand you will be able to stop the leak and restore the system to full working order in a matter of minutes.

Equally, if you have a temporary repair kit, which could include a two-part repair compound, adhesive tape or a pipe clamp, effective emergency measures can be achieved in seconds without having to turn off the water.

Another useful emergency aid is a sheet of tough polythene, which makes excellent temporary glazing or roof cover. Keep some thin nailing strips and wire nails to hand so that the sheet can be anchored quickly to a door or window frame in the event of a breakage.

It is also a good idea to keep a can of aerosol filler handy. This can quickly fill any gap that you discover is letting in the elements. And it can also be used to refix the odd loose clapboard or shingle securely in position.

KEEPING A CHECK

To protect your home and your pocket, give it a regular annual check-up. The most important time to do this is in the fall.

At this time of year the weather should still be mild enough – and dry enough – for any outside jobs to be completed in relative comfort. It is very unpleasant to have to work outside in really cold weather – and it is not always possible or advisable to do so with certain repair materials in adverse or extreme weather conditions.

With the pre-winter check taken care of, you should be fairly confident that the house is able to withstand the worst the weather can throw at it. Every house has to put up with some barrage from the elements. Rain, snow and wind batter the roof, walls, windows and doors while, from below, the all-round attack is completed by moisture in the ground rising to do its worst to the structure.

Make sure you keep this book not only as a basic reference for specific projects but also as a reminder for all the various aspects of your home you should keep your eye on. If you go back through the different sections, you can make a list of the points to watch for when you do your pre-winter inspection.

Get into the habit of carrying out routine maintenance checks and any subsequent work needed so that everything is kept in sound condition. It is a good idea to devote a morning or a day each month to checking and doing small jobs, such as touching up chipped paint, oiling

Your home's log book

As you carry out the gradual repair, restoration and renovation of your home, it makes sense to try to keep track of what you have done by keeping a log book. This will record everything from the materials and fittings you used to the builders and other professionals you employed, and will also be a very useful asset to a future buyer of the property.

You can set up your house log book using a standard A4 or foolscap folder containing lined, blank and graph paper (for drawing scale plans), with divider tabs to split it into sections. Do this either by the type of job involved (building, decorating, plumbing and so on) or by the room or area of the house concerned. The folder (or a matching box file) can be used for manufacturer's leaflets and other useful bits of literature. How detailed your notes are is up to you, but you should at least always record things like quantities of materials used, to save you having to work them out again when you repeat the job.

hinges, testing that shut-off valves are not jammed and other similar aspects of the general 'working' of your home.

Your house is almost certainly going to be the largest investment of your life. For most people it is the tangible proof of the effort they have made to obtain security for themselves and their family. In many ways, it represents their wealth and safeguard against illness, unemployment and other potential pitfalls in life.

Having worked so hard to improve the property – to renovate it and to make it a comfortable and pleasurable place in which to live – you will also have increased its value. Possibly the amount of that increase will surprise even you.

So make sure you safeguard this, the center of family life, by insuring it adequately. If you have any doubts about its worth, get it valued by at least two local real estate agents. It is important to get several estimates if you can, since occasionally a property can unwittingly be over- or undervalued.

Should your insurance cover not represent the true value of the property then, in the event of a claim, you could find yourself not receiving sufficient compensation to meet any necessary repair or rebuilding costs.

Your house is your home and it is there to be enjoyed over the years you remain in it. By working on it, changing it, improving it and caring for it, you will gradually impress your personality on it. With the help of this book, you will also be able to create the home you have always wanted.

Index

A

additions 167–9, 193
air conditioning 186–8
asbestos 31
asphalt 15, 41
attic
    building code 163
    conversion 162–7
    insulation 181, 190–3
    services 165–6
    ventilation 191

B

balloon-frame construction 31, 62
bargeboards 43, 78
baseboard 197
basements 169
bathrooms 25, 150–61
    bath 158
    bidet 161
    condensation 113, 154–5
    lighting 176
    problems 150–7
    redesigning 157–8
    shower 158–61, 166
bedroom lighting 177
bevel-edge siding 76
bidets 161
boilers 18, 182–4
brickwork
    brick veneer 31, 33, 62, 79
    replacing 65–6
    repointing 65
    treating 65–6
    ventilators 68, 196
building code
    attic conversions 163
    carports 209
    chimneys 134, 137
    insulation 191
    loadbearing walls 111
    porches 212
    staircases 104
building paper 192–3

C

cabinets, kitchen, *see* storage units
canlights 121, 173, 175, 179
carcassing, *see* roof
carports 204–9

cars, *see* carports; driveways; garages
ceilings 120–5
    boarded 122, 125
    centerpiece 123–4
    coving 124
    drywall 121, 122–3
    insulation 120
    lath and plaster 121–2
    lowering 124
    sheetrock 121, 122–3
    suspended 122, 125
    timber 122, 125
central heating 18, 180–6
    boilers 182–4
    controls 184–6
    electric 183
    gas-fired 184
    LPG-fired 184
    oil-fired 183–4
    solid-fuel 181, 182
    ventilation 197
    warm air 183
ceramic tiles 128, 155–6
chimneys 44, 134–7
    building code 134, 137
    capping 58, 134
    dampness 58–9
    installing 137
    lining 134–6
    repairing 58–9
    restoring 134–6
    see also fireplaces
cladding
    aluminum 39
    brick veneer 31, 33, 62, 79
    plastic 39
    stone veneer 62, 79
    timber 26, 39, 62, 68, 77–8, 196
    vinyl siding 69, 78–9
clapboarding, *see* cladding
concrete, readymix 216
condensation 113
    basements 169
    bathrooms 154–5
conservatory, *see* sunroom
cork tiles 196
countertops 146–7, 149
coving 124

D

dampness 18–19, 70–9
    chimneys 58–9
    condensation 113, 154–5, 169
    damp-proof course 32, 70–1, 76
    damp-proof membrane 18, 38

damp-proofing 30, 70–9
    exterior walls 32, 38–9, 70–9
    floors 95
    interior walls 113
    penetrating 39, 71
    rising 18, 38, 71–5
    windows 75
diaphragm valve 151–3
dimmers 175
dishwashers 139, 145
doors, exterior 80–6
    draftproofing 198
    fittings 85–6
    replacing 83–5
    security 85–6
doors, interior 119–20
double check valve 139
double glazing 182, 199–201
downspouts 61, 73
draftproofing, *see* insulation
driveways 207
dry rot 19, 23, 45–6, 101–3
drywall 33–5, 62, 121, 122–3

E

eaves boards 43, 78
efflorescence 38, 73
electricity
    central heating 181
    gas compared with 142
    rewiring 18
expanding foam fillers 75
extractor fans 113, 189

F

fascias 43, 78
faucets 141, 149
    mixer 141, 158
felt, *see* roof
fiberglass shingles 41, 55
filler foams 75
finance 26
fireplaces 126–34
    draftproofing 198
    firebacks 129
    firebricks 129
    hearths 129
    installing 136–7
    removing 132–4
    restoring 126–32
    sealing 198
    surrounds 126–9

ventilation 198
see also chimneys
flashings 43, 49, 57–8
floors 94–103
 attic 164–5
 dampness 95
 floorboards 94–9
 gaps 98
 insulation 95, 196–7
 joists 71, 94
 levelling 99
 particle board 97
 replacing 99
 rotten 100–3
 sanding 98
 solid 95, 99
 sunken boards 98
 ventilation 71, 94–5, 198–9
 warped 97–8
fluorescent lighting 173, 175, 178, 179
freezers 140, 144–5

G

garages 204–9
gas
 central heating 181
 electricity compared with 142
 installation 166
glass and glazing 91
 see also double glazing
guttering 17
 leaks 49, 59, 72
 overflowing 22
 repairing 59–61

H

headers 111, 118
heat loss, *see* insulation
heating 180–6
 choosing 181
hot-water tanks 181, 191, 192

I

inspecting property 13–22
insulation 190–201
 additions 193
 attic 181, 190–3
 cavity walls 32
 ceilings 120
 double glazing 182, 199–201
 draftproofing 182, 197–9
 exterior walls 70–9, 181, 194
 floors 95, 196–7
 hot-water tank 181, 191

interior walls 194–6
porches 213
windows 91
ISL lamps 178

J

joists
 floor 71, 94
 roof 49–50, 163

K

kitchens 25–6
 condensation 113
 cooker hoods 144, 175
 countertops 146–7, 149
 design 138–9
 dishwashers 139, 145
 fitting 147–9
 freezers 140, 144–5
 lighting 175–6
 refrigerators 140, 144–5
 sinks 140–1, 149
 storage units 146–7
 stoves 139–40, 142–4
 washing appliances 139, 145–6
 waste disposal 141–2

L

ladders and steps
 attic 166
 safety 52–3, 120
laundry appliances 139, 145–6
lighting 121, 172–9
 bathroom 176
 canlights 121, 173, 175, 179
 ceiling centerpiece 123
 conservatory 177
 corridor 173
 dimmers 175
 dining room 175
 fluorescent 173, 175, 178, 179
 hallway 173
 ISL lamp 178
 kitchen 175–6
 lamps and tubes 177–9
 living room 174
 Luxo lamp 177
 PAR lamp 178
 porch 213
 rise-and-fall 175
 spotlights 121, 173, 175, 179
 stairs 173
 track lighting 121, 177
 trip switch 176

lintels, *see* headers
loadbearing and non-loadbearing walls
 110–11, 118
locks 85–6, 213
LPG (liquefied petroleum gas) 184
Luxo lamp 177

M N O

marble repairs 129
Masonite 150, 196–7
microwave ovens 143
mold 114
oil-fired central heating 181, 183–4

P

paint blisters 71
PAR lamps 178
particle board 97
partitions, 112–13, 118–19
paths 73
patios 73, 214–17
penetrating dampness, *see* dampness
piston valve 151–3
plaster
 damp-proof course and 73
 loose 115
 pitted 117
platform-frame construction 62
plumbing 18
 bathroom 150
 kitchen 139, 146
 leaking 113
porches 210–14
potlights, *see* canlights
purlins 40, 50, 163

R

radiators, *see* central heating
rafters 50, 163
readymix concrete 216
refrigerators 140, 144–5
rise-and-fall lighting 175
rising dampness, *see* dampness
roof
 asphalt 15, 41, 42–3
 built-up 40, 49–50, 55–7, 193–4
 carcassing 40
 construction 39–40, 49–51
 corrugated 42
 coverings 40–3
 felt 42, 56
 fiberglass shingles 41, 55
 flashings 43, 49, 57–8
 flat 40, 49–50, 55–7, 193–4

gable-end 40
gambrel 40
garage 205–6
hipped 40
inspecting 15–16
insulation 190–3
interlocking tiles 41, 51, 53
joists 49–50, 163
leaks 22, 55
lean-to 40, 50
metal sheeting 55
monopitch 40
pitched 40, 50–1
purlins 40, 50, 163
rafters 50, 163
rippling 43
safety 48, 52–3
sagging 43
shingles and shakes 15, 40–1, 50–1, 54
slate 41–2, 50, 54
tiles 41, 51, 53
ventilation 50
windows 165, 167
wood shingles and shakes 15, 40–1

S

safety
    equipment 87
    ladders and steps 120
    roof 48, 52–3
sanders 98
scaffolding 52, 120
sealants 71, 75
security, see locks
shakes 40–1, 51, 54
sheetrock 33–5, 62, 121, 122–3
shingles 40–1, 51, 54, 68
shiplap board 78
showers 158–61, 166
sinks 140–1, 149
slate, see roof
soffits 43, 50, 78
solar power 181
solid-fuel central heating 181, 182–3
spotlights 121, 173, 175, 179
staircases
    building code 104
    creaking 107–8
    installing 166–7
    repairing 104–9
    replacing 109
stone cladding, see cladding
storage units 147–8
storm windows 200
stoves 139–40, 142–4
    woodburning 182
stucco 16, 64, 66–8
stud partitions 112–13, 118–19
sunroom 168–9
    lighting 177

T

termite attack 45, 100–1
tiles
    ceramic 128, 155–6
    cork 196
    interlocking 41, 51
    roof 41, 50–1, 53–5
    slate 41, 50, 54
timber
    clapboard 26, 62, 68, 77–8
    rotten 19, 23, 45, 68–9, 100–3
    shingles 15, 26, 40–1, 62, 68, 77–8
    warped 97
timber-frame construction 33–5
toilets 151–4
tongued-and-grooved board 78, 97
torching felt 56
towers 52, 120
track lighting 121, 177
traps 150
tree problems 37, 64
trip switch 176

V

ventilation 113, 189
    attic 191
    basement 169
    fireplace 198
    floor 71, 94–5, 198–9
    roof 50
ventilators 68, 71, 196
vinyl siding 69, 78–9

W

walls, exterior 30–1, 62–9
    asbestos shingles, 31
    balloon-frame construction 31, 62, 94
    bowing 35–6
    brick veneer 31, 33
    bulging 37–8
    cavity brick 30–1, 32
    checking 16–17, 64–5
    clapboard 26, 62, 68, 77–8
    cracking 36–7, 64, 117
    dampness 32, 38–9, 70–9
    dressed stone 32–3
    insulation 70–9, 181, 194
    natural stone 33
    platform-frame construction 62, 94
    shingles 62, 68, 77–8
    solid brick 31–2, 62, 76–7
    stone veneer 31, 64, 79
    timber-frame 30–1, 62
    vinyl siding 69, 78–9

walls, interior 31, 110–20
    blocking doorway 119–20
    building code 111, 118
    cracks and holes 114–15, 117
    dampness 113
    insulation 194–6
    loadbearing and non-loadbearing 110–11, 118
    partition 112–13, 118–19
    problems 113–18
    removing 118
    types 112–13
waste disposal units 141–2
waste pipes 141–2, 150
wet rot 45, 70, 101
windows 86–91
    cracked sills 73
    dampness 75
    double glazing 182, 199–201
    draftproofing 198
    insulating 91
    replacing 87–91
    roof 165
    storm 200
wood, see timber
wood-burning stoves 182

Z

zoning laws
    carports 209
    garages 206
    porches 212

Acknowledgements

Photographs

Page 10 (top): Four by Five, Superstock. Page 10 (bottom): Darlene Bordwell, The Picture Cube. Page 11 (top): Superstock. Page 11 (bottom): Bonnie McGrath, The Picture Cube. Page 12 (top): Michael Mathers, Peter Arnold Inc. Page 13 (top): John Elk III, Stock Boston. Page 13 (bottom): Michael Mathers, Peter Arnold Inc. Page 14 (bottom): Michael J Howell, The Picture Cube. Page 16 (top and bottom): Superstock. Page 16 (center): W B Finch, Stock Boston. Page 17 (top and center): Superstock. Page 17 (bottom): Elizabeth Whiting Associates. Page 18 (bottom): Four by Five, Superstock. Page 22 (bottom): Eric Neurath, Stock Boston. Page 23 (bottom): Robert Harding Picture Library. Page 24 and 25 (top): Elizabeth Whiting Associates. Page 25 (bottom): Robert Harding Picture Library. Page 36: Superstock. Page 37: Comstock. Page 41 (top): Jeff Dunn, Stock Boston. Page 44 (bottom left): Stephen Swinburne, Stock Boston. Page 44 (bottom right): Robert Harding Picture Library. Page 45 (top and center): Rentokil Ltd. Page 63 (top): Kindra Clineff, The Picture Cube. Page 73: Robert Harding Picture Library. Page 74: Rentokil Ltd. Page 76 (top): External Wall Insulation Association. Page 76 (bottom): National Cavity Insulation Association. Page 77: Comstock. Page 79 (top): B & J McGrath, The Picture Cube. Page 80 (left): Matthew McVay, Stock Boston. Page 80 (center): Richard Pasley, Stock Boston. Page 80 (right): Henryk T Kaiser, The Picture Cube. Page 80 (top right): Jerry Howard, Stock Boston. Page 87 (top left): Mike Mazzaschi, Stock Boston. Page 87 (top center): John Coletti, Stock Boston. Page 100 and 101: Robert Harding Picture Library. Page 103: Rentokil Ltd. Page 104: John Maher, Stock Boston. Page 110: Elizabeth Whiting Associates (Jarvis Woolgar). Page 122: Marshall Cavendish Ltd. Page 123: Elizabeth Whiting Associates. Page 126 (left): Betsy Fuchs, The Picture Cube. Page 126 (bottom): Susan A Anderson, The Picture Cube. Page 127 (left and center): Elizabeth Whiting Associates. Page 127 (right): Thomas Craig, The Picture Cube. Page 129: Marshall Cavendish Ltd. Page 138 (bottom): Keith Scott Morton, Peter Arnold Inc. Page 140 and 141: Franke UK Ltd. Page 142 (top): In-Sink-Erator. Page 143 (top): Robert Harding Picture Library. Page 143 (bottom): Wickes Building Supplies Ltd. Page 144: Magnet plc. Page 145 (top): Elizabeth Whiting Associates. Page 145 (bottom): AEG (UK) Ltd. Page 147 (bottom) to 149: Alno (UK) Ltd. Page 150 (bottom): Shires Bathrooms Ltd. Page 154 (top): Elizabeth Whiting Associates. Page 154 (bottom): Wickes Building Supplies Ltd. Page 155 and 156 (top): Elizabeth Whiting Associates (155: Carolyn Warrender). Page 158 (top): Svedbergs (UK) Ltd. Page 158 (bottom): Armitage Shanks Ltd. Page 159: Robert Harding Picture Library. Page 160 (top): Wickes Building Supplies Ltd. Page 160 (bottom): Svedbergs (UK) Ltd. Page 161 (top): Robert Harding Picture Library. Page 161 (bottom): Carolyn L Bates, f-stop Pictures. Page 162: Keith Scott Morton, Peter Arnold Inc. Page 164: The Velux Co Ltd. Page 165 (top): Owen Markson, Stock Boston. Page 165 (bottom) and 166: The Velux Co Ltd. Page 167 (top): William Johnson, Stock Boston. Page 169 (bottom) and 172: Elizabeth Whiting Associates. Page 173 (top): Marshall Cavendish Ltd. Page 173 (bottom): Elizabeth Whiting Associates. Page 174 (top): Bill Horsman, Stock Boston. Page 174 (bottom): Elizabeth Whiting Associates. Page 175: Superstock. Page 176 (top): Robert Harding Picture Library. Page 176 (bottom): Carolyn L Bates, f-stop Pictures. Page 177: Elizabeth Whiting Associates. Page 178 and 179: Marshall Cavendish Ltd. Page 180: Robert Harding Picture Library. Page 181: Keith Scott Morton, Peter Arnold Inc. Page 184 (top): Potterton Myson Ltd. Page 184 (bottom): Trianco Redfyre Ltd. Page 185: Potterton Myson Ltd. Pages 186 and 187: Carrier Corporation, Syracuse, NY; Bryant Heating & Cooling, Indianapolis, Ind. Page 189: Marshall Cavendish Ltd. Page 190 and 191: Robert Harding Picture Library. Page 198 to 201: Marshall Cavendish Ltd. Page 206 (bottom): Tom Shaner, The Stock Solution. Page 215: Hozelock Ltd. Page 216: Robert Harding Picture Library.

All other special photography by David Markson, LBIPP. Chapter openers by David Parmiter. Styled by Victoria Furbisher.

Illustrations

Pages 30 to 35: Richard Phipps. Page 38: Steve Cross. Page 39: Andrew Green. Page 42: Steve Cross. Pages 44, 48 and 49: Richard Phipps. Pages 50 to 59: Steve Cross. Pages 60 to 68: Ed Stuart. Page 69: Andrew Green. Pages 72 and 74: Rob Shone. Pages 77 and 78: Andrew Green. Page 81: Ed Stuart. Pages 82 to 86 and 88: Rob Shone. Page 89: Ed Stuart. Page 90: Ed Stuart, Rob Shone. Page 91: Rob Shone. Pages 94 to 109: Richard Draper. Pages 111 to 125: Ed Stuart. Pages 128 to 132: Richard Draper. Page 133: Richard Phipps. Pages 134 to 137: Richard Draper. Page 139: Andrew Green. Pages 146 and 151 to 153: Ed Stuart. Pages 157, 164, 182 to 184, 192 to 195, 197, 205 and 217: Andrew Green.